Field Guide to

MUSHROOMS

& other Fungi of South Africa

Gary B Goldman & Marieka Gryzenhout

Principal photographer: Liz Popich

Dedication

Essie, Joshua, Charles and Nomsa, this field guide is for you – thank you for believing in me and making it possible for me to chase my dream. – **Gary B Goldman**

With gratitude to my family for the support and patience provided during the time it took to develop this book ... and whenever I see a mushroom. – **Marieka Gryzenhout**

Published by Struik Nature
(an imprint of Penguin Random House South Africa (Pty) Ltd)
Reg. No. 1953/000441/07
The Estuaries No. 4, Oxbow Crescent, Century Avenue, Century City, 7441
PO Box 1144, Cape Town, 8000 South Africa

www.penguinrandomhouse.co.za
Visit **www.penguinrandomhouse.co.za** and join the Struik Nature Club
for updates, news, events and special offers.

First published in 2019
1 3 5 7 9 10 8 6 4 2

Publisher: Pippa Parker
Managing editor: Roelien Theron
Concept designer: Gillian Black
Designer: Dominic Robson
Proofreader: Thea Grobbelaar

Reproduction by Hirt & Carter Cape (Pty) Ltd
Printed and bound by CTP Printers SA

MIX
Paper from
responsible sources
FSC
www.fsc.org
FSC™ C017578

Print: 9781775846543
Epub: 9781775846604

Front cover: *Aureoboletus gentilis*; **Half-title page:** *Cymatoderma elegans*; **Contents page:** *Amanita pantherina* (all Liz Popich); **Spine:** *Coprinopsis picacea* (Pixabay); **Back cover (from left):** *Amanita foetidissima* (Liz Popich), *Marasmius haematocephalus* (Jean Stephenson), *Panaeolus antillarum* (Liz Popich), *Gymnopilus junonius* (Gary B Goldman)

Disclaimer: Some mushrooms are highly poisonous and can cause illness and even death if eaten. If there is any doubt about the edibility of a species, try not to handle it and **do not** cook or eat it. Ideally, seek the assistance of an expert. The authors and publishers accept no responsibility for readers who do not heed this advice or for any consequences resulting from the use of information contained in this guide.

CONTENTS

SPONSOR'S MESSAGE

For over 50 years Denny Mushrooms has been proudly growing the bulk of mushrooms consumed in South Africa. High in protein and minerals, low in carbohydrates and salt, mushrooms are a natural super food, and an essential part of a balanced diet.

Denny's proud history as a successful local mushroom producer makes it a natural partner for this eagerly awaited book. We fully support the work done by Gary Goldman and Marieka Gryzenhout to bring the fascinating world of fungi to more South Africans. We hope that this work makes wild mushrooms accessible to more South Africans, young and old.

Happy foraging.

Ryan Cotterell
CEO, Denny Mushrooms

ACKNOWLEDGEMENTS

This project may not have come to fruition were it not for the help of many supportive institutions and people.

Dr Riana Jacobs-Venter of the South African National Collection of Fungi (Agricultural Research Council) has been an enthusiastic supporter of this project, and kindly made available data collected on species occurrence by the institution's fungarium. Additional data on distributions came from MushroomMap, part of the Virtual Museum at the Animal Demography Unit at the University of Cape Town. Our thanks go to Prof. Les Underhill, director of the unit, and Megan Loftie-Eaton, project coordinator and moderator of the Mushrooms of Southern Africa Facebook group.

We are grateful for seed funding provided by the Foundational Biodiversity Information Programme, funded by the South African National Biodiversity Institute, the Department of Science and Technology and the National Research Foundation. We also wish to thank Ryan Cotterell, chief executive officer of Denny Mushrooms, for making available a generous sponsorship to assist in the production of this book.

Without the immense contribution of Liz Popich, prolific mushroom photographer and amateur mycologist, we would not have been able to compile such a highly visual guide. The book is all the better for the voluntary contribution of her excellent images. Special thanks also go to Glen van Niekerk, Jean Stephenson, Kelly Gottschalk and Volker Miros for their photographs. Several others contributed images for this project; they are credited alongside their images.

Many other people have shared their knowledge and skills and provided assistance during the course of researching and writing this book. Our sincere thanks go to Michel Beeckman, Simon and Cathy Davis, Olga de Klerk, Johanna and Diana Ferreira, Hugh Glen, Cappy Goldman, Rob Hallock, Dr Tonjock Rosemary Kinge (University of Bamenda, Cameroon), Robert Knuckey, Prof. Gerhard Kost (University of Marburg, Germany), Rob Louw, Patrick Maddon, Sonto Magagula, Dr George G. Ndiritu (Karatina University, Kenya), Liezel Norval-Kruger (Eatsplorer), Alison Paulin, Chamell Pluim (SANParks), Thomas Poole, David Puddu, Fiona Quartermain, Christoph and Felicia Reinold, Bert Reynders, Richard Rose (Elgin Vintners), Dr Leslie Sank, Michael Schnepper, Gregory Schroeder, Myke Scott, Dr Adriaan Smit, Nora Sperling-Thiel (Delheim), Jean and Rico Stephenson, Jenny and Terry Strong, Rod Tullos, Renier van Rensburg, Prof. Bennie Viljoen (University of the Free State) and Johan Christiaan Wagener.

Lastly, we wish to thank the team at Struik Nature – Pippa Parker for her leadership, Roelien Theron for her ability to push the envelope in obtaining the best results, and Dominic Robson for his design work and patience with the many changes throughout. Thanks for your support and dedication to this project.

FOREWORD

Fungi are a diverse group, both biologically and morphologically. Estimates suggest that up to 3.8 million species occur on earth.

They play an invaluable role in all ecosystems, living in a wide range of habitats as saprotrophs that decompose dead or decaying organic matter; as symbionts, which form close associations with other, often much larger, life forms; and as parasites, causing damage and disease in the host. More specifically, they are an important source of food for humans and a vital ingredient in processed foods, traditional and novel medicines, industrial fungal enzymes and compounds. They are also increasingly the subject of research into their psychoactive properties. On the other hand, as pathogens of plants, animals and humans, they can inflict serious harm.

Africa is endowed with a high level of biodiversity. Yet, unlike most other life forms, fungi are almost never included in biodiversity data, nor do they feature in country-specific biological checklists or red lists of threatened species. Proper fungal inventories and databases are largely non-existent and those that are functional contain scant or inadequate information. While the omission of such data results in biodiversity assessments being inherently skewed, it also means that decision makers and the public are never made fully aware of the importance of these life forms.

The problems that affect fungal diversity in Africa, including South Africa, are slash-and-burn agricultural practices, overgrazing, alien plant invasions, reforestation with non-native trees, poor land management, soil degradation and urban encroachment. Given the paucity of fungal data in biodiversity assessments, the impact of these destructive practices on the fungal kingdom remains unknown. The problems are worsened by a serious lack of human capacity in the field of mycology. Other factors that constrain our knowledge of fungi include the dearth of appropriate literature for different audiences, the large numbers of new taxonomic groups that are awaiting description, and the numerous regions and ecological niches that have not yet been explored.

It is estimated that in South Africa alone more than 171,000 fungal species exist, a calculation that is based on the modest assumption that an average of seven fungal species is associated with each of the known plant species. So far, only 780 new species have been reported for the country.

The identification of macrofungi is a difficult task in Africa – not only because of the small number of mycologists working in the field, but also because of the absence of truly comprehensive guides. This book intends to address that gap. The descriptions summarised in its pages – covering ecology, distribution, habitat, species features and edibility – are the result of the work of diligent mycologists and their collaborators. Supported by a myriad attractive, full-colour photographs, this handy field guide will greatly enhance our knowledge of fungal species richness in South Africa.

Importantly, although this book represents a crucial and outstanding contribution to South African mycology, it will also benefit mycologists and citizen scientists throughout the world. We owe Gary Goldman and Marieka Gryzenhout an enormous debt of gratitude for their research and for producing this useful guide on the fascinating world of fungi.

Tonjock Rosemary Kinge (PhD)
Senior Lecturer
Department of Biological Sciences
University of Bamenda, Cameroon

INTRODUCTION

Fungi have been known to humans since the earliest times. Archaeological research has shown that they have been harvested for food and medicine in China for at least 6,000 years. In Central America, the Mayans and Aztecs used hallucinogenic mushrooms to induce a state of trance in healing rituals and religious ceremonies. Other psychoactive mushrooms, notably *Amanita muscaria* (fly agaric), have been at the centre of similar rites in Russia, early Europe and Central Asia.

The rapid development of DNA sequencing technologies has provided sufficient data to suggest that the earliest fungi evolved about 1 billion years ago, accounting for the astonishing diversity of the fungal kingdom. Fungi come in an array of fantastical shapes and sizes, from the familiar, large, fleshy mushrooms to the smallest, single-cell yeasts, and are encountered in all habitat types throughout the world. They are ubiquitous and have intricate interactions with other plants and organisms, forming mutually beneficial relationships with them or detrimental ones, parasitising their hosts and even killing them. Regardless of the damage they may cause, they play a vital role in sustaining life on our planet.

Recent research indicates that between 2.2 and 3.8 million fungal species occur worldwide, yet only about 144,000 of these have been properly documented – less than five per cent of the estimated total number in existence. In South Africa alone, it is believed that more than 171,000 species may exist. Despite this diversity, many related species can look very similar, requiring careful observation to tell them apart. This becomes even more important when foraging for wild mushrooms, as many poisonous fungi can be mistaken for edible ones. The effects of eating a poisonous mushroom may range from a mild upset stomach to organ damage and even death.

This field guide will enable users to identify common and some less common species that occur in South Africa – and, in the process, to learn more about these most curious organisms. The book details the edibility of species and flags those that are harmful or life-threatening. For the nature lover, there may be nothing more rewarding than accurately identifying a species *and* being able to safely harvest it for a special home-cooked meal.

The species covered in this guide are taken from two main fungal groups, the Basidiomycota (pp. 24–333) and the Ascomycota (pp. 334–347). A representative of the Zygomycota (pp. 348–349) is featured here, as it is one of only a few species in this group that can be seen with the naked eye.

In addition to being used in many pharmaceutical and industrial products, mushrooms such as *Coprinellus domesticus* are valued for their edibility.

How to use this book

The species selected for this book are organised according to their most obvious morphological characters (see the table on pp. 21–23) and are arranged according to genus. To make identification easier, some species have been grouped with similar-looking ones rather than strictly in their scientific group. Photographs of most of the fungi are presented at life size or slightly smaller, while others have been magnified to show the features in more detail.

It is not possible to indicate whether species are indigenous to South Africa or introduced because data for this is not adequate. Since the vast majority of species listed here are known from other regions around the globe, it can be assumed that fungi that associate exclusively with non-indigenous trees or plants were introduced with their hosts. Furthermore, although distributions are based on available records, comprehensive surveys still need to be done to accurately map species distribution in the country.

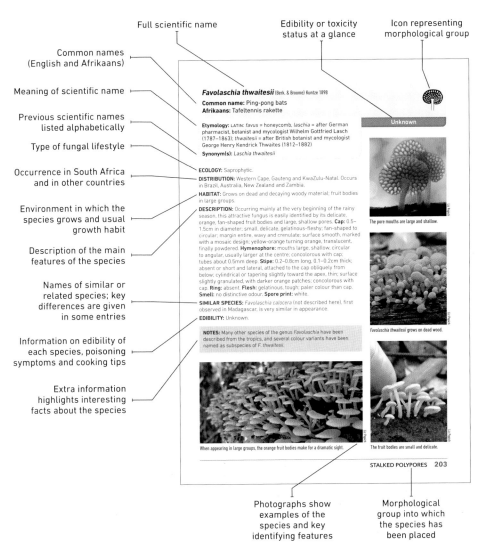

Full scientific name

Edibility or toxicity status at a glance

Icon representing morphological group

Common names (English and Afrikaans)

Meaning of scientific name

Previous scientific names listed alphabetically

Type of fungal lifestyle

Occurrence in South Africa and in other countries

Environment in which the species grows and usual growth habit

Description of the main features of the species

Names of similar or related species; key differences are given in some entries

Information on edibility of each species, poisoning symptoms and cooking tips

Extra information highlights interesting facts about the species

Favolaschia thwaitesii (Berk. & Broome) Kuntze 1898

Common name: Ping-pong bats
Afrikaans: Tafeltennis rakette

Etymology: LATIN: *favus* = honeycomb, *laschia* = after German pharmacist, botanist and mycologist Wilhelm Gottfried Lasch (1787–1863); *thwaitesii* = after British botanist and mycologist George Henry Kendrick Thwaites (1812–1882)
Synonym(s): *Laschia thwaitesii*

ECOLOGY: Saprophytic.
DISTRIBUTION: Western Cape, Gauteng and KwaZulu-Natal. Occurs in Brazil, Australia, New Zealand and Zambia.
HABITAT: Grows on dead and decaying woody material; fruit bodies in large groups.
DESCRIPTION: Occurring mainly at the very beginning of the rainy season, this attractive fungus is easily identified by its delicate, orange, fan-shaped fruit bodies and large, shallow pores. **Cap:** 0.5–1.5cm in diameter; small, delicate, gelatinous-fleshy; fan-shaped to circular; margin entire, wavy and crenulate; surface smooth, marked with a mosaic design; yellow-orange turning orange, translucent, finally powdered. **Hymenophore:** mouths large, shallow, circular to angular, usually larger at the centre; concolorous with cap; tubes about 0.5mm deep. **Stipe:** 0.2–0.8cm long, 0.1–0.2cm thick; absent or short and lateral, attached to the cap obliquely from below; cylindrical or tapering slightly toward the apex, thin; surface slightly granulated; with darker orange patches; concolorous with cap. **Ring:** absent. **Flesh:** gelatinous, tough; paler colour than cap. **Smell:** no distinctive odour. **Spore print:** white.
SIMILAR SPECIES: *Favolaschia calocera* (not described here), first observed in Madagascar, is very similar in appearance.
EDIBILITY: Unknown.

NOTES: Many other species of the genus *Favolaschia* have been described from the tropics, and several colour variants have been named as subspecies of *F. thwaitesii*.

Unknown

The pore mouths are large and shallow.

Favolaschia thwaitesii grows on dead wood.

When appearing in large groups, the orange fruit bodies make for a dramatic sight.

The fruit bodies are small and delicate.

STALKED POLYPORES **203**

Photographs show examples of the species and key identifying features

Morphological group into which the species has been placed

What is a mushroom?

In general, the term 'mushroom' is applied to a fleshy fruit body that has a wide cap with gills underneath and a more or less cylindrical stipe, although the term can broadly be applied to other macrofungi that do not share these characteristics, such as boletes, polypores, brackets, puffballs, earthstars, stinkhorns and many more. These different forms, and their main features, are described in the table detailing morphological groups on pp. 21–23.

A mushroom, in the form of a fruit body, is the visible manifestation of a particular stage in the life cycle of an organism that generally lives below the surface of its habitat for most of the year. Hidden below the soil, inside wood, dung or leaves, or sometimes on the surface of the substrate, is the main body – the **mycelium** – of the fungus: an extensive network of fine, hair-like filaments called **hyphae**, which are the basic building blocks of a fungus. These threads extend at their tips to form branches that develop and spread through or on the substrate. Although the individual strands are invisible to the naked eye, they grow together to form the mycelium, a visible mass that constitutes the vegetative part of the mushroom. The mycelium is responsible for the nutrition and development of the fruit bodies.

The mycelium can be perennial and can survive for centuries; in some parts of the world large fungal organisms that are more than 2,000 years old have been discovered.

In some macrofungi, the mycelium is present as thin, white strands attached to the base. In others, the hyphae form much thicker, root-like mycelial cords or threads, the aggregation of which is called a **rhizomorph**. Microfungi, such as mildew or mould, develop a fine mycelial

PARTS OF A MUSHROOM

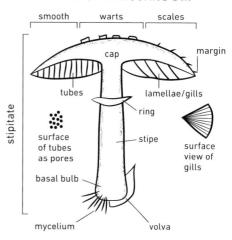

smooth warts scales

cap

margin

tubes

lamellae/gills

ring

stipitate

surface of tubes as pores

stipe

surface view of gills

basal bulb

mycelium

volva

PARTS OF A BRACKET FUNGUS

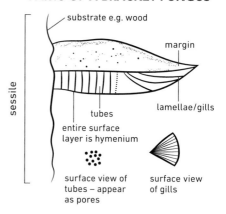

substrate e.g. wood

margin

sessile

tubes

lamellae/gills

entire surface layer is hymenium

surface view of tubes – appear as pores

surface view of gills

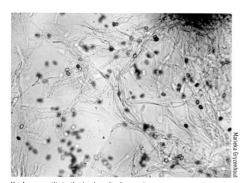

Hyphae constitute the basic unit of a mushroom.

In certain fungi, a rhizomorph forms at the base.

network that can be visible on the surface of the substrate, growing in conditions where there is sufficient moisture and food sources to sustain their growth.

Depending on a range of factors – including sufficient rain and favourable ground temperatures – the fruit body appears at soil level, ready to spread its **spores**.

The **cap** is usually supported on a **stipe** or stalk, although some mushrooms are sessile, being attached directly to the substrate without a stalk. In stalked mushrooms, the stipe is usually attached at the centre of the cap, to one side of it (excentric), or at the edge of the cap (lateral).

On the underside of the cap is the spore-bearing surface, which may be arranged in the form of **gills**, plate-like structures that hang downward, or **tubes**, which end in openings known as **pores**.

In many species, the young fruit body is entirely encased in a membrane called the **universal veil**, giving it the appearance of an egg. When the membrane ruptures, the remnants can be seen on a mature fruit body as a volva, a cup-like appendage at the base of the stipe, or as scales or warts on the surface of the cap.

Some mushrooms also have a second membrane, the **partial veil**, which covers the gills of the developing mushroom. As the cap expands, the membrane breaks away from the margin to expose the gills, allowing the spores to be disseminated. The remains of the partial veil persist as a **ring** of tissue around the stipe.

Macrofungi and microfungi

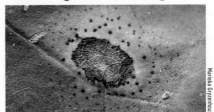
Marieka Gryzenhout

Many microfungi (visible as small black dots around the lesion on this leaf) are pathogens of plants.

Fungi are often divided into two broad groups: macrofungi and microfungi.

Those that produce large spore-bearing structures visible to the naked eye are commonly called macrofungi. A large variety of mushrooms fall into this category, including gilled mushrooms, boletes, brackets, puffballs, stinkhorns and earthstars, to name just a few. Most of the species covered in this book are macrofungi.

Microfungi are typically so small that they can only be observed microscopically. Some, however, are more readily detected by their bright colour or by the large, dense colonies of hyphae that they form on the host surface. They are incredibly diverse, and can be found wherever organic matter occurs – on plants, in the garden, or in the home. Some of the most commonly encountered microfungi are green mould on rotting vegetables, grey fluff on bread, tiny black spots on leaves, and even the grey or green veins in some mouldy cheeses.

Liz Popich

Fragments of the universal veil seen here around the stipe of a developing mushroom.

Liz Popich

The partial veil covers the gills in young mushrooms.

Growth and reproduction

Macrofungi propagate themselves by means of spores (similar to the seeds of plants) formed in special structures on the hymenial, or spore-bearing, surface of the fruit body. The structure of these surfaces, where they are located (externally on the outer surface or inside the fungus) and how the spores are released help to identify the species.

The spores are microscopic and are measured in microns (thousandths of a millimetre). As most spores range between 1 and 30 microns in size, microscopic analysis is required to identify them accurately. They also vary in texture, colour and shape, depending on the species. Spores may be formed sexually in different types of fruit bodies or asexually.

A single fruit body will produce thousands of spores, ensuring that at least some of them will develop into new colonies. Spores cannot move on their own, and are reliant on external processes for their dispersal; once ripe, they can be spread by air currents, wind, water, insects or animals, and each is adapted for its specific means of dispersal. For example, the spores of puffballs are ejected through a pore so that they can be dispersed by

In ink caps like *Coprinellus micaceus* (top left), spores are dispersed in the inky drops that fall to the ground as the cap liquifies. Stinkhorns, such as *Phallus rubicundus* (top right), rely on insects to distribute their spores. The spores of puffballs, including *Lycoperdon perlatum* (above), are released by the pressure of raindrops falling on the fruit body.

air currents; some ink caps distribute their spores by dissolving the gills into a sticky, black liquid; the spores produced in slime can be carried away by water or by insects; and the spore-bearing slime of stinkhorns exudes an odour that attracts flies, which feed on them and inadvertently distribute the spores that cling to them to new locations.

When the fungal spore lands on a suitable substrate and the conditions are favourable, it will germinate by shooting out a germ tube that will grow into the substrate. The germ tube develops into a hypha, which grows and branches to become the mycelium. As long as enough nutrition can be obtained from the substrate and suitable temperature and humidity levels exist, the mycelium will continue to expand the network of hyphae.

Knots develop in the mycelium, and these expand to grow into a mature fruit body on the surface of the substrate. Each species has its own particular set of environmental conditions that will trigger fruiting, with factors such as air temperature, humidity, moisture and type of substrate all playing a role. The dramatic expansion from mycelium to mature fruit body can usually be completed in a matter of hours.

The form of the spore-bearing structures serves as the basis for the subdivision of large fungi into separate groups. The spores of basidiomycetes develop on club-like structures, the basidia, which grow from the hymenium, either inside the fruit body or, more commonly, on the outer surface. Ascomycetes form their spores in sac-like structures called asci, which are sited in a fertile layer on the outer surface, in cups or within the fruit body. Another group of fungi, the Zygomycota, mostly grow in soil, on decaying plant matter or in dung. They differ from other groups in that their spores are created in globose structures called sporangia, each containing hundreds of spores.

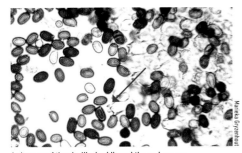

A close-up of the pin-like basidia and the oval spores.

Making a spore print

Although spores are microscopic, they are an important feature used by scientists in the identification of different fungi. The shape, colour, ornamentation and size of the spores are key diagnostic characteristics, and are particularly useful when distinguishing between morphologically similar species. A 'spore print' can be made to show these characteristics.

Choose fresh, mature fruit bodies to make spore prints. Start by removing a wedge-shaped piece from the cap or, alternatively, break off the stipe where it joins the cap and use the whole cap. Place the cap facing down on a piece of paper. Use white paper for dark spores and black paper for white and light-coloured spores (if unsure, use both types of paper).

A rust-brown spore print of a *Gymnopilus* species.

Position a cup or container over the cap and leave it for a few hours or overnight. You can also place a small drop of water on the cap to keep conditions moist and encourage the release of the spores, although this will not yield satisfactory results if the fruit bodies are too old.

After the spores have been released, lift the cap from the paper, taking care not to disturb the layer of spores on the paper. The spore print, which will mirror the shape of the gills or pores, should then be left to dry. Once dry, diagnostic features such as the colour and arrangement of the spores will be visible. However, to accurately describe the characters of the spores, they will need to be examined under a microscope.

If properly protected, spore prints can be stored for several years, making them a valuable resource for future research.

Identifying mushrooms

To positively identify a fungus, take careful note of the key morphological characters of the specimen, as well as the habitat and substrate on which it is growing. Start by observing the shape of the fruit body. Fungi exhibit a dazzling array of forms, all of which serve to protect the spore-producing structures (hymenium) and ensure spore dispersal. The location of the hymenium – on gills, in tubes, on smooth outer surfaces, or concealed inside fruit bodies – determines the form and, to some extent, the distinguishing features of the fungus.

The shape of the cap and the colour and texture of its upper surface (smooth, dry, sticky, scaly, hairy, etc.) also provide useful clues to the identity of a species. Other key characteristics include the colour, shape and spacing of the gills or pores on the undersurface and the attachment to the stipe.

The stipe presents features that can help to distinguish one species from another. The size, shape, texture and colour, as well as the presence of a ring, a volva, or a veil, are important.

The spore colour helps to identify the genus to which a fungus belongs. Look for spore deposits that may cover the surface below the cap, or make a spore print to find out the colour (see p. 11).

Also observe whether the fruit bodies stain or colour when they are touched or cut, and what odour they emit.

To aid accurate identification, mycologists use a number of precise terms to describe the key features of a macrofungus. These are presented in the illustrated glossary on pp. 14–15. Additional terms can be looked up in the glossary at the back of the book on pp. 352–353.

In addition, the table on pp. 21–23 will aid in understanding the main morphological characters of the fungus groups covered in this book.

Boletes have vertical tubes with pore-like openings.

The colour and minute pores of *Pycnoporus sanguineus* distinguish it from other brackets.

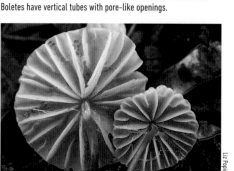

Marasmius species have gills that are well spaced.

The gills of *Leratiomyces* species are closely spaced.

FORMS OF FRUIT BODY

Circular

Fan-shaped

Spathulate/
Spatula-shaped

Oyster-shaped
(longitudinal radial section)

Hoof-shaped/ungulate
(side view)

Bracket-shaped/
shelf-like

TYPES OF STIPE

Central

Excentric

Lateral

CAP SHAPES

Bell-shaped

Globose

Deeply depressed

Depressed

Broadly umbonate

Umbonate

Egg-shaped/ovoid

Conical

Funnel-shaped

Broadly convex

Convex

Hemispherical

Plane/flat

CAP MARGINS (SURFACE VIEW)

Entire

Crenate

Crisped

Undulate /wavy

Lobate /lobed

Appendiculate (with veil remnants)

CAP MARGINS (SECTIONAL VIEW)

Inrolled

Incurved

Decurved

Plane

Upturned

Acute

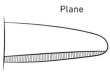
Obtuse

TYPES OF GILL ATTACHMENT

a. Free
b. Adnexed/ narrowly attached

c. Adnate/ broadly attached
d. Notched

e. Notched with decurrent tooth
f. Seceding/separating

Decurrent/ running down stipe

Depressed (tubes)

Distant

Subdistant

Close

Fanned

Crowded

Full and intermediate lengths

Forked

STIPE SHAPES

Cylindrical

Tapering toward base

Tapering downward

Bulbous base

Rooting base

Tapering upward

Club-shaped

The fungal kingdom

Although fungi were once regarded as lower plants, their unique morphology, biology and molecular characters distinguish them from other organisms such as plants and animals.

Fungi have cell walls that are composed of chitin rather than cellulose (the main constituent of plant cells). Chitin is a fibrous substance consisting of a certain type of carbohydrate that is also found in the exoskeleton of insects and in the shells of crabs and lobsters, making fungi more closely related to insects than plants.

Fungi also lack chlorophyll, a green pigment found in all plants, and thus cannot produce their own nutrients by means of photosynthesis. Instead, they excrete enzymes that break down and dissolve living and dead plant and animal matter into simpler nutrients that can be reabsorbed back into the fungal cells. The fungus stores the food reserves in the form of glycogen and lipids, not as carbohydrates (starch), as plants do.

One group of organisms commonly mistaken for fungi is the slime moulds. Initially regarded as fungi, they have now been shown by molecular research to be completely unrelated, and have since been reassigned to the Protista kingdom.

Classification of fungi

To make it easier to understand and study the natural world, scientists have organised all organisms into kingdoms, of which fungi is one. Within each kingdom, there are further subdivisions, based on the similarities and common characteristics of the organisms.

Scientifically, fungi are classified into several phyla, the two largest of which are Basidiomycota (about 50,000 species) and Ascomycota (around 90,000 species). The remaining groups are microscopic, with the better-known ones being Zygomycota, which includes bread moulds, and Chytridiomycota, which contains pathogens that are deadly to amphibians.

The phyla are further broken up into classes, then orders. In the orders, they are grouped into families, genera and species, based on similar features. Each species has its own scientific name, which usually comprises two Latinised or Greek words. The first name denotes the genus, whereas the second identifies the species (for example, *Amanita rubescens*). A third name indicates a subspecies.

To illustrate how scientific classification works, the example below shows the different levels for *Xerocomellus chrysenteron* (gilded bolete).

LEVELS OF CLASSIFICATION

Kingdom – Fungi
Subkingdom – Dikarya
Phylum – Basidiomycota
Class – Agaricomycetes
Order – Boletales
Family – Boletaceae
Genus – *Xerocomellus*
Species – *chrysenteron*

In the past, the classification of fungal species was based purely on morphological and biochemical characteristics. However, more recently, the development of DNA sequencing has led to far-reaching changes in fungal classification. As a result, many species have been reclassified and renamed, and it is likely that, as molecular approaches are applied more widely, many more changes will take place.

Slime moulds, such as *Ceratiomyxa fruticulosa*, become visible when they form large aggregations of single cells (called a plasmodium).

The role of mushrooms in nature

Like all other organisms on earth, fungi play a vital role in any ecosystem. They are closely associated with plants, animals and humans, and the type of relationship they have with their hosts dictates the particular functions they perform in nature.

The manner in which different fungi source food and grow also determines the role they play: **saprophytic** mushrooms grow on dead organic material, removing and recycling natural debris; **mychorrizal** fungi live in mutually beneficial relationships with plants; and **parasitic** fungi prey on plants and animals, helping to control population sizes, but also often destroying their hosts in the process.

Saprophytic fungi

Saprophytic fungi refer to those organisms that feed on dead or decaying plant matter or animal remains. They are extremely beneficial as decomposers of organic material, especially of cellulose and lignin in plants and chitin in insects and other animals, which few other types of organisms can break down. They also play an important role as nature's recyclers, turning dead leaves, branches, logs and roots into humus, minerals and nutrients, which are eventually returned to the soil and utilised by plants.

Although most saprophytic mushrooms are harmless, some species are responsible for structural damage in damp homes and buildings, where they cause rot in woodwork, or for the decay of food. The properties that enable fungi to function and grow can also be exploited in beneficial industrial, pharmaceutical and bioremediation processes, such as breaking down environmental pollutants and rehabilitating contaminated or toxic soil.

Mycorrhizal fungi

Many fungi form symbiotic relationships with living hosts, ranging from the smallest organisms such as algae to massive trees such as oaks. Mycorrhizal fungi exhibit a specific form of symbiosis, involving fungi and the roots of plants. In these mutually beneficial relationships, fungal hyphae penetrate the outer layers of the roots of their host to obtain carbohydrates, using this food to develop an extensive mycelial network in the substrate. In return, the mycelium helps the host plant to absorb water and essential minerals, especially phosphates, to encourage growth. In some species, the hyphae perform an additional function by protecting the roots from pathogens.

Many mushrooms in this group are closely associated with specific host species, and foragers

Many bracket species are saprophytic, breaking down dead organic matter.

will soon learn that certain mushrooms will grow under or near particular trees. Coniferous trees such as pines grow in nutrient-poor soils and benefit from a symbiotic relationship with mycorrhizal species such as *Lactarius deliciosus* (pine ring) and certain species of *Russula* and *Boletus*. Similarly, *Leccinum duriusculum* (poplar bolete) has evolved to coexist with poplar trees, and *Amauroderma rude* (brown stalked polypore) with wattle trees.

Parasitic fungi

Parasitic fungi attack living plants, causing diseases such as leaf spot, leaf blight, mildew and others. Some bracket fungi in particular can cause trunk rot, and eventually death, in living trees. Although this may have a beneficial outcome by killing off other plants to provide more space and nutrients for seedlings, parasitism may also result in the infection of agricultural crops, potentially causing food shortages and significant economic losses.

Some fungi parasitise insects or their larvae or pupae, representing a natural biological method of controlling populations of potentially harmful organisms. A variety of parasitic fungi also occur in humans and animals, leading to conditions such as respiratory tract, skin or nail infections and diseases like ringworm.

Other fungal associations

Many fungi have evolved to form highly specialised relationships with specific hosts.

Lichens are composite organisms, formed by fungi in association with a photosynthetic partner such as green algae or bacteria. Algae are able to use sunlight to photosynthesise carbon dioxide and moisture from the air, enabling them to produce carbohydrates, which are made available to the fungi. The fungi reciprocate by absorbing and retaining water, thus protecting the algae from drying out. This symbiosis allows lichens to survive on some of the most extreme substrates in many different environments, including deserts and the polar regions where nothing else can grow. They play an important role in nature by colonising ecosystems and microhabitats, weathering rocks to release nutrients, providing nourishment for animals, and serving as a gauge of air-pollution levels.

Fascinating symbiotic associations exist between termites and mushrooms of the genus *Termitomyces*. The mushrooms are cultivated and tended in special fungal gardens in the nests of wood-destroying termites. The termites deposit partially digested wood and wood debris in the form of faecal pellets under the mycelia, which extract the nutrients they require to form small nodules of hyphae. The nodules, in turn, serve as food for the termite colony. Depleted fungal gardens are often deposited outside the nest, and fruit bodies of different species may later emerge in the discarded soil. Some species, such as *Termitomyces umkowaan* (I'kowe), emerge from the termite mound to produce large fruit bodies on the surface.

Pycnoporus sanguineus is both saprophytic and parasitic, causing white-rot decay in wood.

Some termites cultivate small fungi inside the nest.

Edible and poisonous mushrooms

Foraging for fungi in nature is a popular pastime for many people. For these enthusiasts the taste and texture of wild mushrooms is incomparable, and more than enough reward for the time and effort it takes to seek out these wonderful delicacies.

For the novice, there are no obvious signs indicating which fungi are edible or inedible, and which are poisonous. By far the majority of fungi are harmless, and the challenge lies in being able to discern edible fungi from those that are poisonous. There is no simple rule of thumb to determine edibility or toxicity, and the only reliable way to establish if a mushroom is edible is to make a positive identification.

Although the number of really dangerous mushrooms is confined to only a few genera, these include some of the most poisonous organisms on earth. The genus *Amanita* contains many deadly species, with the notorious *Amanita phalloides* (death cap) responsible for most cases of fatal mushroom poisoning. Some *Amanita* mushrooms can easily be mistaken for the generally edible *Agaricus* species. The first signs of poisoning from consuming the 'death cap' set in between 5 and 30 hours after consumption. Initial symptoms may include vomiting, diarrhoea and abdominal pains, but once the toxins reach the blood stream, treatment may be too late – and it is likely that the victim will die from kidney or liver failure, or heart damage.

Not all toxic species are deadly poisonous. Some mushrooms contain a variety of harmful compounds that can cause nausea, diarrhoea, abdominal cramps, constricted blood vessels, hallucinations or alcohol-like intoxication. Genera in this group include *Boletus*, *Lactarius*, *Marasmius* and *Russula*. In some cases, the toxins are destroyed in cooking.

The edible *Boletus edulis* (porcini) has a nutty taste.

Other mushrooms affect the central nervous system. These include *Amanita muscaria* (fly agaric) and species of the *Panaeolus* and *Inocybe* genera, which produce toxins that cause blurred vision, profuse sweating, vomiting, hallucinations, delirium and convulsions. These mushrooms are sometimes used intentionally for their hallucinogenic properties. Another genus of hallucinogenic fungi, *Psilocybe*, has been used for sacred rituals in places such as Central America and Russia. There is strong evidence to suggest that psilocybin, the active compound in these mushrooms, may have wider application in the medical field, specifically in the treatment of depression and anxiety.

Microfungi that grow on stored grains and foodstuffs can cause serious illnesses in humans and animals. Although these organisms are not regarded as edible, they are often not visible to the naked eye and may be ingested inadvertently.

It is vital that you heed the warnings about toxicity mentioned in this guide. **If there is any doubt about the edibility of a harvested mushroom, it is best to obtain expert advice and to refrain from eating the specimen.**

If ingested, *Amanita phalloides* is potentially fatal.

Amanita muscaria has hallucinogenic properties.

Foraging for mushrooms

The secret to a successful mushroom hunt lies in knowing one's 'hunting ground'. A thorough knowledge of nearby forests or other areas where mushrooms are likely to grow will help you to locate good specimens before they decay or disappear – or get plucked by fellow mushroom gatherers. There is a good chance that the same species will appear in the same spot each year, so make a point of remembering the locations of previously successful harvests.

It is advisable to begin the hunt early in the morning, before sunlight and warmth dry out freshly erupted specimens – and before other foragers find them. However, there's some benefit in harvesting the more viscid species of mushroom later in the day, when their surface will, to some extent, have dried.

Before setting off, equip yourself with a sharp pocketknife, a small brush to dust off the soil, a large basket or well-ventilated container, and tin foil or wax paper to wrap individual specimens.

When you fill your basket, take care to place the firmer mushrooms at the bottom and the fragile ones on top.

Mushrooms should be removed carefully, making sure that the entire fruit body is dug out. Avoid simply cutting them off at the base, as the parts left behind will rot and infect the mycelium, and no mushrooms will emerge in the area for several weeks.

Try to pick mushrooms in quantities that can be used immediately. Wild mushrooms are best picked, cooked and eaten on the same day. Alternatively, they can be stored in a cardboard box in the fridge for a day or two, depending on the species (the cardboard container may prolong their shelf life). Avoid washing mushrooms with water as they can get soggy. Rather wipe them with a damp cloth.

Mushrooms can be frozen, as long as they are cooked beforehand, but should be eaten within two months of freezing. Some edible mushrooms can be dried for later use; their flavour becomes more intense as they dehydrate.

Tips for foragers

Mushroom poisoning is very unpleasant and could result in death, so learning how to distinguish between poisonous and edible mushrooms is essential for any mushroom collector.

The following guidelines should be observed when collecting mushrooms.

- When starting out as a mushroom collector, it is advisable to apprentice yourself to an experienced and knowledgeable forager or mycology expert.
- Some poisonous mushrooms look very similar to edible ones, so make sure you are familiar with the dangerous species.
- Pick only whole, fresh specimens as some mature mushrooms may cause food poisoning. Avoid mushrooms that smell rotten, look wilted or mouldy, or are infested with insects. If you are in doubt about a mushroom's edibility, do not use it in cooking until it can be identified.
- Store each species separately once picked. Paper bags are preferable to plastic, as the latter will result in rapid deterioration of the mushrooms.
- When in doubt about a mushroom's edibility, wrap it separately from the edible species and store it in a different container for positive identification later.
- Avoid eating raw mushrooms; some may cause unpleasant side effects when consumed. In some species, the harmful compounds can be destroyed during cooking.
- Clean insects and dirt from the mushrooms before cooking them.

As a precaution, the edibility or toxicity of mushrooms featured in this book has been clearly indicated on the species pages.

While collecting mushrooms for the pot can be very satisfying, foragers must make sure they can distinguish between edible and poisonous varieties.

Lastly, remember to obtain a mushroom permit from the relevant parks and reserves authority in your city or town. If you are foraging on private land, always get permission from the landowner.

Photographing mushrooms

Sharp, clear colour photographs that capture all the observable morphological characters of a specimen are an invaluable aid in identifying a fungal species.

It helps to have a camera lens that can take close-range images, and to pay careful attention to lighting. Many fungi are small and grow in dark places such as forests, while others may be found on lawns, in full sunlight; such contrasting situations can result in images that are under- or over-exposed. Although you do not need particularly sophisticated gear, a good macro lens and close-up filter will help to achieve a level of detail not possible with a standard lens. Another option is to photograph the specimen through a 20x magnifying hand lens.

Smartphones are increasingly being used in macro photography, and there are a number of useful tools available to facilitate excellent close-up shots. A high-quality smartphone lens attachment and the phone's in-built magnifier function will go some way to getting a detailed shot of the subject.

It is best to avoid using a flash, which can add an artificial glare to the image. If, however, the light source is not adequate, a ring flash or ring light can be used for illumination and to soften shadows. A reflector will also come in handy to light up the underside of the mushroom. A good tripod is essential to keep your camera or smartphone stable while shooting fungi in the field.

There may be instances when the specimen needs to be removed from the substrate in order to better view all its parts. When digging up a mushroom for study purposes (whether from a log or from the soil), take care to extract the entire mushroom, especially if it has a volva. Avoid breaking the cap or stipe.

The following features should be photographed to facilitate identification:
- top and underside of the cap
- top and side views of the fruit body
- stipe and basal parts, including the volva
- longitudinal cross section, showing the interior and the attachment of the gills, tubes or spines to the stipe
- any discolorations or interesting features
- a spore print (see p. 11)
- where possible, different stages of development, from small button to decaying mushroom
- the habitat, or substrate, upon which the fungus was found.

It is also useful to show the relative size of the specimen. This can be achieved by placing a size bar or a comparative object (such as a coin or a matchbox) next to the mushroom.

Morphological groups of fungi

GROUP	CHARACTERISTICS	REPRESENTATIVE SPECIES
Gills pp. 24–161	Mushrooms with gills on the underside of the cap and a stipe. The gills carry the structures that form the spores.	Marcel Terblanche
Sessile gills pp. 162–171	Mushrooms with gills on the underside of the cap. Stipe is absent and the cap is attached directly by its base to the substrate.	Marieka Gryzenhout
Boletes pp. 172–197	Fleshy mushrooms with a cap and a stipe, and with tubes, instead of gills, on the lower surface of the cap, giving it a sponge-like texture. The closely packed tubes are distinct from the flesh of the cap, and open on the surface as pores.	Gary B Goldman
Stalked polypores pp. 198–211	May or may not have a typical mushroom shape, are usually not fleshy and have pores, ranging from large to minute, on the underside of the cap. The polypores featured in this book have a more or less distinct stipe.	Liz Popich
Brackets pp. 212–245	Form shelves, fans or brackets, are woody, and usually grow from tree trunks or branches. If present, the stipe is rudimentary. The spore-producing surface consists of tubes that open as pores.	Jean Stephenson
Crusts pp. 246–257	Usually flat on the bark (resupinate), occasionally 'peeling off' or looking like paint. Can be soft, spongy to thin, tough, crust-like, or bracket-like. The spore-producing surface can be smooth, wrinkled, veined or warted (no pores or tubes). Although bracket-like, *Stereum* species belong in this group, as their spore-producing surfaces are smooth.	Liz Popich

Bird's nest fungi pp. 258–262 	Small, cup-shaped fruit bodies with spore packets (peridioles) inside. Some species have strands attached to the packets, others have packets immersed in a sticky gel.	
Puffballs, stalked puffballs pp. 263–275 	Round to oval or pear-shaped fruit bodies, with or without a stipe. In stalked species, the stipe terminates at the base of the spore sac and is not part of it. The spores are produced within the fruit body, either in one big sac-like structure or in spore chambers. Depending on the species, the spores are released when the skin of the spore sac disintegrates or when a pore develops.	
Earthstars pp. 276–291 	Round to oval at first, the fruit body's outer layer splits open and curves back in a star-shaped pattern to reveal a round ball in which the spores have developed. The spores are released through a pore, or several pores.	
Stinkhorns pp. 292–313 	Various shapes and sizes (from elongated to branched or lattice-like), but some part is always covered with a greenish, brown or black, putrid-smelling slime that contains the spores. The structures develop from a membraneous sac, which persists at the base of the mature specimen as a volva.	
Clubs pp. 314 	Fruit bodies are more or less club-shaped, erect and unbranched. Spores are formed over the entire surface.	
Corals pp. 315–317 	Simply or intricately branched, the fruit bodies resemble sea corals. In most cases, spores are formed over the entire surface.	

Coral jellies, jellies, jelly ears pp. 318–333	Have a rubbery or gelatinous texture, some displaying a characteristically convoluted shape and others looking like jelly with no definite shape. Some have a cap and stipe, are coral-like or cup-like, while others are flat or bracket-like. The spore-bearing surface is smooth, veined, lobed or toothed.	 *Liz Popich*
Saddles pp. 334–335	Typically saddle-shaped, with a heavily folded cap and a grooved stipe (looking like a mushroom). The spore-bearing structures (asci) are located on the cap surface.	 *Gary B Goldman*
Morels pp. 336	Irregularly lobed, brain-like or honeycomb-like fruit body, with a cap raised on a stipe. The spores are produced in spore-bearing structures on the upper surface.	 *Justin Williams*
Truffles pp. 337–338	Tuber-like, round to oval and occurring underground. The interior may be solid with veins, hollow, or with cavities or canals. The texture inside can be firm or powdery but never gelatinous.	 *Jo Dames*
Flask fungi pp. 339–343	A large and diverse group of ascomycetes, ranging from microscopically small to large enough to see with the naked eye and occurring in a wide range of habitats. The spores are produced in tiny flask-shaped organs called perithecia. These organs can be on their own and appear in a variety of colours, or they can be embedded in larger structures with the mouths of the perithecia protruding from the surface as little dots or bumps.	 *Liz Popich*
Cup fungi pp. 344–347	Flat to disc- or cup-shaped fruit bodies, with or without a stipe. The spore-bearing surface is on the inner layer of the cup.	 *Liz Popich*
Microfungi pp. 344–345	*Pilobolus crystallinus* is included here as a member of the Zygomycota phylum. The spores of *Pilobolus* species are produced in round structures (sporangia) on hyphae that are extensions of the mycelium.	 *Liz Popich*

The gills are free from the stipe and spaced close together under the cap.

The rough, frilly margin is characteristic of *Amanita aureofloccosa*.

Amanita aureofloccosa Bas 1969

Common name: Golden floccose lepidella
Afrikaans: Goud-lepidella

Etymology: ANCIENT GREEK: *amanitai* = a kind of mushroom;
LATIN: *aureus* = gold, *floccose* = covered with woolly tufts

Synonym(s): *Aspidella aurea, A. aureofloccosa, Lepiota aurea,
L. zenkeri*

ECOLOGY: Mycorrhizal.

DISTRIBUTION: First reported in South Africa in Gauteng (Pretoria),
but may be more widespread. Occurs in Brazil, New Zealand and the
Democratic Republic of the Congo.

HABITAT: Grows in grasslands and broadleaved forests; fruit bodies
single or in small groups.

DESCRIPTION: The golden-yellow colour and shaggy appearance
of the fruit body make this a distinctive species. **Cap:** up to 8cm in
diameter; thin-fleshed; plano-convex; margin rough, frilly; surface
covered with fine woolly tufts or minute scales that can easily be
removed; golden yellow to orange-yellow. **Gills:** free, crowded, narrow
to moderately broad, short; white. **Stipe:** up to 14cm long, 0.7–1.8cm
thick; central; cylindrical, tapering upward; surface covered with
woolly tufts or scales; pale yellow at the base and apex, the rest
orange-yellow; hollow. **Ring:** free, somewhat crowded, narrow to
moderately broad; pale yellow, becoming white. **Flesh:** thick, firm;
white. **Smell:** no distinctive odour. **Spore print:** white.

EDIBILITY: Unknown.

The stipe tapers slightly upward.

> **NOTES:** *Amanita aureofloccosa* was originally described as a *Lepiota*
> from a dry forest in the Democratic Republic of the Congo.

Small, woolly tufts cover the cap; they are easily detached, leaving the surface bare.

The stipe surface is tufted to scaly.

The remains of the cuticle can be seen on the smooth, umber-brown surface of the cap.

Marcel Terblanche

Amanita excelsa (Fr.) Bertill. 1866

Common names: Grey spotted amanita, European false blusher
Afrikaans: None

Etymology: ANCIENT GREEK: *amanitai* = a kind of mushroom;
LATIN: *excelsus* = tall, lofty

Synonym(s): *Amanita ampla, A. raphaniodora, A. solida, A. spissa*
var. *excelsa, Venenarius excelsus*

Edible

ECOLOGY: Mycorrhizal.

DISTRIBUTION: Eastern Cape and Gauteng. Occurs in the UK, Europe,
USA, India, China and Zimbabwe (Eastern Highlands).

HABITAT: Grows under coniferous and sometimes broadleaved
trees; fruit bodies single or in small groups.

DESCRIPTION: This large, grey- to brown-capped mushroom has a
very variable appearance. **Cap:** 8–12cm in diameter; fleshy; globose
to hemispherical, becoming flat; margin even, smooth, splitting,
turning upward with age; surface smooth, irregular, with cuticle,
dry; brown-grey to umber-brown. **Gills:** free, crowded, full and
intermediate lengths, thin; white. **Stipe:** 8–10cm long, up to 2.5cm
thick; central; stout, thick, widening downward toward the bulbous
base; striate above the ring, ridges of scales (remains of the volva)
appearing over the upper part of the base below the ring; white
above the ring, ash-grey to pale olive-grey below; fleshy, tough, solid.
Ring: membraneous, persistent; upper part striate, white, lower part
ash-grey to pale olive-grey. **Flesh:** firm, thick; white. **Smell:** faint,
unpleasant odour. **Spore print:** white.

SIMILAR SPECIES: *Amanita rubescens* differs in colour and, unlike
A. excelsa, stains red when cut or bruised. *A. pantherina* has white
pyramidal warts on the cap and a ridge-like rim of volva warts at the
base of the stipe.

EDIBILITY: Edible; however, best avoided since it can easily be
confused with the highly poisonous *Amanita pantherina*.

The surface of the stipe between the ring
and the crowded gills is striate.

The stipe, above the bulbous base, is
covered with downy, ochraceous scales.

The cap cuticle dries and cracks irregularly.

The cap surface of *Amanita foetidissima* is covered with large, thick, soft, irregular scales.

Fragments of the partial veil are visible along the edge of the cap margin.

Amanita foetidissima D.A. Reid & Eicker 1991

Common names: Stinker, stinker lepidella
Afrikaans: Stinksampioen

Etymology: ANCIENT GREEK: *amanitai* = a kind of mushroom;
LATIN: *foetid* = fetid, stinking, *-issimus* = superlative

Synonym(s): *Saproamanita foetidissima*

Unknown

ECOLOGY: Saprophytic.

DISTRIBUTION: Western Cape, Eastern Cape, Gauteng, KwaZulu-Natal and Mpumalanga; appears to be native to South Africa.

HABITAT: Grows in grassy places; fruit bodies single or grouped.

DESCRIPTION: This species is readily recognised by the pale-cream to brownish colour and the coarsely scaled cap and stipe. **Cap:** 0.45–12cm in diameter; fleshy; somewhat conical when young, expanding to convex; margin regular, inrolled, extending slightly beyond the gills, appendiculate (with adhering veil fragments); surface covered with large, thick, soft, irregular scales arranged in more or less concentric circles, slightly sticky, adhering to fingers when handled; pale creamy white to buff, scales cream to buff, occasionally tinged pale brown. **Gills:** free, crowded, full and intermediate lengths, thin, edges entire, up to 0.8cm wide; creamy white or with a pale-pinkish tinge. **Stipe:** 9–18cm long, 1.2–2.2cm thick; central; widening downward to the bulbous, short-rooting base; area below the ring covered with soft, irregular scales, faint rings of wart-like scales appearing on the upper surface of the basal bulb; pale cream to pale buff; fleshy, tough, solid. **Ring:** fixed, membraneous, striate on upper surface, persistent. **Flesh:** firm; creamy white. **Smell:** urine-like odour. **Spore print:** white.

SIMILAR SPECIES: Distinguished from other *Amanita* species by its distinctive odour.

EDIBILITY: Unknown. Since most *Amanita* species are considered poisonous, this species is best regarded as inedible.

The fleshy, somewhat conical, cap is characteristic of young specimens.

NOTES: Heavy rain may wash the scales away, making recognition by sight difficult. Its odour may help you make a positive identification.

The stipe widens toward the bulbous base. In young specimens, the margin is inrolled.

The gills are creamy white or have a pinkish tinge.

Amanita foetidissima, showing different stages of development.

The crowded, whitish gills, skirt-like ring and volva surrounding the bulbous base are distinctive features of *Amanita mappa*.

Amanita mappa Pers. 1797

Common names: False death cap, citrine bulbous amanita, lemon amanita
Afrikaans: Geelhoedamaniet

Etymology: ANCIENT GREEK: *amanitai* = a kind of mushroom;
LATIN: *mappa* = napkin, cloth

Synonym(s): *Amanita bulbosa* var. *citrina*, *A. citrina*,
Amanitina citrina, *Venenarius mappa*

Edible

ECOLOGY: Mycorrhizal.

DISTRIBUTION: First reported in South Africa in the Western Cape and
Mpumalanga, but may be more widespread. Occurs in the UK, Europe,
Canada, USA, Mexico, Costa Rica, Russia, Taiwan, Japan and Australia.

HABITAT: Grows in broadleaved and sometimes coniferous forests;
fruit bodies single or grouped.

DESCRIPTION: The pale lemon-yellow to white cap, patches of
adhering veil remnants, skirt-like stipe ring and bulbous base make
this species easy to identify. **Cap:** 3–8cm in diameter; hemispherical,
then flattening out, upturned when mature; covered with large, or
several smaller, thick, flat, whitish to brownish patches (remnants of
the veil), which may wash off in the rain; ivory to pale lemon-yellow
or greenish yellow, especially near the centre. **Gills:** adnexed, free,
crowded; whitish to very pale cream. **Stipe:** 5–11cm long, 1–2cm
thick; central; cylindrical, tall in proportion to cap, tapering upward,
large basal bulb surrounded by cup-like volva; striated above the
ring; white; hollow. **Ring:** near stipe apex, large, striated, almost
skirt-like, fragile; white. **Flesh:** firm; white. **Smell:** similar to odour of
freshly dug potatoes, radishes or celery. **Spore print:** white.

SIMILAR SPECIES: *Amanita phalloides* has a sac-like volva, which is
less yellow and more greenish. *A. rubescens* and *A. pantherina* also
have scales on the cap.

EDIBILITY: Edible; however, best avoided since it can easily be
confused with the lethal *Amanita phalloides*.

NOTES: According to research at the University of Cambridge, this
mushroom contains the alpha-amanitin toxin. Although the amount
contained in a single specimen is neglible, the toxin may cause harm
if the mushroom were to be ingested in large quantities.

The partial veil persists as a fragile, wavy
ring around the upper section of the stipe.

A young specimen emerges from a
ruptured volva.

Remnants of the unversal veil adhere to
the surface of the cap; they may wash off
in the rain.

The cap is initially hemispherical then flat, becoming upturned at the margin with age.

The scarlet cap, scattered with conspicuous white warts, and the fleshy, central stipe make *Amanita muscaria* (fly agaric) easy to identify.

Gary B Goldman

Amanita muscaria (L.) Lam. 1783

Common names: Fly agaric, fly amanita, fly mushroom
Afrikaans: Vlieëgifswam

Etymology: ANCIENT GREEK: *amanitai* = a kind of mushroom;
LATIN: *musca* = fly, *-aria* = relating to

Synonym(s): *Amanitaria muscaria*, *Venenarius muscarius*

ECOLOGY: Mycorrhizal.

DISTRIBUTION: Widespread in South Africa. Occurs in the UK,
Europe, Canada, USA, Russia and Australia.

HABITAT: Grows in forests, particularly under oak and pine trees;
fruit bodies single or grouped.

DESCRIPTION: The classic storybook mushroom, *Amanita muscaria*'s
bright red, white-warted cap makes it one of the most distinctive
species of fungus. **Cap:** 5–20cm in diameter; fleshy; hemispherical at
first, becoming flat; margin even, usually striate, with adhering white
veil remnants; surface smooth, sticky, covered with white pyramidal
warts that may be removed by rain, cuticle detachable; scarlet to
orange to yellow. **Gills:** free, crowded, full and intermediate lengths;
white. **Stipe:** 10–25cm long, 1.5–2.5cm thick; central; cylindrical or
widening to a bulbous base, covered with shaggy, loose scales and
ridges over the upper half of the base; white to yellowish; firm, solid
or stuffed. **Ring:** membraneous, almost skirt-like, fragile, often drying
and disappearing; white. **Flesh:** soft; white. **Smell:** no distinctive
odour. **Spore print:** white.

SIMILAR SPECIES: *Amanita caeasarea* (not described here).

EDIBILITY: Poisonous; seldom fatal. Has a bitter taste. The toxicity
of *Amanita muscaria* is mistakenly said to be caused by muscarine,
a compound found in many other poisonous mushrooms. Although
A. muscaria contains tiny concentrations of muscarine, it is ibotenic
acid that makes this species toxic. Ibotenic acid also occurs in other
amanitas, sometimes at higher concentrations.

NOTES: Not all poisonings caused by *Amanita* species are accidental:
in many cases, the mushrooms are consumed specifically for their
psychoactive effects, and much has been written about their use in
ceremonial and ritualistic practices in parts of Siberia and elsewhere.

Poisonous

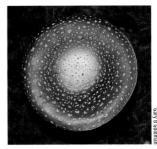

The cap is covered with white warts that may
come off in the rain.

The yellow coloration is usually caused by a
lack of moisture or direct sunlight.

The membraneous ring is attached to the
stipe at the apex.

White spores are visible on the hymenial surface.

The volva is present as several concentric rings at the base of the stipe.

Lenita du Plessis

34   GILLS

Amanita pantherina (DC.) Krombh. 1846

Common names: Panther, warted agaric, panther cap, panther amanita
Afrikaans: Tiersampioen

Etymology: ANCIENT GREEK: *amanitai* = a kind of mushroom; GREEK: *panther* = panther, *-ina* = resembling
Synonym(s): *Amplariella pantherina*

Deadly poisonous

ECOLOGY: Mycorrhizal.

DISTRIBUTION: Widespread in South Africa. Occurs in the UK, Europe, Canada, USA, Russia, Japan and Australia.

HABITAT: Grows under broadleaved and coniferous trees; fruit bodies single, scattered or grouped.

DESCRIPTION: The pale greyish-brown cap that is dotted with white warts or scales, the striate cap margin, the volva rings and the ridges around the basal part of the stipe are the main characteristics of this species. **Cap:** 5–20cm in diameter; fleshy; hemispherical, later flattening; margin even, striate, curving upward; surface smooth, sticky, covered with white pyramidal warts that may be washed away by rain; pale greyish brown, later smoky brown, yellow-brown or brown-olive. **Gills:** free, crowded, thin; white. **Stipe:** 10–25cm long, 1.5–2.5cm thick; central; firm, smooth, widening toward the base, volva enclosing the bulbous base, with white rings and ridges from the volva remaining on the base; white; fleshy, tough, solid turning hollow. **Ring:** tattered, membraneous, persistent; white. **Flesh:** soft; white. **Smell:** no distinctive odour. **Spore print:** white.

SIMILAR SPECIES: *Amanita excelsa, A. rubescens.*

EDIBILITY: Deadly poisonous. This species causes nausea, vomiting and unconsciousness 1–3 hours after eating. Can result in death if left untreated. Poisoning in *Amanita pantherina* is caused by the compound ibotenic acid, of which *A. pantherina* has a higher concentration than *A. muscaria*.

White, pyramidal warts appear in concentric rings on the caps of young specimens.

Amanita pantherina specimens, showing the thick, central stipe, bulbous base and volva.

The gills are not attached to the stipe.

Glen van Niekerk

Amanita phalloides, known as the death cap, is the most deadly poisonous species in the fungi kingdom.

Gary B Goldman

A young specimen, its cap already turning from white to greenish olive-yellow, emerges from the soil.

Amanita phalloides (Vaill. ex Fr.) Link 1833

Common names: Death cap, death cup, poison amanita
Afrikaans: Duiwelsbrood, slangkos

Etymology: ANCIENT GREEK: *amanitai* = a kind of mushroom; LATIN: *phallus* = swollen, puffed up, phallus-like; *-oides* = likeness

Synonym(s): *Agaricus phalloides, Amanitina phalloides, Venenarius phalloides*

Deadly poisonous

ECOLOGY: Mycorrhizal.

DISTRIBUTION: Widespread in South Africa. Occurs in the UK, Europe, Canada, USA, Russia, Japan, Australia and New Zealand.

HABITAT: Grows in forests, particularly under oak and conifer trees, sometimes under poplar trees; fruit bodies single or scattered.

DESCRIPTION: The smooth greenish-yellow to olive cap, sometimes with veil remnants, the ring near the stipe apex, and the large white volva are characteristic of this mushroom. **Cap:** 5–15cm in diameter; fleshy; subglobose, becoming convex then flattened; margin even, downturned, splitting, can have adhering veil fragments; surface smooth, sticky when wet, like satin when dry, can be streaked with radiating dark fibrils; white becoming greenish olive-yellow, smoky brown to olive. **Gills:** free, crowded, full and intermediate lengths, thin; white. **Stipe:** 5–15cm long, 0.8–2cm thick; central; cylindrical, widening into a bulbous base which is enclosed in a large, white volva; smooth or fairly banded; white; fleshy, tough, solid becoming hollow. **Ring:** near the stipe apex, membraneous, persistent; white. **Flesh:** thin; white with a faint yellowish flush under the skin. **Smell:** sweet when young, unpleasant fetid odour when older. **Spore print:** white.

SIMILAR SPECIES: *Amanita mappa, Volvariella speciosa*, which has a prominent volva.

EDIBILITY: Deadly; highly toxic, responsible for the majority of fatal mushroom poisonings worldwide. The type of amatoxins found in *Amanita phalloides* are phallotoxins and amanitins. Amatoxin poisoning from *A. phalloides* occurs in four phases. Initially, in the first 8–12 hours after consumption, there are no signs of poisoning (in severe cases, the onset time can be 6 hours or less; in mild cases it can take 2–3 days). In the second phase, which may last for up to 48 hours, the patient experiences severe abdominal pain and cramping, vomiting and watery diarrhoea. Symptoms subside for about 24 hours during the third phase, the patient assuming the ordeal is over. In the fourth, sometimes fatal, phase, the abdominal pain returns, progressively accompanied by bloody diarrhoea, the onset of jaundice, possible kidney failure, convulsions, coma, and, in approximately 10–15% of victims, death.

NOTES: It is estimated that ingesting half a cap of this mushroom is enough to result in death. Toxicity is *not* reduced by cooking, freezing or drying the mushroom.

The membraneous ring and prominent volva are identifying features.

The cap is subglobose in younger specimens.

The cap flattens with age.

Loose, cotton-like scales cover the cap of the developing *Amanita praeclara*, giving it a fluffy appearance.

The gills are narrowly attached to the stipe.

Amanita praeclara (A. Pearson) Bas. 1969

Common name: Playing field lepidella
Afrikaans: Speelveld-lepidella

Etymology: ANCIENT GREEK: *amanitai* = a kind of mushroom; LATIN: *praeclārus* = very bright

Synonym(s): *Aspidella praeclara*, *Lepiota praeclara*, *Saproamanita praeclara*

ECOLOGY: Saprophytic.

KNOWN DISTRIBUTION: To date, found only in South Africa (Western Cape and Gauteng), suggesting it is native to the country.

HABITAT: Grows in grassy areas; fruit bodies often in fairy rings.

DESCRIPTION: The large, almost fluffy-looking, white to pale-yellow cap and stipe are unmistakable, making it easy to identify this species. **Cap:** 1–10cm in diameter; thick-fleshed; globose to plano-convex, sometimes slightly depressed at the centre; margin fringed with remains of the veil; surface covered with fine hairs to minute scales, smooth or with some poorly delimited felted to warty elevated patches over the centre when older, young specimens covered with white hair-like filaments or woolly tufts; white, staining pale yellow. **Gills:** adnexed to free, crowded to subdistant, thin, rather broad, straight or ventricose; white to cream, staining pale yellow, butter-coloured when older. **Stipe:** 7–13cm long, less than 0.1–2cm thick; central; cylindrical, smooth, glabrous; white; solid, firm. **Ring:** forming near the apex, broad, membraneous, covered with woolly tufts, pendent, margin torn; white. **Flesh:** cap white with a marshmallow texture; stipe white, lemon-coloured when cut. **Smell:** no distinctive odour; stipe has a soapy smell. **Spore print:** white.

SIMILAR SPECIES: *Amanita thiersii* (not described here), found in the USA, has a similar appearance.

EDIBILITY: Edible.

The cap of the young fungus is composed of minute, hair-like filaments.

The ring is covered with woolly tufts.

Felted to warty patches appear over the centre of the cap in older specimens.

The cap can grow up to 16cm in diameter.

Amanita rubescens may grow on relatively poor soil in broadleaved and coniferous woodlands.

The cap surface is covered with patches of irregular, loose scales.

Amanita rubescens <small>Pers. 1797</small>

Common names: Blusher, blushing amanita, false panther, pearl mushroom
Afrikaans: Vals tieramaniet

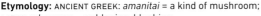

Etymology: ANCIENT GREEK: *amanitai* = a kind of mushroom; LATIN: *rubescens* = reddening, blushing

Synonym(s): *Amplariella rubescens*, *Limacium rubescens*

Edible

ECOLOGY: Mycorrhizal.

DISTRIBUTION: Widespread in South Africa. Occurs in the UK, Europe, Canada, USA, Russia, Japan and Australia.

HABITAT: Grows in broadleaved and coniferous forests; fruit bodies single, scattered or grouped.

DESCRIPTION: The reddish colours of the fruit body, the slightly greenish, striate, pendulous ring, and the tendency of the flesh to turn pink when cut or bruised are characteristic. **Cap:** 6–15cm in diameter; hemispherical turning flat; margin even, smooth to faintly striate; surface smooth, patches of irregular, loose scales; russet-pink to rose-brown to red-brown to pink-fawn. **Gills:** free, crowded, full and intermediate lengths, thin, soft; pure white, staining russet-pink when bruised. **Stipe:** 6–14cm long, 0.5–1.5cm thick; basal bulb with volva of several concentric warty rings; white with flushes of cap colour. **Ring:** membranous; white, staining red. **Flesh:** soft; white, orange-red beneath cuticle. **Smell:** no distinctive odour. **Spore print:** white.

The stipe is white with flushes of the cap colour.

SIMILAR SPECIES: *Amanita excelsa* and the poisonous *A. pantherina*, which, unlike this species, do not blush when cut or bruised.

EDIBILITY: Edible when cooked, but poisonous when raw. *Amanita rubescens* contains a hemolytic toxin which can cause anaemia if eaten raw. The toxin is eliminated during cooking. In Gauteng, this mushroom soon becomes infested with maggots, and it is best to cook it as soon as possible after picking.

> **NOTES:** Differences in the size of the fruit body, coloration and character of the scales on the cap make this mushroom very variable.

The volva persists as a sheath around the basal bulb.

Sited toward the apex of the stipe, the ring is membraneous and white.

The cap margin is smooth to faintly striate.

Amanita veldiei can be identified by the prominent white warts that cover the shiny cap and the tall stipe.

Amanita veldiei D.A. Reid & Eicker 1991

Common name: Veldie's lepidella
Afrikaans: Veldie se lepidella

Etymology: ANCIENT GREEK: *amanitai* = a kind of mushroom; *veldiei* = after ecologist Dr Veldie (J.V.) van Greuning (1940–present)
Synonym(s): None

Unknown

ECOLOGY: Mycorrhizal.

DISTRIBUTION: Gauteng (Pretoria); appears to be native to South Africa. Also occurs in Zambia.

HABITAT: Grows under indigenous broadleaved trees; fruit bodies single or grouped, sometimes in fairy rings.

DESCRIPTION: The shiny cap covered with prominent whitish warts, the tall white stipe and the persistent ring make this mushroom easy to recognise. **Cap:** 4–6cm in diameter; thick, fleshy; shallowly convex to plane; margin fringed with tooth-like veil remnants, extending beyond the gill edges; surface shiny, covered with thick, whitish warts which are broader and more conspicuous around the centre, turning into cobwebby fibrils toward the margin; white. **Gills:** free, very narrow at both ends; flesh-coloured to dirty cream. **Stipe:** 12.5–13cm long, 0.6–1.1cm thick; spindle-shaped, narrowing slightly upward; basal bulb up to 2.2cm thick, top of the bulb covered with fine white fibres; smooth above the well-formed ring, covered with fibrillose warts below the ring, most prominent toward the base; white. **Ring:** on upper part of stipe, membraneous, skirt-like, persistent. **Flesh:** firm; thick; white. **Smell:** no distinctive odour. **Spore print:** white.

SIMILAR SPECIES: *Amanita zangii* from tropical China, *A. hesleri* from the USA (neither of which is described here).

EDIBILITY: Unknown.

The gills are very narrowly attached at the stipe and margin.

Young specimens of *Amanita veldiei*.

The gills are flesh-coloured to dirty cream.

Woolly, wart-like, white tufts cover the stipe below the ring.

Initially spherical with an inrolled margin, the cap of *Agaricus arvensis* expands until it is almost flat.

Agaricus arvensis Schaeff. 1774

Common names: Horse mushroom, snowball mushroom
Afrikaans: Perdesampioen

Etymology: GREEK: *agaric* = mushroom; LATIN: *arvensis* = belonging to a field

Synonym(s): *Pratella arvensis*, *Psalliota arvensis*, *P. fissurata*, *P. leucotricha*

ECOLOGY: Saprophytic.

DISTRIBUTION: Widespread in South Africa. Occurs in the UK, Europe, Canada, USA, Russia, Japan, Australia and New Zealand.

HABITAT: Grows in grassy, well-composted pastures, lawns and similar places after good rains in autumn; fruit bodies single or grouped, sometimes in fairy rings.

DESCRIPTION: Although this species shares some features with *Agaricus campestris*, the cogwheel-like ridges on the expanding ring are characteristic. **Cap:** 8–15cm in diameter, up to 20cm; convex, becoming flat; young cap is smooth with inrolled margin; yellow to off-white, stains orange-yellow to ochre. **Gills:** free, crowded; white, then pale pink, finally dark chocolate-brown. **Stipe:** 8–12cm long, 1.2–2cm thick; broadens slightly at the base, but not bulbous; smooth; yellowish; hollow. **Ring:** prominent, pendant double ring, the lower one splitting into a star shape, scales on the underside. **Flesh:** thick, firm; white. **Smell:** aniseed odour. **Spore print:** dark purplish brown.

SIMILAR SPECIES: *Agaricus xanthodermus*, which bruises yellow when cut. Also similar to *A. campestris*, but *A. arvensis* can be distinguished by the larger and more robust fruit body, prominent ring and distinctive aniseed smell.

EDIBILITY: Edible; excellent flavour.

> **NOTES:** The gills remain white for a long period, causing confusion with mushrooms of the *Parasola* genus.

The stipe broadens slightly at the base.

The gills are free from the stipe.

The ring is formed from the partial veil, here seen covering the gills of a young specimen.

The large fruit body of *Agaricus augustus* and the fleshy stipe, which widens toward the base, are distinctive.

Liz Popich

Agaricus augustus Fr. 1838

Common name: Prince
Afrikaans: Prins

Etymology: GREEK: *agaric* = mushroom; LATIN: *augustus* = majestic, august

Synonym(s): *Fungus augustus, Pratella augusta, Psalliota augusta*

ECOLOGY: Saprophytic.

DISTRIBUTION: Western Cape, Eastern Cape and Gauteng, possibly more widespread. Occurs in the UK, Europe, USA, Russia, Australia, New Zealand and Nigeria.

HABITAT: Grows in rich soil in all types of forest, in parks and in garden compost; fruit bodies single or grouped.

DESCRIPTION: This species may be recognised by the large creamy cap densely covered with small brownish scales, the large, hanging ring and a distinctive almond odour. **Cap:** 8–15cm, up to 20cm in diameter; fleshy; broad ovoid to hemispherical at first, expanding to convex, with a central depression; margin even, somewhat inrolled; surface covered with fibrous scales in more or less concentric rings, merged into a continuous disc at the centre; yellowish to reddish brown. **Gills:** free, crowded, full and intermediate lengths, thin; whitish for a long time, darkening to creamy buff and finally reddish brown, lighter along the edges. **Stipe:** 5–12cm long, 1.5–3.5cm thick; central; cylindrical or widening downward to the bulbous base; smooth above the ring, fleshy toward the base; pink-brown. **Ring:** large, hanging. **Flesh:** thick, firm; white, unchanged when cut, but slowly stains yellow when bruised, becoming reddish with age. **Smell:** strong odour of almonds. **Spore print:** brownish black cocoa.

SIMILAR SPECIES: Most *Agaricus* species are similar, differing only in size. *A. augustus* is one of the largest.

EDIBILITY: Edible; excellent flavour, tastes of almond. Contains a high degree of cadmium, which does little harm but is best eaten in small quantities. *Agaricus* species should not be eaten raw.

NOTES: The gills remain white for a long period, causing confusion with mushrooms of the *Parasola* genus.

Edible

The cap is hemispherical at first.

The cap surface is densely covered with fibrous scales.

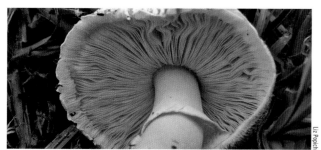

The gills are white at first, becoming pale pink and then dark brown with age.

A partial veil covers the gills.

Agaricus bisporus (J.E. Lange) Imbach 1946

Common names: Cultivated mushroom, button mushroom, portabellini
Afrikaans: Gekweekte sampioen

Etymology: GREEK: *agaric* = mushroom; LATIN: *bi-* = with two, *spora* = spore

Synonym(s): *Agaricus brunnescens, A. campestris* var. *hortensis, A. cookeianus, Psalliota bispora*

ECOLOGY: Saprophytic.

DISTRIBUTION: Widespread in South Africa. Occurs in the UK, Europe, Canada, USA, Russia, Australia and New Zealand.

HABITAT: Grows on compost, manure heaps, rotting garden waste and heavily composted open soil; fruit bodies single or grouped.

DESCRIPTION: This species is found in most food shops around the world. Since it is difficult to distinguish in the wild, the gills need to be examined microscopically. **Cap:** 8–15cm in diameter; fleshy; hemispherical at first, becoming convex then flat; margin regular, projecting slightly beyond the gills; surface smooth, dry, with radiating fibrils uniting into small scales arranged concentrically around the centre, but larger and more scattered toward the margin; white to dark brown. **Gills:** free, crowded, full and intermediate lengths, thin, edges entire; dirty pinkish, darkening to pinkish beige, finally purplish brown. **Stipe:** 3–6.5cm long, 1.2–1.8cm thick; central; cylindrical, with rhizoids attached to the base; white, darkening later, turning pale yellow-brown when handled; fleshy, tough, solid at first, later hollow. **Ring:** narrow, membraneous, persistent, with a double margin. **Flesh:** firm, thick; white, turning faint pinkish brown on bruising. **Smell:** mushroomy odour, lightly anise to almond. **Spore print:** cocoa to violet-brown.

SIMILAR SPECIES: Has been confused with *Amanita phalloides*.

EDIBILITY: Edible; full of flavour. Available throughout the year, it is one of the most commercially cultivated mushroom species in the western world, with different strains of the species resulting in variations in colour and size. It dries well, either whole or cut.

NOTES: This species has two spores per basidium instead of the usual four, differentiating it from other species in the genus.

Button mushrooms are widely available in stores.

A younger stage of the button mushroom, portabellini, is harvested before the gills are formed.

Agaricus bisporus, showing different stages of development.

Although widely available in shops, button mushrooms do occur in the wild.

Agaricus bitorquis (Quél.) Sacc. 1887

Common names: Pavement mushroom, sidewalk mushroom, spring agaric, banded agaric
Afrikaans: Sypaadjie-sampioen

Etymology: GREEK: *agaric* = mushroom; LATIN: *bi-* = with two, *torquis* = twisted necklace

Synonym(s): *Agaricus campestris* subsp. *bitorquis*, *Pratella bitorquis*, *Psalliota bitorquis*

ECOLOGY: Saprophytic.

DISTRIBUTION: Gauteng (Pretoria), possibly more widespread. Occurs in the UK, Europe, Canada, USA, Russia, Australia and New Zealand.

HABITAT: Grows in gardens and parks, along footpaths, at roadsides and on grass verges; fruit bodies grouped, sometimes fused together at the base of the stipe.

DESCRIPTION: The white, thick, fleshy cap, the brown gills and the two rings on the short stipe distinguish this species. **Cap:** 4–10cm in diameter; thick, fleshy; convex, soon flattened or slightly depressed, distinct shoulder; margin even, smooth, with ragged veil remnants, consistently and persistently inrolled; surface silky, smooth, with small, pale-brown scales over the centre, often covered with soil; white, pale brownish. **Gills:** free, crowded, full and intermediate lengths, narrow, thin, edges entire; pale greyish pink at first, gradually darkening to brownish black with whitish edges. **Stipe:** 2.5–6.5cm long, 1–3.5cm thick; short, pointed at the base; white, silky; fleshy, tough, solid. **Ring:** two separate rings, both upturned, lower one narrower and just above soil level, resembling the edge of a volva. **Flesh:** firm, thick; white, faintly pinkish when cut. **Smell:** pleasant mushroomy odour. **Spore print:** dark brown.

SIMILAR SPECIES: Other *Agaricus* species, but *A. bitorquis* has two rings.

EDIBILITY: Edible; tough but with a strong, pleasant flavour. Occasionally cultivated commercially.

> **NOTES:** Known as the pavement mushroom because of its ability to grow through hard-packed soil and even tarred pavements.

Edible

The white cap has small, brownish scales over the centre.

In older specimens the gills are dark brown.

A cross section, showing the inrolled margin and the short, fleshy stipe, which tapers at the base.

The rose-pink gills and the delicate ring are characteristic of young *Agaricus campestris* mushrooms.

Liz Popich

Agaricus campestris Fr. 1753

Common names: Field mushroom, meadow mushroom, pink bottom
Afrikaans: Veldsampioen, kampernoelie

Etymology: GREEK: *agaric* = mushroom; LATIN: *campestris* = growing in a field

Synonym(s): *Agaricus campester, A. edulis, Fungus campestris, Pratella campestris, Psalliota campestris*

ECOLOGY: Saprophytic.

DISTRIBUTION: Widespread in South Africa. Occurs in the UK, Europe, Canada, USA, Mexico, Brazil, Chile, Russia, Japan, Australia and New Zealand.

HABITAT: Grows on lawns and soil; fruit bodies single or grouped, often in fairy rings.

DESCRIPTION: The smooth, silky, white fruit body, the bright, pinkish gills, which soon darken to brown, and the very delicate ring on the white stipe make this species easy to identify. **Cap:** 3–10cm; fleshy; spherical when young, then convex, later plane; margin even; surface dry, smooth, silky or covered with fine scales; white to pearl-grey or beige, sometimes reddish brown. **Gills:** free, crowded, full and intermediate lengths, thin; whitish at first, very soon rosy pink, darkening to chocolate-brown, finally almost black. **Stipe:** 3–10cm long, 1–2cm thick; central; cylindrical, firm, more or less even or swollen at the base; white. **Ring:** membraneous, halfway up or in the middle of the stipe, sometimes disappearing partly or entirely in older fruit bodies; white. **Flesh:** thick, soft; white, turning brownish when bruised. **Smell:** pleasant mushroomy odour. **Spore print:** chocolate-brown.

SIMILAR SPECIES: Most of the *Agaricus* species are similar, appearing as a white mushroom with brown gills. An exception is *A. xanthodermus*, which bruises yellow when cut.

EDIBILITY: Edible. It is best consumed fresh when the cap is closed and the gills are still pink. Older specimens can be used in soups, stews and sauces.

NOTES: This mushroom is not commercially cultivated on account of its rapid maturation and short shelf life.

The cap of the young mushroom is spherical.

As the mushroom develops, the cap expands, becoming convex then plane.

The gills of the mature mushroom are almost black.

Agaricus crocopeplus Berk. & Broome 1871

Common name: Golden fleece mushroom
Afrikaans: Goudvlies-sampioen

Etymology: GREEK: *agaric* = mushroom; *croc* = saffron, *peplos* = robe, coat
Synonym(s): *Fungus crocopeplus, Stropharia crocopepla*

Edible

ECOLOGY: Saprophytic.

DISTRIBUTION: First reported in South Africa in Gauteng (Pretoria), but may be more widespread. Occurs in India, Sri Lanka, Thailand, Malaysia, Democratic Republic of the Congo, Tanzania, Zambia and Swaziland.

HABITAT: Grows in evergreen forests; fruit bodies single.

DESCRIPTION: This species is readily recognised by the small, brilliantly orange-yellow scales on the surface of the cap and lower part of the stipe and the gills which darken as the mushroom matures. **Cap:** 2–5cm in diameter; hemispherical to flattened; margin inrolled; surface shaggy, covered with fleecy, powdery scales; orange-yellow. **Gills:** free; white at first, becoming pink, finally dark brown. **Stipe:** 2–9cm long, 0.5–1.5cm thick; surface fleecy-scaly below ring. **Ring:** delicate. **Flesh:** firm; off-white. **Smell:** no distinctive odour. **Spore print:** dark brown.

SIMILAR SPECIES: *Agaricus trisulphuratus* (not described here).

EDIBILITY: Edible.

The orange-yellow scales on the surface of the cap give it a shaggy appearance.

NOTES: Although individual specimens may not immediately be recognised as species of *Agaricus*, *A. crocopeplus* is identifiable by the darkening of its gills as it matures, a typical feature of this genus.

Hemispherical and orange at first, the cap becomes flat to expose the brown gills.

Like the cap, the stipe is fleecy-scaly.

Agaricus diminutivus Peck 1874

Common name: Diminutive agaric
Afrikaans: Klein agarikus

Etymology: GREEK: *agaric* = mushroom; LATIN: *diminutivus* = diminutive, extremely or unusually small

Synonym(s): *Fungus diminutivus*

ECOLOGY: Saprophytic.

DISTRIBUTION: Gauteng (Pretoria), possibly more widespread. Occurs in Canada, USA and Japan.

HABITAT: Grows on grass patches and in humus on the forest floor; fruit bodies single, widely scattered or in small groups.

DESCRIPTION: The purplish-brown gills and spores, the whitish cap and the stipe, which has a persistent ring, are identifying features of this small mushroom. **Cap:** 1.5–3.5cm in diameter; fleshy, fragile; convex, maturing to flat, sometimes with a brown disc at the centre; margin even, smooth; surface silky, with red to brown fibrils; white to grey, later darkened by spores. **Gills:** free, crowded, full and intermediate lengths; whitish at first, then becoming deep pinkish, finally dark purplish brown. **Stipe:** 2–5cm long, 0.3–0.5cm thick; cylindrical, sometimes with a slight basal bulb; smooth or fibrillose; white; fleshy-tough, stuffed, becoming hollow. **Ring:** delicate, persistent; white. **Flesh:** thin, whitish. **Smell:** mild aniseed to almond odour. **Spore print:** purple-brown to dark brown or chocolate-brown.

SIMILAR SPECIES: Its diminutive size distinguishes it from other *Agaricus* species.

EDIBILITY: Edible; too small to be of culinary use.

Fruit bodies grow singly or in small groups.

The cap of the young mushroom is convex.

The crowded gills are whitish before becoming deep pinkish and finally dark purplish brown.

At maturity, the silky cap may develop a brownish disc at the centre.

Agaricus placomyces Peck 1878

Common name: Flat-top agaric
Afrikaans: Plat sampioen

Etymology: GREEK: *agaric* = mushroom; *plac* = flat, round plate, *myces* = fungus

Synonym(s): *Fungus placomyces, Psalliota placomyces*

Poisonous

ECOLOGY: Saprophytic.

DISTRIBUTION: Western Cape, Eastern Cape and Gauteng, possibly more widespread. Occurs in the UK, Canada, USA, Brazil, Chile, Australia and New Zealand.

HABITAT: Grows in coniferous and broadleaved forests, but is rare; fruit bodies single or scattered.

DESCRIPTION: Distinguishing features include the blackish scales over the ivory-white cap surface, gills that remain greyish pink before finally turning blackish brown, and a stipe that bruises yellow. **Cap:** 5–8cm in diameter; fleshy; convex, becoming flat with a depressed centre; margin even, initially slightly inrolled; surface covered with blackish-brown fibrillose scales which form an unbroken disc at the centre; ivory-white underneath scales, charcoal-brown at the centre, stains yellow when bruised. **Gills:** free, crowded; dusty salmon-pink, remaining this colour for longer than most other *Agaricus* species before finally becoming blackish brown. **Stipe:** 5–7cm long, 1–1.5cm thick; cylindrical, with a bulbous base; greyish white; hollow. **Ring:** fairly near the apex, membraneous. **Flesh:** thin, firm; white, staining yellow when cut or bruised. **Smell:** strongly unpleasant odour. **Spore print:** dark brown.

SIMILAR SPECIES: Any of the *Agaricus* species that stain yellow.

EDIBILITY: Poisonous to some people. Ingesting this mushroom affects different people in different ways. Some of the symptoms are gastrointestinal irritation, stomach cramps, sweating, flushing and vomiting. While the impact is rarely serious, the symptoms can be highly unpleasant.

The greyish-white stipe is cylindrical, ending in a bulbous base.

The gills are initially a dusty salmon-pink colour, becoming blackish brown over time.

The expanded cap has a depressed charcoal-brown centre.

Agaricus semotus (Fr.) 1863

Common names: Rosy wood mushroom, yellow-bulbed mushroom
Afrikaans: Geelbolsampioen

Etymology: GREEK: *agaric* = mushroom; LATIN: *semotus* = distant, removed, separated

Synonym(s): *Fungus semotus, Pratella semota, Psalliota semota*

ECOLOGY: Saprophytic.

DISTRIBUTION: Western Cape, Eastern Cape and Gauteng, possibly more widespread. Occurs in the UK, Europe, Canada, USA, Brazil, Russia, Australia and New Zealand.

HABITAT: Grows in grassy clearings and on the outside edges of coniferous forests; fruit bodies single or in small groups.

DESCRIPTION: The egg-shaped, flat-topped fruit body of the button stage is a distinctive feature. **Cap:** 2–5cm in diameter; flat-topped and cylindrical at first, becoming shallowly convex with a flattened centre; margin even; surface smooth, silky, with minute fibres radiating from the tawny reddish centre, small, flaky, yellowing scales near the margin; white, fibres becoming pink to lilac to reddish with age. **Gills:** free, broad, crowded; whitish to lilac drab, then dingy purplish and finally light greyish brown. **Stipe:** 3–6cm long, 0.4–0.8cm thick; white, yellow at the bulbous base.
Ring: double, thin, narrow, skirt-like, membraneous; whitish then brownish. **Flesh:** white, becoming tinged with reddish brown, base bruising yellow. **Smell:** strong odour of aniseed, sometimes mixed with smell of bitter almond. **Spore print:** brown.

The partial veil ruptures to expose the gills.

SIMILAR SPECIES: Any of the *Agaricus* species that stain yellow.

EDIBILITY: Poisonous to some people. It can cause stomach cramps, sweating, flushing and vomiting; symptoms are short-lived and not fatal. Although there is disagreement about its edibility, it is probably best to avoid this mushroom.

The mature cap is shallowly convex with a flattened centre.

The fruit bodies of *Agaricus semotus* appear singly or in small groups.

The gills turn purplish and then light greyish brown with age.

The gills of this young *Agaricus silvaticus* mushroom are protected by a partial veil, a temporary structure of tissue also called the inner veil.

Liz Popich

Agaricus silvaticus Schaeff. 1774

Common names: Scaly forest mushroom, forest agaric, bleeding wood mushroom, red-staining mushroom
Afrikaans: Skubberige bossampioen

Etymology: GREEK: *agaric* = mushroom; LATIN: *silvaticus* = belonging to the woods
Synonym(s): *Agaricus haemorrhoidarius, A. laceratus, A. sanguinarius, A. vinosobrunneus*

ECOLOGY: Saprophytic.

DISTRIBUTION: Western Cape, Eastern Cape, Gauteng and KwaZulu-Natal, possibly more widespread. Occurs in the UK, Europe, Canada, USA, Mexico, Brazil, Russia, South Korea and Japan.

HABITAT: Grows on conifer debris in forests and parks; fruit bodies grouped or in rings on pine needles.

DESCRIPTION: The orange-brown, scaly cap and flesh that turns red when cut help to identify this species. **Cap:** 5–10cm in diameter; fleshy; bell-shaped to convex, expanding to almost plane with a slight, flat, central umbo; margin regular; surface densely covered with fine fibrillar scales; scales brownish orange to caramel-brown, base underneath the scales slightly lighter. **Gills:** free, crowded, full and intermediate lengths, thin, edges entire; pale grey, turning rose-pink and finally chocolate-brown. **Stipe:** 4–13cm long, 0.5–1.5cm thick; central; long-cylindrical with a bulbous base; smooth or mostly scaly; white to pale brownish; fleshy-tough, solid at first, later hollow. **Ring:** hanging, skirt-like, pronounced; white to pale brown. **Flesh:** firm, medium to thick; whitish, stains red if bruised or cut. **Smell:** pleasant mushroomy odour. **Spore print:** purplish brown to chocolate-brown to dull brown.

SIMILAR SPECIES: Similar to most *Agaricus* species, but *A. silvaticus* bruises carmine-red when cut.

EDIBILITY: Edible; tasty, but rather tough and chewy; best used in stews.

Edible

The crowded gills, hanging ring and bulbous base are characteristic.

The flesh stains red when bruised or cut.

Fine fibrous scales cover the cap.

The stipe of *Agaricus xanthodermus* widens into a bulbous base.

Liz Popich

Agaricus xanthodermus Genev. 1876

Common names: Yellow stainer, yellow-staining mushroom
Afrikaans: Geelvleksampioen

Etymology: GREEK: *agaric* = mushroom; *xanthos* = various shades of yellow, *derma* = skin

Synonym(s): *Agaricus jodoformicus, Pratella xanthoderma, Psalliota flavescens, P. xanthoderma*

ECOLOGY: Saprophytic.

DISTRIBUTION: Western Cape and Gauteng, possibly more widespread. Occurs in the UK, Europe, Canada, USA, Mexico, Russia, Australia and New Zealand.

HABITAT: Grows in open forests, parks, gardens and on grass; fruit bodies single or grouped.

DESCRIPTION: This species may be distinguished by the yellow-staining flesh, which has an odour of carbolic acid. **Cap:** 6–12cm in diameter; subglobose-cylindrical to convex to flattened; margin incurved; surface smooth, cracking radially with age into grey scales; cream to tan or grey, stains yellow when bruised. **Gills:** free, crowded, full and intermediate lengths; white, turning pink, then dark brown when mature. **Stipe:** 6–12cm long, 0.8–1.5cm thick; central; slender, widening into a bulbous base; cream, staining yellow when bruised; solid turning hollow. **Ring:** double ring on the upper part of stipe. **Flesh:** firm; white, staining yellow when bruised. **Smell:** odour similar to benzene (carbolic acid). **Spore print:** black-brown.

SIMILAR SPECIES: May be mistaken for the edible *Agaricus arvensis.*

EDIBILITY: Poisonous. A gastrointestinal irritant, this species causes nausea, vomiting, headaches, profuse sweating and diarrhoea within 4 hours after eating.

NOTES: In South Africa, white and grey varieties of this species – *Agaricus xanthodermus* var. *lepiotoides* and *A. xanthodermus* var. *meleagriodes* – are also poisonous.

The gills are crowded and free from the stipe.

The white flesh bruises bright yellow when damaged or cut.

In this young specimen, the gills are temporarily covered with a partial veil.

Coniolepiota spongodes (Berk. & Broome) Vellinga 2011

Common names: None
Afrikaans: None

Etymology: GREEK: *kônos* = cone, pine cone, *lepis* = scale;
LATIN: *spongiola* = little sponge
Synonym(s): *Agaricus spongodes*, *Lepiota spongodes*

Unknown

ECOLOGY: Saprophytic.

DISTRIBUTION: First reported in South Africa in Gauteng and KwaZulu-Natal, but may be more widespread. Occurs in India, Bangladesh, Thailand, Sri Lanka, Malaysia, Singapore, China and the Philippines.

HABITAT: Grows along roadsides in forests; fruit bodies single or in small groups of two.

DESCRIPTION: This species is characterised by its grey-lilac to purple floccose cap and crowded, cream to yellow gills. **Cap:** 4–8cm in diameter; plano-convex to flattened; margin slightly incurved; surface floccose, covered with lilac to purple-grey powdery warts (remains of the veil) in young specimens, warts densely arranged at the centre, becoming spread out toward the margin, sometimes remaining in the centre but disappearing in the outer zone to reveal a pallid to whitish background, powdery warts sometimes hanging over the margin; lilac to purple-grey, whitish background. **Gills:** free, crowded; creamy white to pale yellowish. **Stipe:** 2.5–5cm long, 0.6–1cm thick; central; cylindrical, usually slightly tapering upward, base slightly swollen and covered with whitish mycelium; glabrous; pallid white at the apex, remaining parts covered with powdery lilac warts; hollow. **Ring:** thin, membraneous, detachable. **Flesh:** dull white to slightly pale purplish. **Smell:** unknown. **Spore print:** white.

EDIBILITY: Unknown.

The gills are remote from the stipe and densely arrranged.

NOTES: The genus is monotopic, containing only the single species, *Coniolepiota spongodes*, first reported from Thailand.

In this young specimen, the cap is covered with woolly tufts.

The cap is flattened in older specimens.

The cap surface becomes lilac to purple-grey as the velar warts begin to disappear.

Leucoagaricus bisporus Heinem. 1973

Common names: None
Afrikaans: None

Etymology: GREEK: *leukos* = white, *agaric* = mushroom;
LATIN: *bisporus* = with two spores

Synonym(s): None

ECOLOGY: Saprophytic.

DISTRIBUTION: Gauteng, KwaZulu-Natal and Mpumalanga, possibly more widespread. Occurs in Brazil and Democratic Republic of the Congo.

HABITAT: Grows on decaying plant material; fruit bodies single or clustered.

DESCRIPTION: The pale-coloured fruit body, more deeply coloured umbo, striate cap margin, tall stipe and flesh that turns reddish when cut characterise this species. **Cap:** 2.5–6.5cm in diameter; fleshy; conical becoming bell-shaped, with a prominent, flattened umbo; margin even or wavy, striate, downturned, slightly ragged; surface silky, with small, more or less concentrically arranged cream-coloured scales; cream to pale yellow, tan over the umbo. **Gills:** free, crowded, full and intermediate lengths, thin; white to pale yellow, becoming darker. **Stipe:** 2.5–6cm long, 0.6–1.2cm thick, widening downward to 1–3cm thick; central; cylindrical, smooth, can have a slightly bulbous base, fused to other stipes with rhizoids below soil level; cream white to pale fawn, darkens when handled, turns reddish when bruised; fleshy, tough, hollow. **Ring:** fixed, membraneous, funnel-shaped, persistent; whitish above, buffy brown from adhering soil below. **Flesh:** firm; white, discolours red when bruised or cut. **Smell:** unknown. **Spore print:** white to pale yellow.

SIMILAR SPECIES: *Agaricus* species, *Amanita phaloides*.

EDIBILITY: Suspect.

The young cap is conical to bell-shaped.

Pale yellow at first, the umbo turns tan as the mushroom ages.

The cap surface is covered with scales that are more or less concentrically arranged.

The stipe has a slightly bulbous base.

Leucoagaricus leucothites has a delicate, movable ring around the stipe.

Leucoagaricus leucothites (Vittad.) Wasser 1977

Common names: Smooth parasol, smooth lepiota, chalk-top, white dapperling, off-white parasol
Afrikaans: Gladde sambreel

Etymology: GREEK: *leukos* = white, *agaric* = mushroom; *leukos* = white, *-ites* = pertaining to

Synonym(s): *Lepiota cretacea, L. leucothites, Leuoagaricus naucinus, L. subcretaceus*

ECOLOGY: Saprophytic.

DISTRIBUTION: Western Cape, Eastern Cape, Gauteng and Free State, possibly more widespread. Occurs in the UK, Europe, USA, Russia, India, Japan, Australia, New Zealand and Tenerife.

HABITAT: Grows in grasslands, open fields, gardens and on the side of the road after good rains; fruit bodies in small groups or fairy rings.

DESCRIPTION: The movable ring, the pale-pinkish mature gills that never turn brown, and the absence of a volva help to distinguish this species. **Cap:** 4–10cm in diameter; fleshy; oval to nearly round at first, then expanding to broadly convex and finally to plane, sometimes with a slight umbo; margin even, smooth, initially inrolled, occasionally with adhering veil remnants; surface smooth, matt, sometimes cracking with age; silvery white, buff or smoky with age. **Gills:** free, crowded; white when young, becoming pale pink with age. **Stipe:** 6–10cm long, 0.6–1.5cm thick; central; swollen at the base, tapering upward; silky, smooth, slightly striate on lower part; white; firm, stuffed at first, hollow. **Ring:** prominent, membraneous with frilly edges, slides up and down stipe easily, often disappearing with age. **Flesh:** firm; white when young, becoming spongy with age. **Smell:** pleasant odour. **Spore print:** white, or with a slight pink tinge.

SIMILAR SPECIES: Sometimes mistaken for the similar-looking *Agaricus campestris* and for some *Amanita* species.

EDIBILITY: Edible; excellent flavour.

Edible

The young cap is oval to nearly round.

A young specimen, showing the partial veil separating from the margin.

Leucoagaricus leucothites, showing the free gills, swollen base and prominent ring.

A slight umbo may appear on the cap surface.

Leucoagaricus rubrotinctus (Peck) Singer 1948

Common names: Ruby dapperling, little red lepiota, red-eyed parasol
Afrikaans: Rooi-oog sambreel

Etymology: GREEK: *leukos* = white, *agaric* = mushroom;
LATIN: *ruber* = red, *tinctus* = coloured

Synonym(s): *Lepiota rubrotincta*

ECOLOGY: Saprophytic.

DISTRIBUTION: First reported in South Africa in Gauteng and KwaZulu-Natal, but may be more widespread. Occurs in Canada, USA, Mexico, Costa Rica, Brazil, Chile, Argentina, Japan, Australia and New Zealand.

HABITAT: Grows in forests on humus, especially after the first good rain; fruit bodies single or in small groups.

DESCRIPTION: The pinkish to orangish-brown cap and the evenly darker centre, along with the absence of any staining of the flesh, make this species relatively easy to identify. **Cap:** 2–6cm in diameter; convex, later becoming flattened; surface smooth, fibrillose, becoming cracked when expanded, exposing the whitish to pale-tan ground colour, sometimes scaly; pinkish to orangish or reddish-brown, centre of the cap darker than the margin. **Gills:** free, close; white. **Stipe:** 4–12cm long, 0.3–1cm thick; central; more or less cylindrical, usually slender or thicker below, often extending fairly deep into humus; smooth; white, discolouring with age; later hollow. **Ring:** thin, fragile, membraneous, persistent; white, edge sometimes reddish. **Flesh:** thin; white, not bruising when cut. **Smell:** no distinctive odour. **Spore print:** white.

SIMILAR SPECIES: *Leucoagaricus cristata* looks similar, but is much smaller, and *L. rubrotinctoides* is browner in colour (neither of which is described here).

EDIBILITY: Suspect.

NOTES: This species was first described as *Agaricus rubrotinctus* in 1884 by American mycologist Charles Horton Peck. It was reclassified as a species of the genus *Leucoagaricus* by the German-born mycologist and taxonomist, Rolf Singer, in 1948.

A small group of young mushrooms on forest humus.

The cap is convex in younger specimens.

The gills are free from the stipe.

As the mushroom expands, the cap surface becomes cracked.

Leucocoprinus birnbaumii (Corda) Singer 1962

Common names: Lemon-yellow lepiota, flowerpot parasol, yellow parasol, yellow-pleated parasol
Afrikaans: Geelsambreel

Etymology: GREEK: *leukos* = white, *coprinus* = pertaining to dung, manure; *birnbaumii* = after a Czech gardener, Birnbaum, who found this mushroom in his hothouse in 1839

Synonym(s): *Bolbitus birnbaumii*, *Lepiota aurea*, *L. coprinoides*, *L. pseudolicmophora*, *Leucocoprinus luteus*

ECOLOGY: Saprophytic.

DISTRIBUTION: Gauteng and KwaZulu-Natal, possibly more widespread. Occurs in the UK, Europe, Canada, USA, Mexico, Guatemala, Costa Rica, Brazil, Japan, China, Indonesia, Australia and New Zealand.

HABITAT: Grows in rich compost soil, decaying wood debris and potting soil; fruit bodies single or grouped.

DESCRIPTION: The small fruit body is quite conspicuous and readily recognisable by its uniform lemon-yellow colour and the powdery cap and stipe surfaces. **Cap:** 1.5–4cm in diameter; thin, fragile; bell-shaped, becoming conical to almost flat, with a rounded umbo; margin grooved, eventually turning upward; surface powdery, covered with small scales; lemon-yellow, fading with age. **Gills:** free, crowded, full and intermediate lengths; lemon-yellow fading to yellow-white. **Stipe:** 2–6cm long, 0.2–0.4cm thick; central; widening toward the base; covered with yellow powdery granules; tough, solid. **Ring:** membraneous, movable, often disappearing. **Flesh:** thin; lemon-yellow. **Smell:** no distinctive odour. **Spore print:** white to light yellowish.

SIMILAR SPECIES: *Leucocoprinus fragilissimus.*

EDIBILITY: Poisonous. If eaten, it can cause a severe upset stomach.

NOTES: This mushroom was first described as *Agaricus luteus* in 1788 by the British botanist and mycologist, James Bolton. Its name was later changed, as that name had already been assigned.

Poisonous

A tiny muhsroom, *Leucocoprinus birnbaumii* may occur in groups.

Small scales cover the powdery cap surface.

The conical cap and rounded umbo are distinctive.

The lemon-yellow coloration of the fruit body is characteristic.

The gills are of varying lengths, and free from the stipe.

Liz Popich

Leucocoprinus fragilissimus is characterised by a fragile stipe and a delicately grooved cap.

Leucocoprinus fragilissimus (Berk. & M.A. Curtis) Pat. 1900

Common name: Fragile dapperling
Afrikaans: Delikate sampioen

Etymology: GREEK: *leucos* = white, *coprinus* = pertaining to dung, manure; LATIN: *fragilis* = fragile, weak, brittle, frail, perishable, *-issimus* = most (most fragile)

Synonym(s): *Hiatula fragilissima, Lepiota fragilissima*

ECOLOGY: Saprophytic.

DISTRIBUTION: First reported in South Africa in Gauteng and KwaZulu-Natal, possibly more widespread. Occurs in Europe, Canada, USA, Mexico, Guatemala, Bolivia, Paraguay, Hong Kong, Australia and New Zealand.

HABITAT: Grows in humus, very decayed plant matter and compost in tropical and subtropical forests; fruit bodies single or scattered.

DESCRIPTION: The fragile fruit body and stipe, the deeply grooved white cap with its yellow centre, and the flimsy ring make this species relatively easy to recognise. **Cap:** 1.5–3.5cm in diameter; fragile; bell-shaped when young, becoming convex and nearly flat with age, with a small, central, deep-yellow protrusion; surface deeply grooved from margin to centre; pale yellow to nearly white, centre yellowish. **Gills:** free, distant, often dissolving in hot weather; pale yellow. **Stipe:** 2–7cm long, 0.1–0.2cm thick; exceedingly fragile; cylindrical above the small basal bulb; bald, coated with tiny yellow scales; pale yellow, fading to nearly white. **Ring:** thin, fragile, sometimes disappearing; yellow. **Flesh:** insubstantial; yellowish. **Smell:** no distinctive odour. **Spore print:** white.

SIMILAR SPECIES: *Leucocoprinus birnbaumii*.

EDIBILITY: Suspect; possibly poisonous.

> **NOTES:** This species was first documented by French mycologist Narcisse Théophile Patouillard in 1900.

The young fungus has a bell-shaped cap.

A small protrusion at the centre of the cap distinguishes the mature mushroom.

The cap surface is deeply grooved from the margin to the centre.

Leucocoprinus fragilissimus is short-lived and collapses soon after the cap has expanded.

The cap of *Macrolepiota zeyheri* takes the shape of a small umbrella, the inspiration for its common name 'white parasol'.

As the mushroom matures, the cap surface breaks up into loose, brown scales toward the centre but remains intact around the umbo.

Macrolepiota zeyheri (Berk. & Singer) Heinem. 1962

Common name: White parasol
Afrikaans: Sambreelsampioen, witsambreel

Etymology: GREEK: *macros* = large, *lepis* = scale, *-ota* = possessing; *zeyheri* = after German botanist Karl Ludwig Philipp Zeyher (1799–1858)

Synonym(s): *Agaricus zeyheri, Lepiota zeyheri, Leucocoprinus zeyheri*

ECOLOGY: Saprophytic.

DISTRIBUTION: To date, found only in South Africa, suggesting it is native to the country.

HABITAT: Grows in grasslands, fields and pastures; fruit bodies scattered.

DESCRIPTION: The large, white fruit body is characteristic of this species. **Cap:** 5–20cm in diameter; globose at first, then umbrella-shaped, umbo small or depressed; margin even, smooth, with adhering remnants of the veil; surface covered with white concentric scales when young, later breaking up into loose, brown scales, but remaining intact around the umbo; white, cream or brown, umbo clay-brown **Gills:** free, crowded, full and intermediate lengths, separated from the stipe by a collar, thin, soft, fragile, with fringed edges; white drying to pale tan. **Stipe:** 8–25cm long, 1–2cm thick; central; cylindrical, slender, with a bulbous base; firm, smooth or with scales, striate; white, turning brown once handled; tough, hollow. **Ring:** large, double, upper part membraneous and shaggy, skirt-like, movable, persistent; white or creamy white. **Flesh:** white, may turn salmon in older specimens. **Smell:** mild mushroomy odour. **Spore print:** white to pale pink when fresh, later pale pinkish buff.

SIMILAR SPECIES: May be confused with *Chlorophyllum molybdites*, which has similar gills, but with a greenish tint. Also similar to *Amanita foetidissima*, which smells of urine, and *Macrolepiota rhacodes* (not described here).

EDIBILITY: Edible; flavour variable, especially in older specimens. Delicious when flaked and lightly fried in butter.

NOTES: The travelling German botanical collector, Karl Ludwig Philipp Zeyher, discovered this mushroom in Uitenhage, in the Eastern Cape, in 1825. He sent the mushroom to Kew Gardens in the UK, where it was later named in his honour.

A large membraneous ring persists toward the apex of the stipe.

Remnants of the veil can be seen along the margin of the cap.

This mushroom grows in grassy areas.

Chlorophyllum molybdites can be identified by the white to creamy cap surface covered with scattered brown scales.

Chlorophyllum molybdites (G. Mey.) Massee 1898

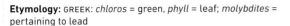

Common names: False parasol, green-lined parasol, Morgan's lepiota
Afrikaans: Vals sambreelsampioen

Etymology: GREEK: *chloros* = green, *phyll* = leaf; *molybdites* = pertaining to lead

Synonym(s): *Agaricus congolensis, Lepiota morganii, Leucocoprinus molybdites, Macrolepiota molybdites*

ECOLOGY: Saprophytic.

DISTRIBUTION: Gauteng and KwaZulu-Natal, possibly more widespread. Occurs in Europe, USA, Mexico, Brazil, Japan, Hong Kong, Australia, Norfolk Island, Tenerife, Democratic Republic of the Congo and Zambia.

HABITAT: Grows on lawns and in grassy areas; fruit bodies grouped, sometimes in fairy rings.

DESCRIPTION: This mushroom can be recognised by the large, irregular, amber-brown scales over the white cap surface, the stipe that widens downward to the basal bulb, and the marked greenish coloration of the mature gills (often only apparent the day after the specimen first appears). **Cap:** 10–25cm in diameter; fleshy; subglobose to hemispherical to convex, with a central umbo; margin even, striate, sometimes splitting, occasionally turning upward in wet weather; surface initially covered with a tough, brown skin that breaks up into coarse, irregular, brown scales as the cap expands; white to creamy, umbo brown. **Gills:** free, crowded, full and intermediate lengths, thin, fragile; white turning greenish to dull olive-green with age. **Stipe:** 8–20cm long, 1–2.5cm thick; central; swollen at the base, tapering upward; silky; white, darkening to brownish below the ring, staining reddish brown when cut or wounded. **Ring:** conspicuous, movable, often with a thickened brown margin. **Flesh:** thick, firm; white. **Smell:** unknown. **Spore print:** pale to bright green turning dull sordid green.

SIMILAR SPECIES: Can be confused with the edible *Macrolepiota zeyheri*, which grows in similar localities.

EDIBILITY: Poisonous; not fatal. A gastrointestinal irritant, this species causes nausea and diarrhoea, with symptoms lasting up to 3 days.

Poisonous

Liz Popich

The budding mushroom is covered with a tough, brown skin that breaks up into scales as the fruit body grows.

Liz Popich

A young specimen of *Chlorophyllum molybdites*.

Liz Popich

Initially white, the gills turn greenish to dull olive-green with age.

Liz Popich

Initially pale, the narrowly attached gills darken to cinnamon or rust-brown.

Bolbitius titubans (Bull.) Fr. 1838

Common names: Sunny side up, yellow field cap, yellow cow-pat mushroom
Afrikaans: Geelveldmus

Etymology: GREEK: *bolbitius* = having the quality of a bulb;
LATIN: *titubans* = to stagger
Synonym(s): *Bolbitius vitellinus*

Inedible

ECOLOGY: Saprophytic.

KNOWN DISTRIBUTION: Widespread in South Africa. Occurs in the UK, Europe, USA, Brazil, Japan, Australia and New Zealand.

HABITAT: Grows on lawns and herbivore dung, occasionally on woodchip mulch; fruit bodies scattered or clustered; lasting little more than 24 hours after appearing – one of the most short-lived of all mushrooms.

DESCRIPTION: Although variable in size, the strongly grooved, slimy cap and the dark, rust-coloured gills (pale at first) are identifying features. **Cap:** 2–6cm in diameter; fleshy; conical to bell-shaped to flattened; margin striate almost to the centre; surface slightly viscid when young, dry, shiny when old; lemon-yellow to egg-yolk yellow, fading to brownish grey at the margin with age. **Gills:** adnexed, crowded, edges entire; pale yellow, darkening to cinnamon or rust colour. **Stipe:** 3–10cm long, 0.2–0.5cm thick; central; slender, cylindrical or tapering slightly upward; powdery; pale yellow; fragile, soft, hollow. **Ring:** absent. **Flesh:** thin, membraneous. **Smell:** no distinctive odour. **Spore print:** rust-orange to rust-brown.

SIMILAR SPECIES: *Parasola plicatilis* (not described here).

EDIBILITY: Inedible, but harmless.

> **NOTES:** As its scientific name suggests, this mushroom tends to lean and eventually fall in a manner that is best described as a 'slow-motion stagger'. *Bolbitius vitellinus* was traditionally a separate species from *B. titubans* because of its thicker flesh, less striate cap and whiter stipe. Mycologists have since synonymised the two species; since *titubans* is the older name, it takes precedence.

Bolbitius titubans is found in well-fertilised soil and on dung.

Marginal striations become visible as the cap develops.

The caps of young specimens are distinctively egg-shaped.

Viscid at first, the cap soon begins to fade and dry out.

The slender, yellowish stipe tapers upward.

Panaeolina foenisecii (Pers.) Maire 1933

Common names: Mower's mushroom, haymaker, brown mottlegill, brown hay mushroom, brown hay cap
Afrikaans: Graskappie

Etymology: GREEK: *panaeolus* = variegated, LATIN: *-īna* = similar to; LATIN: *foenisecii* = pertaining to haymaking

Synonym(s): *Panaeolus foenisecii, Psathyra foenisecii, Psathyrella foenisecii*

ECOLOGY: Saprophytic.

DISTRIBUTION: Widespread in South Africa. Occurs in the UK, Europe, USA, Mexico, Russia, Australia and New Zealand.

HABITAT: Grows on lawns or in soil, not on dung; fruit bodies grouped or scattered.

DESCRIPTION: This small mushroom can be recognised by its conical to convex cap and the gills that become a mottled darkish brown as the spores mature. **Cap:** 1.5–3cm in diameter; conical at first, becoming convex to almost flat; surface dry, smooth, hygrophanous; as the cap dehydrates the surface appears zoned and cracked; grey-brown to red-brown, buff when dry. **Gills:** adnate to adnexed, close; dark brown to purple-black with lighter edges, becoming mottled as spores mature. **Stipe:** 4–6cm long, 0.2–0.3cm thick; slender; surface smooth, powdery, slightly striate; white to light brown; fragile, hollow. **Ring:** absent. **Flesh:** thin, fragile. **Smell:** nutty, slightly unpleasant odour. **Spore print:** dark brown to purple-brown.

SIMILAR SPECIES: *Panaeolus subbalteatus*.

EDIBILITY: Inedible.

The expanding cap changes from conical to convex before almost flattening out.

The gills are dark brown to purple-black, becoming mottled as the spores mature.

Panaeolina foenisecii is widespread and often fruits in large numbers.

Panaeolus subbalteatus (Berk. & Boone) Sacc. 1887

Common names: Banded mottlegill, dark-rimmed mottlegill, weed panaeolus, dark-banded dung mushroom
Afrikaans: Geringde kappie

Etymology: GREEK: *panaeolus* = variegated; LATIN: *sub* = less, *balteatus* = girdled

Synonym(s): *Panaeolus cinctulus, P. fimicola* var. *cinctulus*

ECOLOGY: Saprophytic.

DISTRIBUTION: First reported in South Africa in Gauteng (Pretoria), but may be more widespread. Occurs in the UK, Europe, Canada, USA, Mexico, Russia and New Zealand.

HABITAT: Grows on herbivore manure, compost and fertilised lawns; fruit bodies grouped or in small scattered clumps.

DESCRIPTION: A small reddish-brown mushroom, this species has a darker grey-brown marginal zone when slightly dry. **Cap:** 1.5–3cm in diameter; convex to bluntly conical, becoming broadly convex to broadly umbonate to flattened or with an uplifted margin; surface smooth or wrinkled, sometimes slightly fissured in older specimens, not viscid; colour variable, brown to reddish brown or cinnamon-brown when wet, fading as it dries to tan, buff or even whitish (from spores), often with a reddish-brown to brown or dark-grey marginal zone when slightly dry. **Gills:** adnate to adnexed, close, broad; cream-coloured when young, pale watery brown or reddish brown, darkening gradually to black; edges whitish and slightly fringed, vertical faces usually mottled when fully mature. **Stipe:** 2–8cm long, 0.2–0.7cm thick; central; cylindrical or tapering at either end; brown to reddish brown, but often appearing whitish and powdery, or dusted grey by spores, upper part often paler; usually striate; base and mycelium occasionally staining faintly bluish when bruised or cut; hollow. **Ring:** absent. **Flesh:** thin; cinnamon-brown to cream-coloured. **Smell:** slightly starchy odour. **Spore print:** jet-black.

SIMILAR SPECIES: *Panaeolina foenisecii*.

EDIBILITY: Inedible; tastes like flour when fresh and salty when dried. Its hallucinogenic properties, derived from moderate to low levels of psilocybin, have made it one of the more popular 'recreational' species (commonly known as 'magic mushrooms') in use today. It is easily cultivated. The legal status of psilocybin mushrooms varies worldwide; in South Africa it is listed as a Class A drug, along with cocaine, tik, heroin and ecstasy.

NOTES: This is one of the major mushroom 'weeds' in cultivated mushroom beds around the world.

The gills, which darken as the mushroom matures, are broadly to narrowly attached to the stipe.

These mushrooms grow in clumps on well-fertilised lawns.

A darker band is present along the margin, but disappears as the mushroom dries out.

The sticky cap, pale gills and flaky upper stipe of *Hebeloma crustuliniforme* are diagnostic.

Hebeloma crustuliniforme (Bull.) Quél. 1872

Common names: Poison pie, fairy cakes, weeping fairy cake
Afrikaans: Radysswam

Etymology: ANCIENT GREEK: *hebe* = youth, *-loma* = fringe; LATIN: *crustulum* = thin bread crust, pastry, *-forme* = in the shape of

Synonym(s): *Hebelomatis crustuliniformis, Hylophila crustuliniformis*

ECOLOGY: Mycorrhizal.

DISTRIBUTION: Western Cape, possibly more widespread. Occurs in the UK, Europe, USA, Mexico, Costa Rica, Russia, Australia, New Zealand and Tenerife.

HABITAT: Grows in association with coniferous and broadleaved trees; fruit bodies single, grouped or in fairy rings.

DESCRIPTION: This mushroom is readily recognised by its cream to brownish sticky cap, pale gills, flaky upper stipe and radishy odour. **Cap:** 2–7cm in diameter; fleshy; convex, flattening out; surface slightly viscid when wet; pale to pinkish beige, darker at the centre, buff to almost white at the margin. **Gills:** adnate, close to crowded, full and intermediate lengths; grey or clay. **Stipe:** 4–7cm long, 0.5–1.5cm thick; central; cylindrical or somewhat flattened, or narrowing slightly upward; mealy over the upper part, smooth and finely striate over the lower part; whitish, darkening to brownish toward the base; hollow. **Ring:** absent. **Flesh:** white. **Smell:** radish- or turnip-like odour. **Spore print:** rust to snuff-brown.

SIMILAR SPECIES: Distinguished microscopically from other *Hebeloma* species by spore size and shape, reactions in iodine reagents, and subtle differences in size, cap colour and ecology. Other *Hebeloma* species have a similar smell of radishes, sometimes with a hint of cocoa.

EDIBILITY: Poisonous. The odour of radish and the fact that the gills turn brown are signs that this species should be avoided. It contains small amounts of hemolysin, which causes gastroenteritis.

NOTES: In young specimens, the gills exude drops of clear liquid at the edges in which mature spores are later trapped; when dry, the drops form a dark spotting visible on the gill edges.

Hebeloma crustuliniforme occurs in pine plantations and under broadleaved trees.

The gills are closely arranged and broadly attached to the stipe.

The fleshy cap is buff-coloured with a white margin.

Short and full-length gills are interspersed.

The thick, pink gills of *Laccaria laccata* turn white and powdery when the spores mature.

Jean Stephenson

Laccaria laccata (Scop.) Cooke 1884

Common names: Deceiver, waxy laccaria, painted gill
Afrikaans: Verkulswam

Etymology: PERSIAN: *laccaria* = varnish, lacquer; FRENCH: *laccata* = varnished, coated with lacquer

Synonym(s): *Collybia laccata, Omphalia laccata, Russuliopsis laccata*

ECOLOGY: Mycorrhizal.

DISTRIBUTION: Western Cape, Eastern Cape, Gauteng and KwaZulu-Natal, possibly more widespread. Occurs in the UK, Europe, USA, Mexico, Brazil, Costa Rica, China, Australia, New Zealand and Tenerife.

HABITAT: Grows in leaf litter under trees, especially pines, often on damp or poor soil; fruit bodies grouped.

DESCRIPTION: The variability in the colour and appearance of the fruit bodies has earned this species the name 'deceiver'.
Cap: 0.6–6cm in diameter; fleshy; convex becoming flat, can be depressed; margin striate, wavy, downturned, then turning upward; surface smooth, flaky when dry; tawny to red when wet, ochraceous yellow when dry. **Gills:** adnate, notched, subdistant, margin toothed; pink, becoming white and powdery when the spores mature.
Stipe: 3.5–10cm long, 0.6–1cm thick; central; cylindrical, tall, robust, slightly swollen at the base; smooth, can be flattened and twisted; concolorous with cap, base white; tough, hollow, often compressed.
Ring: absent; **Flesh:** thin, soft; red-brown. **Smell:** no distinctive odour.
Spore print: white.

SIMILAR SPECIES: *Laccaria tortilis, Lactarius hepaticus.*

EDIBILITY: Edible.

> **NOTES:** Due to its variable appearance and colour, this species is known as the 'deceiver'. Also considered by mushroom collectors to be a 'mushroom weed' because of its abundance and plain stature.

Two specimens, in different stages of development.

The gills are spaced somewhat far apart.

The fruit bodies appear in groups, commonly in leaf litter under pine trees.

The cap, often depressed in the centre, is convex before becoming flat.

The mature mushroom has a flattened cap and wavy margin.

Laccaria tortilis (Bolton) Cooke 1884

Common name: Twisted deceiver
Afrikaans: Gedraaide bedriëer

Etymology: PERSIAN: *laccaria* = varnish, lacquer; LATIN: *tortilis* = ability to twist

Synonym(s): *Collybia tortilis, Omphalia tortilis*

Edible

ECOLOGY: Mycorrhizal.

DISTRIBUTION: First reported in South Africa in Gauteng (Pretoria), but may be more widespread. Occurs in the UK, Europe, Canada, USA, Russia, Japan, Australia and New Zealand.

HABITAT: Grows on soil in damp forests, often along banks of streams or ponds; fruit bodies grouped.

DESCRIPTION: The small, translucent fruit body, irregularly wavy margin and light-pink, distant gills are distinctive. **Cap:** 0.3–1.5cm in diameter; hemispherical to flattened, sometimes bell-shaped, centrally depressed; margin irregularly wavy; surface smooth, translucent, striate from margin to centre when moist; pale pinkish brown to reddish brown, darker at the centre, drying pale flesh-pink. **Gills:** adnate, distant; pale pink. **Stipe:** 0.8–2cm long, 0.1–0.2cm thick; cylindrical, with fine, white basal mycelium; concolorous with cap; hollow with age. **Ring:** absent. **Flesh:** thin; concolorous with cap. **Smell:** no distinctive odour. **Spore print:** white.

SIMILAR SPECIES: Its larger size distinguishes *Laccaria laccata* from *L. tortilis.*

EDIBILITY: Edible; too small to be of culinary value.

The cap is pale pinkish brown, darkening toward the centre.

The pinkish gills are spaced far apart, and are attached to the stipe along their entire width.

A tiny mushroom, this species can reach a height of 2cm.

Laccaria tortilis grows on bare, moist soil in damp forests.

Hygrocybe chlorophana (Fr.) Wünsche 1877

Common names: Golden wax cap, lemon wax cap
Afrikaans: Goudwasmus

Etymology: GREEK: *hygros* = wet, moist, *kybe* = head; *chlorophana* = light greenish yellow

Synonym(s): *Godfrinia chlorophana*, *Hygroporus chlorophanus*

ECOLOGY: Saprophytic.

DISTRIBUTION: First reported in South Africa in Gauteng (Pretoria), but may be more widespread. Occurs in the UK, Europe, Canada, USA, Mexico, Brazil, Russia, Japan, Australia, New Zealand and Tenerife.

HABITAT: Grows in grassy areas, along edges of forests, beside hedges, and in gardens; fruit bodies grouped or in fairy rings.

DESCRIPTION: The golden to lemon-yellow colour, slimy cap and stipe, and whitish to yellowish gills make this species easy to recognise. **Cap:** 2–3.5cm in diameter; convex to flattened, becoming slightly depressed, with a central umbo; margin slightly wavy, striated toward the centre; surface viscid; rich, golden orange-yellow to shades of pale sulphur-yellow, greyish yellow with age. **Gills:** adnexed, distant, broad, fleshy, fragile; colour paler than that of the cap. **Stipe:** 4–5cm long, 0.3–1cm thick; central; cylindrical; smooth, grooved, sticky when wet, upper part powdery; concolorous with cap. **Ring:** absent. **Flesh:** soft; whitish to pale yellow. **Smell:** no distinctive odour. **Spore print:** white.

SIMILAR SPECIES: Has the same yellow colour as *Hygrocybe flavescens*, *H. obrussea* and *H. ceracea* (none described here).

EDIBILITY: Edible; has a mild flavour, but the flesh is watery and somewhat insubstantial.

> **NOTES:** Many mycologists differentiate *Hygrocybe chlorophana* from the slightly larger *H. flavescens* by the moistness of the stipe. In this species, the stipe is viscid, whereas in *H. flavescens* it is dry to moist.

The cap of the developing mushrooms is viscid when damp.

The cylindrical stipe is slightly grooved.

Broad and spaced far apart, the gills are slightly paler in colour than the cap and stipe.

The gills are narrowly attached to the stipe.

The wavy margin is distinctive.

A small frog perches on the viscid cap of a specimen of *Hygrocybe conica*.

Liz Popich

Hygrocybe conica (Schaeff.) P. Kumm. 1871

Common names: Blackening wax cap, conical slimy cap, witch's hat, conical wax cap
Afrikaans: Verkoolwaslamel

Etymology: GREEK: *hygros* = wet, moist, *kybe* = head; *conic* = conical, cone-shaped

Synonym(s): *Godfrinia conica, Hygrocybe riparia, H. trista, Hygrophorus conicus*

ECOLOGY: Saprophytic.

DISTRIBUTION: Western Cape and Gauteng, possibly more widespread. Occurs in the UK, Europe, Canada, USA, Russia, Japan, Australia, New Zealand and Tenerife.

HABITAT: Grows in grassy areas, except those that have been heavily fertilised; fruit bodies single or in small groups, sometimes in fairy rings.

DESCRIPTION: Both the bright red, waxy cap and the yellowish stipe of this delicate mushroom turn black with bruising and age, making it relatively easy to identify. **Cap:** 2–3.5cm in diameter; fleshy; conical to bell-shaped; margin irregularly lobed, turning upward and splitting; surface smooth, slightly slimy when wet, waxy; bright orange to scarlet, blackening with age. **Gills:** almost free to adnexed, sinuate, distant, thick, wavy; pale yellow turning black. **Stipe:** 4–5cm long, 0.3–1cm thick; central; cylindrical, longitudinal fibres, grooved, streaked with age; yellow with scarlet tints, white above the base; firm, hollow. **Ring:** absent. **Flesh:** blackens with age or when handled. **Smell:** no distinctive odour. **Spore print:** white.

SIMILAR SPECIES: *Leratiomyces ceres, Hygrocybe nigrescens* (not described here). *H. nigrescens,* also commonly known as 'blackening wax cap', is very similar, but has a slight colour and cap variation.

EDIBILITY: Edible; has a mild flavour, but the flesh is watery and insubstantial.

Young fruit bodies emerge from the soil.

The young fruit body is easily recognised by its orange cap and yellow stipe.

The margin turns upward, exposing the brightly coloured gills.

The fruit body becomes black with age.

The furrowed cap is supported by a rigid, black stipe that resembles horsehair.

Gymnopus androsaceus (L.) Della Magg. & Trassin. 2014

Common names: Horsehair fungus, horsehair parachute, horsehair mummy cap
Afrikaans: Haarsteelswam

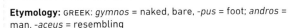

Etymology: GREEK: *gymnos* = naked, bare, *-pus* = foot; *andros* = man, *-aceus* = resembling

Synonym(s): *Androsaceus androsaceus, Marasmius androsaceus, Merulius androsaceus, Setulipes androsaceus*

ECOLOGY: Saprophytic.

DISTRIBUTION: Western Cape, Eastern Cape and Gauteng, possibly more widespread. Occurs in the UK, Europe, Canada, USA, Colombia, Brazil, Chile, Russia, Japan, Australia and New Zealand.

HABITAT: Grows on plant litter, especially on twigs, pine needles and leaves; fruit bodies grouped.

DESCRIPTION: Minute in size, the tiny fruit body is characterised by a delicately wrinkled cap and a tall, thin stipe. **Cap:** 0.3–1cm in diameter; thin, membraneous, delicate; convex becoming flattened, occasionally with a depressed centre; margin lobed; surface radially grooved or furrowed; clay-brown with a pink hue, darker at the centre. **Gills:** adnate, distant, narrow, well-spaced; concolorous with or lighter than the cap. **Stipe:** 2.5–5cm long, less than 0.1cm thick; central; long, slender, rigid; connected to the substrate by black, horsehair-like mycelial threads; surface smooth, shiny; black; tough, fibrous, solid. **Ring:** absent. **Flesh:** very thin; white in the cap, dark in stipe. **Smell:** no distinctive odour. **Spore print:** white.

SIMILAR SPECIES: Resembles *Marasmius rotula*, but the gills do not form a collarium (collar) on the stipe.

EDIBILITY: Inedible; too fragile and thin to be useful in cooking.

NOTES: This species derives its common name 'horsehair fungus' from the network of black, shiny, tough strands around the base of the stipe. These strands, resembling the hair of a horse's tail, extend outward to bind the stipe to a loose bundle of litter under the group of fruit bodies.

Gymnopus androsaceus grows on plant litter such as leaves, pine needles and twigs.

Barely a centimetre wide, the cap is thin and fragile.

The long, slender stipes are attached to the substrate by fine, black mycelial threads.

Fruit bodies of *Marasmiellus candidus* can grow singly or gregariously, depending on environmental conditions.

Marasmiellus candidus (Fr.) E. Horak 1987

Common names: Blackfoot parachute, black-footed marasmius
Afrikaans: None

Etymology: GREEK: *marasmos* = wasting away, withered, *-ellus* = diminutive; LATIN: *candidus* = clear, transparent, white

Synonym(s): *Marasmius albocorticis*, *M. albus-corticis*, *M. candidus*, *M. magnisporus*

ECOLOGY: Saprophytic.

DISTRIBUTION: First reported in South Africa in Gauteng (Pretoria), but may be more widespread. Occurs in the USA, Mexico, Costa Rica, Puerto Rico, Bolivia, Japan and Australia.

HABITAT: Grows on twigs, small logs and similar litter in broadleaved and coniferous forests; fruit bodies single or scattered.

DESCRIPTION: The striking contrast between the white cap and black stipe makes this a distinctive mushroom. **Cap:** 0.5–1.8cm in diameter; thin, membraneous, fragile; convex to flattened, with a slightly depressed centre when young; surface shiny, dry, slightly radially wrinkled; translucent white. **Gills:** decurrent, very distant, becoming irregular and wavy or vein-like; white, developing pinkish or yellowish stains with age. **Stipe:** 0.5–3cm long, 0.05–0.1cm thick; central; cylindrical or slightly tapering at either end; dry, covered with soft, woolly hairs; white, becoming brown to blackish from the base upward. **Flesh:** thin; whitish. **Smell:** no distinctive odour. **Spore print:** white.

SIMILAR SPECIES: *Tetrapyrgos nigripes* (not described here).

EDIBILITY: Inedible.

A tiny mushroom with a striking contrast between the white cap and the black stipe.

The lower surface appears vein-like.

The gills are widely spaced apart and broader where they are attached to the stipe.

Marasmius bekolacongoli occurs in indigenous forests in South Africa and elsewhere on the African continent.

Jean Stephenson

Marasmius bekolacongoli Beeli 1928

Common names: None
Afrikaans: None

Etymology: GREEK: *marasmos* = wasting away, withered; *bekolacongoli* = after the Congo (modern-day Democratic Republic of the Congo)
Synonym(s): None

Unknown

ECOLOGY: Saprophytic.

DISTRIBUTION: First reported in South Africa in the Western Cape, Eastern Cape (Wild Coast) and KwaZulu-Natal, but may be more widespread. Possibly native to Africa; occurs in Nigeria, Cameroon, Gabon, Uganda, Rwanda, Burundi, Democratic Republic of the Congo, Tanzania, Kenya, Zambia, Malawi, Zimbabwe and Madagascar.

HABITAT: Grows on humus in indigenous forests; fruit bodies single or in small groups.

DESCRIPTION: The unusually large fruit body distinguishes this from other *Marasmius* species. **Cap:** up to 10cm in diameter; bell-shaped to convex; surface smooth, very strongly grooved, pleated; translucent, violet to violet-brown at the umbo and on radial ridges, yellowish white to lemon to lilac-brown in the depressions. **Gills:** almost free, very distant; whitish. **Stipe:** up to 15cm long; central; thin, with a white mycelial base; pale yellow to yellowish beige, lower part light brown. **Ring:** absent. **Flesh:** thin; pale. **Smell:** unknown. **Spore print:** white to cream.

EDIBILITY: Unknown.

The tall, thin stipe grows up to 15cm.

Marasmius bekolacongoli is broadly bell-shaped with a violet to violet-brown umbo and similarly tinted depressions.

The whitish gills are spaced far apart.

Growing on a decaying tree trunk, these specimens of *Marasmius haematocephalus* resemble small parachutes.

Jean Stephenson

Marasmius haematocephalus (Mont.) Fr. 1838

Common names: Rosy parachute, red horsehair parachute, blood-red marasmius
Afrikaans: Roosvalskermpie

Etymology: GREEK: *marasmos* = wasting away, withered; *haimatos* = blood red, *cephal* = head

Synonym(s): *Agaricus haematocephalus*, *Chamaeceras haematocephalus*

ECOLOGY: Saprophytic.

DISTRIBUTION: First reported in South Africa in Gauteng and KwaZulu-Natal, but may be more widespread. Occurs in the USA, Mexico, Costa Rica, Puerto Rico, Cuba, Colombia, Ecuador, Suriname, French Guiana, Brazil, Sri Lanka, Vietnam, Malaysia, China, Indonesia, Papua New Guinea, Australia, New Zealand, Sierra Leone, Côte d'Ivoire, Ghana, Benin, Nigeria, Cameroon, Gabon, Uganda, Democratic Republic of the Congo, Tanzania, Kenya, Zimbabwe and Madagascar.

HABITAT: Grows on fallen branches, twigs, leaves, sometimes on dung; fruit bodies in small groups.

DESCRIPTION: This delicate mushroom can be identified by the deep-magenta to red colour of the cap and the dark, slender stipe. **Cap:** 0.1–0.9cm in diameter; very thin; bell-shaped then convex, finally almost plane; margin crenate; surface glabrous, membraneous, finely hairy, radially grooved, pleated; ruby to deep red. **Gills:** narrowly adnexed, distant; pallid. **Stipe:** 2.5–5cm long, less than 0.1cm thick; central; cylindrical, very slender; glabrous; umber or blackish; hollow. **Ring:** absent. **Flesh:** thin. **Smell:** no distinctive odour. **Spore print:** white to pale yellowish.

SIMILAR SPECIES: The fruit body of *Marasmius pulcherripes* (not described here) is reddish.

EDIBILITY: Inedible; far too small to be useful in cooking.

Jean Stephenson

The colour of the long, slender stipe is umber to blackish toward the base.

Liz Popich

Bell-shaped and thin, the cap becomes plane as the fruit body matures.

Liz Popich

The gills are pinkish, often with red edges.

Liz Popich

A small group of fruit bodies growing on herbivore dung.

Marasmius rotula (Scop.) Fr. 1838

Common names: Collared parachute, wheel mushroom, little pinwheel, common wheel mummy cap
Afrikaans: Wieletjie

Etymology: GREEK: *marasmos* = wasting away, withered;
LATIN: *rotula* = small wheel

Synonym(s): *Agaricus rotula, Androsaceus rotula, Chamaeceras rotula, Merulius collariatus, Micromphale collariatum*

ECOLOGY: Saprophytic.

DISTRIBUTION: Gauteng, possibly more widespread. Occurs in the UK, Europe, USA, Brazil, Russia, Australia, New Zealand, Madagascar and Mascarene Islands.

HABITAT: Grows on sticks and woody debris in broadleaved forests, occasionally on coniferous wood; fruit bodies single or clustered.

Marasmius rotula grows on woody debris.

DESCRIPTION: The gills of this species are attached to a collar (collarium) around the stipe, rather than to the stipe. **Cap:** 0.5–2cm in diameter; broadly convex, soon developing a navel-like central depression, usually appearing to have a flat top and squarish sides when viewed from the side; surface bald, dry, radially grooved, pleated; whitish, brownish in the depressions. **Gills:** attached to a tiny collar that encircles the stipe, distant; ivory to yellowish white. **Stipe:** 1.5–4cm long, 0.1cm thick; central; cylindrical; wiry; dry, shiny, sometimes with stiff hairs at the base; pale at first, soon dark brown to black, except at the apex, upper stipe off-white. **Ring:** absent. **Flesh:** thin, almost nonexistent; white in the cap, brown in the stipe. **Smell:** no distinctive odour. **Spore print:** white or off-white.

The fruit bodies turn brown with age.

SIMILAR SPECIES: *Marasmius bulliardii* (not described here), *Gymnopus androsaceus.*

EDIBILITY: Inedible; too small for culinary use.

Ivory to yellow-white, the gills are attached to a ring (collarium).

The broadly convex cap is marked by a brownish central depression.

Marasmius siccus (Schwein.) Fr. 1838

Common names: Orange pinwheel, orange beach umbrella
Afrikaans: Oranjewiel

Etymology: GREEK: *marasmos* = wasting away, withered;
LATIN: *siccus* = dry

Synonym(s): *Agaricus siccus, Chamaeceras siccus*

ECOLOGY: Saprophytic.

DISTRIBUTION: Gauteng, possibly more widespread. Occurs in Scandinavia, USA, Russia, Japan and Australia.

HABITAT: Grows on leaf humus in coniferous and broadleaved forests; fruit bodies in small groups or scattered.

DESCRIPTION: The orangish colour of the bell-shaped cap and the white to pale-yellowish gills are characteristic. **Cap:** 0.5–3cm in diameter; convex at first, soon becoming broadly convex to broadly bell-shaped, with a shallow central depression or a low, rounded, narrow hump; surface dry, dull, opaque, smooth at first, but soon roughened or minutely velvety, conspicuously pleated; orange, fading with age. **Gills:** adnate, free, very distant; white to pale yellowish, rarely with a brownish-orange edge. **Stipe:** 2.5–6.5cm long, 0.1cm thick; central; cylindrical, long, wiry, with basal mycelium; surface dry, bald; yellowish along the upper part, dark red to brown toward the base; tough, hollow. **Ring:** absent. **Flesh:** very thin, insubstantial, fragile to flexible, almost nonexistent; white. **Smell:** no distinctive odour. **Spore print:** white.

SIMILAR SPECIES: Often confused with other *Marasmius* species.

EDIBILITY: Inedible; too small for culinary use.

The gills are spaced far apart.

The pleated surface is conspicous.

The cap becomes broadly bell-shaped and develops a shallow central depression.

The stipe is yellowish along the upper part and dark red toward the base.

Amparoina spinosissima (Singer) Singer 1958

Common name: Tiny spiny-stalked mycena
Afrikaans: Doringstem-sampioentjie

Etymology: *amparoina* = after Amparo Heidi, the daughter, of mycologist Rolf Singer (1906–1994); LATIN: s*pinatus* = spiny, *-issimus* = most, very

Synonym(s): *Marasmius spinosissimus, Mycena spinosissima*

ECOLOGY: Saprophytic.

KNOWN DISTRIBUTION: First reported in South Africa in Gauteng, but may be more widespread. Occurs in the USA, Mexico, Costa Rica, Puerto Rico, Colombia, Ecuador, Brazil, Argentina, India, Japan and New Caledonia.

HABITAT: Grows on decaying twigs; fruit bodies scattered or clustered.

DESCRIPTION: This small, delicate mushroom is easily recognised by its overall whitish appearance; in young specimens, the surface of the cap is covered in spines that disappear as the fruit body matures. **Cap:** 0.20–0.55cm in diameter; initially conical, becoming broadly bell-shaped; entirely covered in the early stage with a universal veil of pale-greenish or ivory-coloured, erect or curved, conic, deterstile warts and spines that disappear first from the middle, then from the margin, and finally from the entire cap; margin straight with spiny veil fragments, becoming plane and wavy or finely torn with age; surface dry, very thin, striate, covered with white, powdery granules, becoming slightly corrugated toward the margin; white to whitish. **Gills:** adnexed, fairly close, ventricose; white. **Stipe:** 2–3.8cm long, 0.05–0.10cm thick; central; cylindrical, slightly tapering; surface dry, almost smooth at the apex, densely powdery to hairy toward the base; translucent white; hollow. **Ring:** absent. **Flesh:** very thin; translucent white. **Smell:** no distinctive odour. **Spore print:** white.

EDIBILITY: Unknown.

NOTES: This mushroom was named *Marasmius spinosissima* by mycologist Rolf Singer in 1951, who had originally found the species in Argentina in 1949. It was assigned to the *Amparoina* genus in 1958.

The stipe is hairy and covered with minute, white, powdery granules, giving it a frosted appearance.

The gills are slightly swollen.

The cap covering of greenish to ivory-coloured spines and warts disappears as the mushroom matures.

The young fruit body is covered in spines and warts.

A developing fruit body.

Cruentomycena viscidocruenta (Cleland) R.H. Petersen & Kovalenko 2008

Common name: Ruby bonnet
Afrikaans: Rooikappie

Etymology: LATIN: *cruento* = to make bloody, ANCIENT GREEK: *mykēs* = fungus; LATIN: *viscidus* = sticky, *cruentus* = to make bloody

Synonym(s): *Mycena coccinea, M. coccineus, M. viscidocruenta*

ECOLOGY: Saprophytic.

DISTRIBUTION: First reported in South Africa in the Western Cape, Eastern Cape and Gauteng, but may be more widespread. Occurs in Australia and New Zealand.

HABITAT: Attached to small sticks and leaves in moist locations; fruit bodies in small groups.

DESCRIPTION: The blood-red cap and stipe make it easy to identify this tiny mushroom. **Cap:** 0.1–0.7cm in diameter; hemispherical, flattening as it matures, centre depressed; margin striate; surface viscid when wet, glossy and sticky, radially grooved in mature specimens; blood red, translucent. **Gills:** adnate, distant; red, paler than cap. **Stipe:** 1–3cm long, 0.2–0.6cm thick; central; gelatinous, quite viscid when wet, drops of gluten visible on stipe of very fresh specimens; red; fragile, slender, hollow. **Ring:** absent. **Flesh:** thin; red. **Smell:** no distinctive odour. **Spore print:** white.

EDIBILITY: Unknown.

A small group of fruit bodies on a twig.

The red gills are distinctive.

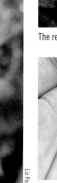

Bright red in colour, the cap is hemispherical before becoming flattened with age.

A minute mushroom, the cap width ranges between 0.1 and 0.7cm.

The young buds of *Cyptotrama asprata* resemble small pompoms.

Jean Stephenson

Cyptotrama asprata (Berk.) Redhead & Ginns 1980

Common names: Golden coincap, golden scruffy collybia
Afrikaans: Harige goudmus

Etymology: GREEK: *kypto* = stooped forward, LATIN: *trama* = something thin; LATIN: *asper* = rough, thorny, *-ata* = possessing

Synonym(s): *Armillaria asprata, Collybia chrysopepla, Cyptotrama chrysopepla, Gymnopus chrysopeplus*

ECOLOGY: Saprophytic.

DISTRIBUTION: Western Cape, Eastern Cape, Gauteng, KwaZulu-Natal and Mpumalanga, possibly more widespread. Occurs in Europe, Canada, USA, Mexico, Costa Rica, Puerto Rica, Cuba, Brazil, Russia, India, Thailand, Taiwan, Japan, South Korea, China, Australia, New Zealand, Madagascar and tropical East Africa.

HABITAT: Grows on fallen and dead brances of broadleaved trees; prefers damp conditions; fruit bodies scattered in groups.

DESCRIPTION: This small, bright-yellow to orange mushroom is easily identified by the coarsely scaled cap. **Cap:** 0.5–2.5cm in diameter; thin, fleshy; globose, becoming convex to almost flat, young buds look like pompons; margin even to slightly undulate, striate; surface scaly to granular-mealy, scales darker and denser at the centre but falling off to leave a dry, smooth, bright yellow-orange surface; golden at first, then bright yellow. **Gills:** adnate to slightly decurrent, subdistant, broad; white. **Stipe:** 1–5cm long, 0.15–0.3cm thick; central; cylindrical, ring-like ridge on the upper half, with the part above the ridge smooth and white with fine hairs, rough with scales below the ridge; solid, fairly tough, cartilaginous. **Ring:** absent. **Flesh:** very thin; white. **Smell:** no distinctive odour. **Spore print:** white.

SIMILAR SPECIES: *Pholiota* species (not described here), which are distinguished by a brown spore print.

EDIBILITY: Unknown.

NOTES: This species is involved in the conversion of dead wood and woody debris to humus.

The cap is covered with coarse scales.

The broad, white gills are adnate, meeting the stipe at nearly a right angle.

A young mushroom emerges from a substrate of rotting wood.

The young cap is golden at first before becoming bright yellow.

Cyptotrama asprata occurs in groups on dead broadleaved trees.

In humid conditions the cap of *Hymenopellis radicata* becomes sticky.

Hymenopellis radicata (Relhan) R.H. Petersen 2010

Common names: Deep rooter, rooting shank
Afrikaans: Wortelstoeltjie

Etymology: GREEK: *hymenos* = membraneous, LATIN: *-pellis* = skin; LATIN: *radicatus* = rooted

Synonym(s): *Collybia radicata*, *Mucidula radicata*, *Oudemansiella radicata*, *Xerula radicata*

ECOLOGY: Saprophytic.

DISTRIBUTION: Gauteng (Pretoria), possibly more widespread. Occurs in the UK, Europe, USA, Brazil, Russia, Japan, Australia and New Zealand.

HABITAT: Grows near stumps and dying broadleaved trees in forests; sometimes attached to dead buried roots; fruit bodies single or scattered.

DESCRIPTION: The tough, slender stipe, sticky yellowish-brown cap, and pure-white gills of this tall mushroom aid identification.
Cap: 2.5–10cm in diameter; bell-shaped to convex, then flattened with broad umbo; surface sticky, greasy, wrinkled, veined, viscid when humid; whitish, ochre to brown. **Gills:** adnate, each with a decurrent tooth, medium spaced; pale cream, often with brown edges.
Stipe: 5–15cm long, 0.5–1cm thick; central; slender, long, cylindrical, often twisted, with a root-like extension of the stipe (pseudorhiza); surface covered with fine, white hairs causing a velvety appearance, longitudinally striate; white at the apex, darkening toward the base to almost the same colour as the cap; rigid, fibrous, tough. **Ring:** absent.
Flesh: soft, watery, fibrous in the stipe; off-white. **Smell:** mealy odour. **Spore print:** white to pale cream.

EDIBILITY: Inedible.

In older specimens, the cap is upturned and the margin wavy.

With a bit of care and digging, the rooting stipe can be excavated.

Full-length gills are interspersed with shorter ones that radiate from the margin.

A broad umbo is visible on the flattened cap.

Pluteus romellii (Britzelm.) Sacc. 1895

Common names: Goldleaf shield, yellow-stemmed pluteus
Afrikaans: None

Etymology: LATIN: *pluteus* = shield, easel; *romellii* = after
Swedish mycologist Lars Rommel (1854–1927)

Synonym(s): *Pluteus lutescens, P. splendidus, P. sternbergii*

Unknown

ECOLOGY: Saprophytic.

DISTRIBUTION: First reported in South Africa in Gauteng (Pretoria),
but may be more widespread. Occurs in the UK, Europe, Canada,
USA, Colombia, Russia, Japan and Australia.

HABITAT: Grows on decaying wood or woody debris of broadleaved
trees; fruit bodies single or in small groups.

DESCRIPTION: Fragile and beautiful, this fungus is easily identified
by the yellow stipe, brownish to olive cap, free gills and pinkish
spores. **Cap:** 2.5–5cm in diameter; convex to flat, sometimes
with an umbo; margin striate; surface wrinkled over the centre;
yellowish brown to olive-brown. **Gills:** free, crowded, full and
intermediate lengths, swollen around the middle; pale yellowish,
pink at maturity. **Stipe:** 2–4cm in height, 0.2–0.6cm thick; more or
less cylindrical, often twisted, sometimes broadening at the base;
longitudinally striate; yellow at the base, pale yellow toward the
apex; fragile. **Ring:** absent. **Flesh:** cap firm and translucent white;
stipe thin and yellow. **Smell:** no distinctive odour. **Spore print:** pink
to dull salmon-pink.

EDIBILITY: Unknown.

More or less cylindrical, the stipe is yellow at
the base and pale yellow in the upper part.

The stipe is more or less cylindrical, but
broadens toward the base.

The gills are pale yellowish at first, becoming pink at maturity.

An umbo sometimes forms over the
centre of the cap.

Pluteus salicinus (Pers.) P. Kumm. 1871

Common names: Willow shield, knackers' crumpet, Illinois backwoods shroom
Afrikaans: None

Etymology: LATIN: *pluteus* = shield, easel; *salicinus* = pertaining to willow trees

Synonym(s): *Rhodosporus salicinus*

Edible

ECOLOGY: Saprophytic.

DISTRIBUTION: Gauteng (Pretoria), possibly more widespread. Occurs in the UK, Europe, Canada, USA, Russia and New Zealand.

HABITAT: Grows on dead wood; fruit bodies grouped or clustered.

DESCRIPTION: This species is readily identified by the prominent rounded umbo and the grey-green to olive-green coloration of the cap. **Cap:** 2.5–5cm in diameter; fleshy, thin; conical, expanding to bell-shaped, then flattening, sometimes with a broad, rounded umbo; margin even, downturned, striate; surface smooth at first, becoming minutely scaly over the umbo, minute, dark fibrils radiate toward the margin; dull greenish, bluish or olive-grey, paler toward the margin, which acquires fawnish tints as spores mature. **Gills:** free, close, full and intermediate lengths, edges entire, broad; creamy white at first, changing to brownish pink or salmon. **Stipe:** 0.55–0.90cm long, 0.4–0.8cm thick; central; long, cylindrical, slightly bulbous base; faintly striate, with fine blackish fibrils on the lower parts; creamy white; firm, solid. **Ring:** absent. **Flesh:** thin; creamy white, greyish under cap cuticle. **Smell:** faint mushroomy odour. **Spore print:** pinkish grey to pale brownish pink.

EDIBILITY: Edible; needs to be parboiled before cooking.

Smooth at first, the cap becomes minutely scaly over the umbo.

The stipe is cylindrical, becoming slightly bulbous at the base.

The expanded cap has a broad, rounded umbo.

The closely spaced gills change from white to brownish pink with age.

Growing to about 1cm in diameter, the caps of *Coprinellus disseminatus* are creamy white when young and grey in maturity.

Coprinellus disseminatus (Pers.) J.E. Lange 1938

Common names: Fairies' bonnets, little helmet, fairy ink cap
Afrikaans: Bondelinkmus

Etymology: GREEK: *coprinus* = pertaining to dung, *-ellus* = diminutive; *dissemino* = to sow, *-atus* = resembling

Synonym(s): *Coprinarius disseminatus, Coprinus disseminatus, Psathyrella gyroflexa, Pseudocoprinus disseminatus*

ECOLOGY: Saprophytic.

DISTRIBUTION: Western Cape, Gauteng and KwaZulu-Natal, possibly more widespread. Occurs in the UK, Europe, Canada, USA, Brazil, Russia, Japan, Australia and New Zealand.

HABITAT: Grows on woody material and decaying stumps or on adjoining soil; fruit bodies characteristically clustered in very large groups.

DESCRIPTION: This mushroom can be recognised by its cap shape and greyish-black gills. **Cap:** up to 1cm in diameter; fragile; egg-shaped to hemispherical; margin even; surface pleated or grooved, covered with fine hairs and grains that are visible through a magnifying glass, pleats clearly visible on young caps; cream to white becoming buff to grey, paler when young, colour darker in the centre. **Gills:** adnate, distant; white turning grey to black; do not deliquesce. **Stipe:** 2–4cm long, 0.5–2mm thick; central; slender, short, cylindrical, delicate; fungus spreads from wood to adjoining soil by means of tough strands of matted brownish-red mycelium at the base; white; hollow. **Ring:** absent. **Flesh:** thin, membraneous; white. **Smell:** no distinctive odour. **Spore print:** umber to black-brown.

SIMILAR SPECIES: *Termitomyces microcarpus, Parasola plicatilis* (not described here).

EDIBILITY: Edible; has a mild taste. The fruit bodies virtually disappear during cooking, making them unsuitable for culinary purposes.

NOTES: This is an extremely fragile mushroom, and the caps quickly crumble when handled.

Edible

The caps are broadly egg-shaped to hemispherical.

The fruit bodies are characteristically clustered in very large groups.

Coprinellus domesticus (Bolton) Vilgalys, Hopple & Jacq. Johnson 2001

Common names: Fire-rug ink cap, domestic inky cap
Afrikaans: Mat-inkmus

Etymology: GREEK: *coprinus* = pertaining to dung, *-ellus* = diminutive; LATIN: *domesticus* = belonging to a household

Synonym(s): *Coprinus domesticus*

ECOLOGY: Saprophytic.

DISTRIBUTION: First reported in South Africa in Gauteng (Pretoria), but may be more widespread. Occurs in the UK, Europe, USA, Russia and Japan.

HABITAT: Grows on dead wood of broadleaved trees, on compost and vegetable debris and sometimes in damp cellars, also found behind loose bathroom tiles and in other damp areas; fruit bodies ocassionally single, in large groups or clustered.

DESCRIPTION: The fruit body of this light-brown fungus grows out of a mat of orange to brown fibres that are attached to the substrate, making it instantly recognisable. **Cap:** 1–3cm in diameter; egg-shaped at first, later expanding to convex and then bell-shaped; splitting at the margin; surface powdered at first with whitish or buff veil remnants, later smooth and becoming grooved from margin to centre; pale buff with a tawny centre. **Gills:** free or adnate, crowded; white, turning grey to reddish grey, then black and inky when deliquescing. **Stipe:** 4–10cm long, 0.2–1cm thick; central; swollen, ridged at the base; often arising from a reddish to orange mat of mycelium, called an ozonium, around the base; white, tinged buff toward the base. **Ring:** absent. **Flesh:** thin. **Smell:** no distinctive odour. **Spore print:** dark brown.

SIMILAR SPECIES: *Coprinellus radians* (not described here) also grows from an orange to brown mycelium mat. *C. micaceus* may look very similar.

EDIBILITY: Edible; very flavourful when cooked.

Edible

The crowded gills become black and inky when decaying.

Liz Popich

Fine grooves stretch from the margin of the cap to the centre.

Liz Popich

The common name of this species, 'fire-rug ink cap', is derived from the reddish to orange mat of mycelium, called an ozonium.

Jean Stephenson

Whitish to buff veil remnants collect on the cap surface, giving it a powdery appearance.

Liz Popich

Coprinellus heptemerus (M. Lange & A.H. Sm.) Vilgalys, Hopple & Jacq. Johnson 2001

Common names: None
Afrikaans: None

Etymology: GREEK: *coprinus* = pertaining to dung, *-ellus* = diminutive; *hepta* = seven, *meros* = parts
Synonym(s): *Coprinus heptemerus*

ECOLOGY: Saprophytic.

DISTRIBUTION: First reported in South Africa in Gauteng (Pretoria), but may be more widespread. Occurs in the UK, Europe, Canada, USA, Japan, Australia and New Zealand.

HABITAT: Grows on herbivore dung; fruit bodies in small groups or clustered.

DESCRIPTION: The tiny white fruit body and the long, thin, translucent white stipe are distinctive. **Cap:** 1.5–3cm in diameter; ovoid at first, expanding to bell-shaped, becoming radially grooved; margin thin, translucent; brown, yellow-brown to dark brown at the centre, margin whitish grey. **Gills:** adnexed or free, moderately spaced to distant; whitish at first, turning black; sometimes deliquescent. **Stipe:** 1–5cm long, 0.05–0.10cm thick; central; downy; translucent or white. **Ring:** absent. **Flesh:** almost nonexistent. **Smell:** unknown. **Spore print:** black.

EDIBILITY: Inedible.

The cap is radially grooved.

The stipe is downy and translucent.

A small group of fruit bodies on herbivore dung.

Whitish at first, the gills turn black, sometimes becoming liquid.

A dense cluster of fruit bodies grows in soil adjacent to a decaying tree stump.

Glen van Niekerk

Coprinellus micaceus (Bull.) Vilgalys, Hopple & Jacq. Johnson 2001

Common names: Glistening ink cap, mica cap
Afrikaans: Glinsterinkmus

Etymology: GREEK: *coprinus* = pertaining to dung, *-ellus* = diminutive; LATIN: *mica* = crumb, morsel, *-eus* = similar to

Synonym(s): *Coprinus micaceus*

ECOLOGY: Saprophytic.

DISTRIBUTION: Widespread in South Africa. Occurs in the UK, Europe, Canada, USA, Russia, Australia and New Zealand.

HABITAT: Commonly grows in soil, on decaying stumps or wood and on lawns; fruit bodies in dense clusters.

DESCRIPTION: This mushroom can be recognised by the glistening mica-like particles that cover the surface of the small, brownish young caps. **Cap:** 1–3.5cm in diameter; conical to bell- or egg-shaped; margin striate, curving inward, splitting easily; surface slightly pleated or striate, smooth, sprinkled at first with minute, glistening, whitish particles (universal veil remnants), which often disappear with age; beige to slightly light brown, centre darker. **Gills:** free but touching the stipe, close; white, turning light brown to grey, finally brown-black when deliquescing. **Stipe:** 2–5cm long, 0.3–0.6cm thick; central; cylindrical, slightly wider toward the base; surface smooth, silky; white to yellowish beige; hollow, brittle. **Ring:** absent. **Flesh:** soft; pale yellow. **Smell:** odourless to slightly mushroomy. **Spore print:** brown-black.

SIMILAR SPECIES: There are a number of similar-looking species that can only be distinguished by microscopic examination.

EDIBILITY: Edible. These mushrooms should always be cooked as they can be mildly poisonous if eaten raw, causing an upset stomach in some people.

Remnants of the veil appear as whitish particles on the caps.

> **NOTES:** Where these mushrooms grow along roadsides or on polluted land, they may be contaminated with heavy metals such as cadmium and lead, making them potentially poisonous. These heavy metals can become concentrated in the mycelium, causing high concentrations of toxins in the fruit bodies.

Older fruit bodies become inky at the margins before decomposing.

White at first, the gills turn light brown to grey, finally becoming brown-black.

Coprinopsis nivea (Pers.) Redhead, Vilgalys & Moncalvo 2001

Common names: Snowy ink cap, snowy white ink cap
Afrikaans: Sneeu-inkmus

Etymology: GREEK: *coprinus* = pertaining to dung, LATIN: *-opsis* = resembling; LATIN: *niveus* = snowy

Synonym(s): *Coprinus latisporus, C. niveus*

ECOLOGY: Saprophytic.

DISTRIBUTION: Western Cape, Gauteng, KwaZulu-Natal, possibly more widespread. Occurs in the UK, Europe, Canada, USA, Australia and New Zealand.

HABITAT: Grows on fresh herbivore dung, sometimes also on wet or fertilised ground or composted grass; fruit bodies clustered.

DESCRIPTION: The snow-white coloration, mealy veil remnants on the cap, and very large spores make this a distinctive mushroom. **Cap:** 0.2–2.5cm in diameter; initially egg-shaped, then conical, finally flattening out; margin split and curled over on itself; surface covered with fine mealy scales (remnants of veil); white. **Gills:** adnexed, crowded; white then flesh-coloured, finally blackish and deliquescent. **Stipe:** 0.2–3.8cm long, 0.1–0.3cm thick; cylindrical, narrowing toward the apex; densely covered in cottony fibres that tend to disappear; white; hollow. **Ring:** consists of fine mealy scales around the base of the stipe. **Flesh:** thin; white. **Smell:** no distinctive odour. **Spore print:** black.

EDIBILITY: Inedible.

The cap margin is curved back.

The cap is tiny compared to a finger.

Tiny veil fragments are visible on the cap surface.

A young specimen.

The cap is ribbed and the margin somewhat tufty.

Coprinopsis picacea (Bull.) Redhead, Vilgalys & Moncalvo 2001

Common name: Magpie ink cap
Afrikaans: Ekster-inkmus

Etymology: GREEK: *coprinus* = pertaining to dung, LATIN: *-opsis* = resembling; LATIN: *picacea* = pertaining to a magpie

Synonym(s): *Coprinus picaceus*

ECOLOGY: Saprophytic.

DISTRIBUTION: Western Cape, Gauteng, possibly more widespread. Occurs in the UK, Europe, Canada, USA, Russia and Australia.

HABITAT: Grows among leaf litter in broadleaved forests, sometimes under pines, also among sawdust and woodchips; fruit bodies single or in small groups.

DESCRIPTION: This unmistakable ink cap has a black-and-white pattern on the bell-shaped cap, caused by the veil breaking up into scales as the cap expands. **Cap:** 2–6cm in diameter; conical to broadly bell-shaped when expanded; covered in whitish patches of veil remnants; white then sepia-grey, finally black. **Gills:** white at first, rapidly purplish, then black when deliquescing. **Stipe:** 9–20cm long, 0.6–1.3cm thick; central; cylindrical, tapering toward the apex, bulbous base; woolly or fine fleecy covering; white; hollow. **Ring:** absent. **Flesh:** thin; white. **Smell:** fetid odour, said to smell of naphthalene. **Spore print:** black.

SIMILAR SPECIES: When young, this mushroom looks similar to *Coprinus comatus*.

EDIBILITY: Inedible.

NOTES: The cap is covered with a white veil that tears as the mushroom grows, leaving large light-coloured patches that contrast with the brownish-black surface of the cap. This coloration resembles that of a magpie, a bird of the Corvidae (crow) family – hence the common name of 'magpie ink cap'.

Coprinopsis picacea grows among leaf litter.

The cap is covered by white patches of veil, which easily rub off.

The entire cap becomes liquid within a few hours of fruiting.

The gills are white at first, but quickly become purple then black.

Coprinus comatus has a white, scaly, barrel-shaped cap, which turns inky from the margin toward the apex of the cap.

Coprinus comatus (O.F. Müll.) Pers. 1797

Common names: Shaggy ink cap, lawyer's wig, shaggy mane
Afrikaans: Wolhaarinkmus

Etymology: GREEK: *coprinus* = living on dung; *comatus* = with dense hair, hairy

Synonym(s): None

ECOLOGY: Saprophytic.

DISTRIBUTION: Widespread in South Africa. Occurs in the UK, Europe, Canada, USA, Argentina, Brazil, Peru, Chile, Colombia, Japan, Australia and New Zealand.

HABITAT: Grows in rich soil in gardens, by roadsides, along paths, in cultivated fields and on rubbish dumps; has been known to force its way up through tar on pathways and through the surface of tennis courts constructed on old rubbish dumps; fruit bodies single or clustered, often in large numbers.

DESCRIPTION: The unusual shape of the fruit body and the characteristic deliquescence into a black liquid make this species easy to identify. **Cap:** 2–5cm in diameter; fleshy; cylindrical and elongate at first, with the margin connected to the stipe by a ring, expanding to barrel-shaped, maturing to a narrow bell shape once the margin is released from the stipe; surface breaks up into broad scales; margin curling outward; white to creamy white, with pale-yellowish to brown tips and white to light-brown scales; brittle and thin prior to deliquescing. **Gills:** free or adnexed, crowded; white turning pink to grey, black when deliquescing. **Stipe:** 10–20cm long, 1cm thick; central; cylindrical, widening to a slightly bulbous base, almost asparagus-like; white; tough, hollow. **Ring:** if present, the ring is moveable; loose, often falling to the base of the stipe; white. **Flesh:** soft; white, turns pink. **Smell:** faint, pleasant odour. **Spore print:** black.

SIMILAR SPECIES: Can be distinguished from other ink caps by its characteristically long, slender shape.

EDIBILITY: Edible. This fungus is good to eat, having a delicate flavour when in a young state before the spores ripen and deliquescence begins.

> **NOTES:** The gills of ink caps change into black liquid as a means of distributing spores. The fluid can be used as ink by storing it in a bottle with a preservative such as formalin (in a formalin–ink ratio of 1 to 20). The ink will begin to smell rancid after a few days if a preservative is not added.

Edible

Glen van Niekerk

Younger specimens can be identified by their elongated egg shape.

Glen van Niekerk

A cluster of mature fruit bodies start to deliquesce.

Gary B Goldman

The stipe is almost all that remains after the fruit body has matured.

Agrocybe pedaides has a thin cap and slender stipe. Evidence of the partial veil usually disappears within a few hours of the mushroom emerging from the substrate.

Agrocybe pediades (Fr.) Fayod 1889

Common names: Common field cap, half-globe mushroom, lawn cap, grass agrocybe, common agrocybe
Afrikaans: Graskoepeltjie

Etymology: GREEK: *agros* = field, *kybe* = head, cap; *pedion* = a plain, level country

Synonym(s): *Agrocybe semiorbicularis, A. splendida, Naucoria subpediades, Pseudodeconica semiorbicularis*

ECOLOGY: Saprophytic.

DISTRIBUTION: Gauteng (Pretoria) and KwaZulu-Natal, possibly more widespread. Occurs in the UK, Europe, USA, Brazil, Chile, Argentina, Russia, Japan, Australia and New Zealand.

HABITAT: Grows in lawns, grassy places and open fields, also on matured mulch; fruit bodies scattered or grouped.

DESCRIPTION: The colour and size of this mushroom are variable, but the thin, sticky cap and skinny stipe help with identification.
Cap: 1–2.5cm in diameter; thin, fleshy; hemispherical becoming convex; margin even, downturned; surface smooth, becomes slightly greasy in wet weather; yellowish to ochraceous to tan, darker at the centre. **Gills:** adnate, well-spaced, full and intermediate lengths, edges entire, broad; pale ochraceous turning to dark cinnamon.
Stipe: 2.5–7.5cm long, 0.2–0.3cm thick; central; cylindrical, slender, solid, straight; surface shiny, smooth, with a few fine hairs; concolorous with cap or paler; tough, stuffed to hollow with age.
Ring: absent. **Flesh:** thin; yellowish, darkening toward the base of the stipe. **Smell:** mealy odour. **Spore print:** tobacco-brown.

EDIBILITY: Although considered edibile, this species is not recommended for eating because of the danger of confusing it with other small brown mushrooms, some of which are poisonous.

Edible

The gills are relatively densely arranged, with the spaces between them easily visible.

The cap is yellowish to ochraceous above the margin and darker at the centre.

The stipe is solid and usually straight.

The thick, central stipe widens slightly at the base.

Gymnopilus junonius (Fr.) P.D. Orton 1960

Common names: Orange tuft, laughing jack, giant gymnopilus, spectacular rustgill, giant flame cap
Afrikaans: Pragbondelswam

Etymology: GREEK: *gymnos* = naked, LATIN: *pilus* = a hair; *junonius* = pertaining to Juno (Roman goddess, wife of Jupiter)

Synonym(s): *Fulvidula spectabilis*, *Gymnopilus spectabilis*, *G. spectabilis* var. *junonius*, *Pholiota gigantea*

ECOLOGY: Saprophytic.

DISTRIBUTION: Western Cape, Eastern Cape, Gauteng and KwaZulu-Natal, possibly more widespread. Occurs in the UK, Europe, USA, Costa Rica, Russia, Japan, Australia and New Zealand.

HABITAT: Grows at ground level on unhealthy or dying broadleaved or conifer trees; fruit bodies single or grouped and clustered in overlapping clumps.

Fruit bodies cluster in overlapping clumps.

DESCRIPTION: The large orange fruit body, prominent stipe ring, and thread-like veil at the margin make this an easily identifiable species. **Cap:** 5–20cm in diameter; fleshy; convex, with a slight umbo; margin even to undulate, smooth, inrolled when young, turning down; fibrillose veil in young specimens; surface smooth, dry, covered with small orange-yellow fibrils or scales; bright tawny to yellow, darkening to orange. **Gills:** adnexed, crowded, full and intermediate lengths, broad, thin; yellow, ageing to rust-brown. **Stipe:** 3–10cm long, 1–2cm thick; central; the base of the stipe widens slightly; surface smooth or scaly; tawny yellow to ochre with tawny orange fibrils, deposited spores turn it rusty; thick, solid, sturdy. **Ring:** membraneous, near the upper part of the stipe; concolorous with the rest of the fruit body, becoming rust-coloured. **Flesh:** firm; pale yellow to ochre, reddening when touched. **Smell:** mild to slightly pleasant odour. **Spore print:** rust-orange.

SIMILAR SPECIES: Other *Gymnopilus* species, *Omphalotus olearius*, *Lactarius deliciosus*.

EDIBILITY: Inedible; has a bitter taste.

A young *Gymnopilus junonius* specimen.

NOTES: *Gymnopilus* species cause a brown rot. Other *Gymnopilus* species found in South Africa (but not described here) are *G. penetrans*, *G. hybridus* and *G. sapineus*, which are all orange in colour but considerably smaller.

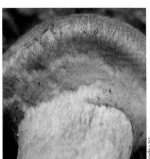

A young cap, showing the thread-like veil beneath the cap.

Liz Popich

The fruit bodies of *Omphalotus olearius* appear in clusters on dead or dying trees and stumps.

Omphalotus olearius (DC.) Singer 1948

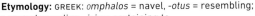

Common names: Copper trumpet, jack o'lantern, lantern funnel
Afrikaans: Vals chantarelle

Etymology: GREEK: *omphalos* = navel, *-otus* = resembling;
LATIN: *olea* = olive, *-icis* = pertaining to

Synonym(s): *Clitocybe olearia, Omphalotus olearius* var. *illudens, Pleurotus olearius*

ECOLOGY: Mycorrhizal.

DISTRIBUTION: Western Cape and Gauteng, possibly more widespread. Occurs in Europe, USA, Mexico and Australia.

HABITAT: Grows on the wood of deciduous trees; fruit bodies single or clustered.

DESCRIPTION: This bright orange-gilled mushroom can be mistaken for a chanterelle. **Cap:** 6–14cm in diameter; compact, fleshy; dome-shaped at first, then flat to finally funnel-shaped; margin wavy, incurved; surface covered with fine hairs or innate, small scales composed of fibrils; pale yellow, orange to dark coppery orange, with darker markings. **Gills:** decurrent, crowded, unequal, bioluminescent; olive to bright yellow-orange. **Stipe:** 6–15cm long, 0.8–2cm thick; central to exentric; striate, fibrillose; concolorous with cap; tough, solid, spongy. **Ring:** absent. **Flesh:** yellowish, darkening toward the base of the stipe. **Smell:** no distinctive odour. **Spore print:** whitish.

SIMILAR SPECIES: The fruit bodies of *Lactarius deliciosus, Gymnopilus junonius* and *Chantharellus cibarius* (not described here) share a similar orange colour, but this species can be distinguished by its prominent decurrent gills.

EDIBILITY: Poisonous; causes severe cramps, vomiting and diarrhoea.

NOTES: In the dark, the gills of fresh fruit bodies emit a greenish bioluminescent glow.

The bright orange gills and copper-orange cap are distinctive.

Intially dome-shaped, the cap becomes funnel-shaped and the margin wavy.

The fruit body is attached to the substrate by a short, excentric stipe.

The gills are strongly decurrent, running down the upper part of the stipe.

Deconica coprophila (Bull.) P. Kumm 1871

Common names: Dung-loving psilocybe, dung-loving deconica
Afrikaans: Mis-sampioen

Etymology: LATIN: *de-* = indicating the undoing of an action, GREEK: *conic* = cone-like; GREEK: *coprophila* = living on or growing in dung

Synonym(s): *Geophila coprophila, Psilocybe coprophila, Stropharia coprophila*

The gills are few, and spaced far apart.

ECOLOGY: Saprophytic.

DISTRIBUTION: Eastern Cape, Gauteng and KwaZulu-Natal, possibly more widespread. Occurs in the UK, Europe, USA, India, Australia and New Zealand.

HABITAT: Grows on herbivore dung; fruit bodies grouped or clustered.

DESCRIPTION: This small, short-lived mushroom can be recognised by the smooth, shiny, brownish cap, dark-brownish gills and violet-tinted spores. **Cap:** 0.5–2.5cm in diameter; thin; fleshy; hemispherical to broadly bell-shaped, often umbonate; margin even, smooth, slightly inturned; surface smooth, shiny, viscid, cuticle peeling easily; tan to pale reddish brown. **Gills:** adnexed, distant, full and intermediate lengths, broad, thin, edges entire; pale grey-brown at first, darkening to dark brown. **Stipe:** 2.5–4cm long, 0.1–0.3cm thick; central; cylindrical, straight to sometimes curved at the base; smooth, dry, covered with fine, cottony tufts near the base; surface often scaly when young, becoming fibrillose; whitish to dingy yellow-brown; fragile. **Ring:** absent. **Flesh:** very thin; concolorous with cap. **Smell:** faint mealy odour. **Spore print:** violaceous brown.

EDIBILITY: Suspect.

The cap surface is smooth, shiny and viscid.

NOTES: The genus *Deconica* was formerly considered synonymous with *Psilocybe*, but following molecular studies *Psilocybe* was divided into two clades, one generally containing the bluing and hallucinogenic species (*Psilocybe*), the other (*Deconica*) incorporating the non-bluing, non-hallucinogenic species.

The broadly bell-shaped caps are fringed with whitish scales.

This fungus grows on the dung of herbivores.

Leratiomyces ceres (Cooke & Massee) Spooner & Bridge 2008

Common names: Redlead roundhead, orange naematoloma
Afrikaans: Rooi-slymmus

Etymology: *leratio* = after French botanist Auguste-Joseph Le Rat (1872–1910), ANCIENT GREEK: *mykes* = mushroom; LATIN: *cere* = waxen

Synonym(s): *Naematoloma aurantiacum, Psilocybe squamosa* var. *aurantiaca, Stropharia aurantiaca*

Poisonous

ECOLOGY: Saprophytic.

DISTRIBUTION: Western Cape, Gauteng and Mpumalanga, possibly more widespread. Occurs in the UK, Europe, Canada, Mexico, Australia and New Zealand.

HABITAT: Grows under broadleaved trees where there is an abundance of woody debris such as woodchips and sawdust, often after tree felling; fruit bodies scattered or grouped.

DESCRIPTION: This easily recognisable fungus turns bright red and slimy when wet. **Cap:** 1–5cm in diameter; semiglobose to convex, sometimes with a slight umbo; margin smooth, can have white veil remnants; surface smooth; slimy and bright red when wet, becoming browner with age. **Gills:** adnate to adnexed or notched, close, full and intermediate lengths; creamy becoming dark green-yellow or brown. **Stipe:** 2–10cm long, 0.1–0.6cm thick; central; thin, cylindrical, can be bent, base often swollen, attached to the substrate by yellow mycelium; surface covered with fibres; off-white, streaked brown toward the base; hollow. **Ring:** disappears or leaves remnants. **Flesh:** reddish yellow. **Smell:** no distinctive odour. **Spore print:** dark purple-brown.

EDIBILITY: Poisonous; causes an upset stomach.

Initially creamy, the gills change colour to become dark green-yellow or brown.

White remnants of the veil hang down from the cap margin.

The fully expanded cap sometimes has a slight umbo.

The cap surface is smooth, slimy and bright red when wet.

Young specimens of *Hypholoma fasciculare* have fleshy, convex caps and sulphur-yellow stipes.

Liz Popich

Hypholoma fasciculare (Huds.) P. Kumm. 1871

Common names: Sulphur tuft, common sulphur head, dwarf sulphur head
Afrikaans: Swawelkop

Etymology: GREEK: *hyphé* = tissue, spiderweb, *lōma* = margin, border; LATIN: *fasciculare* = in bundles or clusters

Synonym(s): *Dryophila fascicularis, Geophila fascicularis, Psilocybe fasciculare*

Poisonous

ECOLOGY: Saprophytic.

DISTRIBUTION: Western Cape, Eastern Cape and Gauteng, possibly more widespread. Occurs in the UK, Europe, Canada, USA, Costa Rica, Brazil, Japan, Australia and New Zealand.

HABITAT: Occurs on dead wood of broadleaved and coniferous trees; fruit bodies in small and large clusters.

DESCRIPTION: The bright sulphur colour, greenish tint of the mature gills, dark spores and clustered growth habitat are the main characteristics of this attractive mushroom. **Cap:** 1–5cm in diameter; fleshy; convex to slightly umbonate, expanding to plane; margin smooth, wavy, downturned, becoming ragged with partial veil fragments; chrome-yellow at margin, tawny orange toward the centre. **Gills:** adnexed, crowded, full and intermediate lengths, thin; sulphur-yellow with greenish tint, becoming greyish black to chocolate with age. **Stipe:** 5–15cm long, 0.2–1cm thick; central; widening slightly toward the base, often curved or bent; smooth over the upper part, fibrillose toward the base; sulphur-yellow with a tawny brown streaked zone, particularly toward the base; firm, solid, later hollow. **Ring:** faint ring zone, often darkened by trapped spores; pale yellow. **Flesh:** thin, firm; yellowish cream, darker in the stipe; unchanging when cut. **Smell:** mushroomy odour. **Spore print:** violet-brown.

EDIBILITY: Poisonous; causing vomiting, diarrhoea and convulsions.

NOTES: This mushroom causes a white rot in wood, and helps in the decomposing of dead wood in forests.

Initially sulphur-yellow with a greenish tint, the gills soon become greyish black.

Some specimens have curved or bent stipes.

The fruit bodies appear in clusters on rotten wood.

The cap is tawny orange toward the centre.

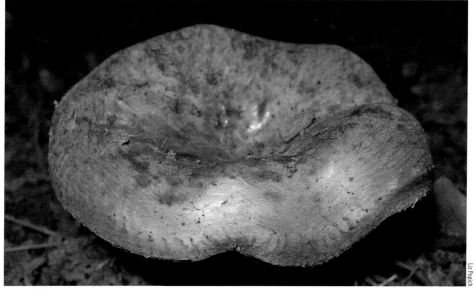

Deadly poisonous, *Paxillus involutus* can be recognised by its funnel shape, decurrent gills, and strongly inrolled margin.

The cap surface is shiny and smooth, except along the margin, where it is ribbed.

Paxillus involutus (Batsch) Fr. 1838

Common names: Brown roll-rim, felty peg, poison pax, inrolled pax, involute paxillus, time-bomb toadstool
Afrikaans: Gesteelde krulsoom

Etymology: LATIN: *paxillus* = peg, small stake; *involut* = roll up
Synonym(s): *Omphalia involuta, Rhymovis involuta*

Deadly poisonous

ECOLOGY: Mycorrhizal.

DISTRIBUTION: Western Cape, Eastern Cape and Gauteng, possibly more widespread. Occurs in the UK, Europe, Canada, USA, Chile, Russia, China, Japan, Australia and New Zealand.

HABITAT: Grows in coniferous and broadleaved forests; fruit bodies single or scattered.

DESCRIPTION: This deadly poisonous mushroom is identifiable by the dull-brown colours of its somewhat hollow cap, strongly inrolled margin, and brownish, decurrent gills. **Cap:** 4–10cm in diameter; fleshy; convex to hollow or funnel-shaped, turning flat and then depressed at the centre; margin woolly and strongly inrolled; surface shiny and smooth, except toward the edge, which is often ribbed and downy, glutinous when wet; ochre to tawny yellow, turning brown. **Gills:** decurrent, crowded, forking, thin; yellow turning olive-yellow to brown, stains brown where touched; soft and easy to remove. **Stipe:** 4–6cm long, 0.8–1.5cm thick; central, can be excentric; cylindrical or widening upward; smooth, felty; concolorous with cap or lighter, often streaky; fleshy, tough, solid. **Ring:** absent. **Flesh:** thick, firm; pale yellow to ochraceous buff, stipe turns brown when cut or bruised. **Smell:** mushroomy odour. **Spore print:** rust to sienna to ochre-brown.

SIMILAR SPECIES: Can be confused with the well-known *Lactarius deliciosus* (pine ring), as the ochre to tawny yellow cap is close in coloration to some specimens of the edible *L. deliciosus*.

EDIBILITY: Deadly poisonous. Although once considered edible, it is known to cause potentially fatal autoimmune hemolysis anaemia. An antigen in the mushroom triggers the immune system to attack red blood cells, resulting in potentially fatal complications such as shock, acute kidney injury and acute respiratory failure. It is known to affect even those who consumed the mushroom years previously without any ill effects at the time. *Paxillus involutus* was responsible for the death of German mycologist Julius Schäffer in 1944.

Liz Popich

The densely arranged gills are attached to the stipe.

Liz Popich

As the mushroom matures, the cap flattens out and forms a depression at the centre.

Xanthagaricus luteolosporus (Heinem.) Little Flower, Hosag. & T.K. Abraham 1997

Common names: None
Afrikaans: None

Etymology: GREEK: *xanthos* = yellowness, *agaric* = mushroom; LATIN: *luteolus* = yellow, GREEK: *spora* = seeds, spores
Synonym(s): *Hymenagaricus luteolosporus*

Unknown

ECOLOGY: Saprophytic.

DISTRIBUTION: Gauteng, KwaZulu-Natal and Mpumalanga, possibly more widespread. Occurs in India and Sri Lanka.

HABITAT: Grows on decaying wood debris in soil under trees and on lawns; fruit bodies densely clustered.

DESCRIPTION: This mushroom is readily recognised by the striking appearance of the densely clustered fruit bodies, the yellow caps covered with dark-brown, wart-like scales, and the pinkish-grey gills that later turn black. **Cap:** 2–5cm in diameter; fleshy; bell-shaped, turning convex-umbonate; margin regular, slightly incurved with veil remnants, smooth; surface dry, covered with numerous concentric, small brown scales concentrated toward the centre; dull yellow, umbo covered by a brown disc. **Gills:** free, close, full and intermediate lengths, thin; pink-grey turning purple-brown. **Stipe:** 4–8cm long, 0.5–1cm thick; central; cylindrical, long, slender, curved or sinuous; fibrous, the upper part silky, the lower part slightly scaly, membraneous; pale grey-yellow, scales brown. **Ring:** persistent, high on stipe. **Flesh:** pale grey-yellow to pale brown in the stipe. **Smell:** unknown. **Spore print:** black.

SIMILAR SPECIES: *Hypholoma fasciculare* also appears in clusters.

EDIBILITY: Unknown.

NOTES: A genus of fungi in the family Agaricaceae, *Xanthagaricus* contains 22 species found mainly in tropical regions. *Xanthagaricus* was originally described in 1984 by Belgian mycologist Paul Heinemann as a subgenus of *Hymenagaricus*, but in 1997 its status was raised to independent genus.

Glen van Niekerk

A ring persists near the top of the stipe.

Liz Popich

Glen van Niekerk

The cap is covered with small brown scales, which are concentrated toward the centre.

The fruit bodies are densely clustered.

Heliocybe sulcata (Berk.) Redhead & Ginns 1985

Common names: Daisy mushroom, parachute flower, fence saw blade
Afrikaans: Madeliefiesampioen

Etymology: GREEK: *helios* = sun, *kybe* = head; LATIN: *sulcata* = furrowed

Synonym(s): *Lentinus sulcatus, Neolentinus sulcatus, Pleurotus sulcatus*

ECOLOGY: Saprophytic.

DISTRIBUTION: First reported in South Africa in Gauteng (Pretoria), but may be more widespread. Occurs in Europe, Canada, USA, Mexico, Guatemala, Russia and Mongolia.

HABITAT: Grows on decorticated logs of conifer and broadleaved trees in dry areas; fruit bodies single or grouped.

DESCRIPTION: The resemblance of the fruit body to a daisy and the absence of a ring on the stipe are identifying features of this mushroom. **Cap:** 1–3cm in diameter; convex to flat; margin saw-toothed at maturity; surface dry, noticeably furrowed, covered with radiating scales; orange-brown, centre darker brown. **Gills:** adnexed to adnate, close, relatively broad, unequal; whitish. **Stipe:** 1–3cm long, 0.2–0.6cm thick; central; cylindrical, scaly near the base; pinkish tan; solid. **Ring:** absent. **Flesh:** very firm, fibrous; whitish or creamy. **Smell:** mild mealy odour. **Spore print:** white.

EDIBILITY: Inedible.

NOTES: Microscopically it differs from *Neolentinus* species by the absence of clamp connections – the rounded structures that are formed at the point where hyphae cells divide.

Heliocybe sulcata grows in dry areas on logs that are free of bark.

The gills are relatively broad and the margin edges become saw-toothed at maturity.

The cap is noticeably furrowed with orange-brown radiating scales.

In this old specimen of *Lentinus sajor-caju*, the fruit body has become thin and leathery.

Liz Popich

Lentinus sajor-caju (Fr.) Fr. 1838

Common name: Funnel woodcap
Afrikaans: Tregterhoutswam

Etymology: LATIN: *lentus* = tough, tenacious, pliant, *-inus* = resembles; the origin of the specific name is unknown

Synonym(s): *Pleurotus sajor-caju*

ECOLOGY: Saprophytic.

DISTRIBUTION: Western Cape, Eastern Cape, Gauteng, KwaZulu-Natal and Mpumulanga, possibly more widespread. Occurs in Japan, the Philippines, southeastern Asia, New Zealand, Cameroon and sub-Saharan Africa.

HABITAT: Grows on dead wood of broadleaved trees; fruit bodies single, grouped or scattered.

DESCRIPTION: This species is recognised by its large, conspicuous, mostly funnel-shaped fruit body set upon a short stipe. **Cap:** 5–14cm in diameter; soft-leathery, becoming tough, drying hard-horny; convex and deeply depressed, turning cup- to funnel-shaped; margin inrolled, later straight, smooth, wavy; surface smooth, dry, finally radially striate, can be covered with small, dark scales; colour varies from white to cream, pale ochraceous to brown, darker in the centre. **Gills:** decurrent, dense, full and intermediate lengths; white to concolorous with cap. **Stipe:** 0.8–3cm long, 0.5–1.5cm thick; central to excentric or occasionally lateral; short, cylindrical; concolorous with cap; tough, solid. **Ring:** persistent, near the apex, but disappearing; white to yellowish brown or blackish. **Flesh:** firm, tough but pliable, hard when dry; white. **Smell:** no distinctive odour. **Spore print:** white.

SIMILAR SPECIES: Mushroom cultivators have mistakenly called a variety of oyster mushroom *Pleurotus sajor-caju*, now known as *Pleurotus pulmonarius* (not described here). The true *Pleurotus sajor-caju* was returned to the genus *Lentinus* by Pegler in 1975, and is now called *Lentinus sajor-caju*.

EDIBILITY: Edible; best eaten while the mushrooms are young and fresh, otherwise very tough.

NOTES: This species plays an active role in the decay of dead wood in which it causes a white rot.

The cap is deeply depressed at the centre.

The cap margin is inrolled, wavy and smooth.

The fruit bodies appear singly, scattered or grouped on dead wood of broadleaved trees.

The funnel-shaped cap is supported by a short, thick stipe.

Lentinus strigosus (Schwein.) Fr. 1838

Common names: Ruddy panus, hairy panus, rough fan
Afrikaans: Harige waaierswam

Etymology: LATIN: *lentus* = tough, tenacious, pliant, *-inus* = resembling; *strigosus* = thin, scraggy

Synonym(s): *Lentinus substrigosus, Panus fragilis, P. rudis*

ECOLOGY: Saprophytic.

DISTRIBUTION: Gauteng and KwaZulu-Natal, possibly more widespread. Occurs in the UK, Europe, USA, Mexico, Costa Rica, Venezuela, Colombia, Russia, Japan, the Philippines, Australia, New Zealand and Madagascar.

HABITAT: Grows on rotting stumps and logs of broadleaved trees; fruit bodies grouped.

DESCRIPTION: The hairy cap and stipe, tough texture and short, lateral to excentric stipe make this mushroom easily identifiable. When young, it is usually tinged purple. **Cap:** 2.5–8cm in diameter; fan- or wedge-shaped to somewhat irregular in outline, convex becoming plane or depressed; margin inrolled, often lobed; surface dry, covered with dense, coarse, stiff, velvety hairs; reddish brown to tan, but often violet when fresh and wet. **Gills:** decurrent, close, narrow, edges entire; white, creamy or concolorous with cap. **Stipe:** 0.8–3cm long, 0.5–1.5cm thick; lateral to excentric; short, stout; hairy; more or less concolorous with cap; tough, solid. **Ring:** absent. **Flesh:** tough, thin; white. **Smell:** no distinctive odour. **Spore print:** white or yellowish.

SIMILAR SPECIES: *Phyllotopsis nidulans* (not described here) is also laterally attached and hairy-capped, but its orange-yellow colour differentiates it from *Lentinus strigosus*.

EDIBILITY: Inedible; too hairy, hard and bitter to be of culinary value.

The gills are attached to a short stipe.

The cap is reddish brown in colour.

The cap margin is inrolled and often lobed.

Coarse, stiff velvety hairs cover the cap.

Lentinus stuppeus Klotzsch 1833

Common names: Bluegum woodcap, hairy woodcap
Afrikaans: Bloekomhoutswam

Etymology: LATIN: *lentus* = tough, tenacious, pliant, *-inus* = resembling; *stuppeus* = covered with matted hair
Synonym(s): *Panus stupeus*, *P. stuppeus*

ECOLOGY: Saprophytic.

DISTRIBUTION: Eastern Cape, Gauteng and KwaZulu-Natal, possibly more widespread. May be native to Africa; occurs in tropical parts of East Africa.

HABITAT: Grows on dead or decaying broadleaved trees; fruit bodies in small groups.

DESCRIPTION: The fruit body may be recognised by its dark, tough, hairy cap with a strongly inrolled margin and a relatively thin stipe. **Cap:** 2.5–8cm in diameter; tough, leathery; depressed to funnel-shaped; margin strongly inrolled; surface densely covered with hair, but less hairy over the centre; dark red to brown to black. **Gills:** decurrent and anastomosing at the stipe apex, crowded, full and intermediate lengths, edges toothed; pale yellow-buff. **Stipe:** 0.8–3cm long, 0.5–1.5cm thick; central; cylindrical, relatively short, thin, widening toward the apex; densely covered with brown hairs at the apex, small yellow-brown scales elsewhere, hairy at the base; tough, solid. **Ring:** absent. **Flesh:** tough, fibrous; white to beige. **Smell:** no distinctive odour. **Spore print:** cream.

SIMILAR SPECIES: Other *Lentinus* species, *Polyporus* species.

EDIBILITY: Inedible; too tough to be of culinary value.

NOTES: Causes a white rot in wood of broadleaved trees.

The gills form a toothed edge at the margin.

Densely hairy, the cap turns brown to black with age.

The cap has a strongly inrolled margin.

Less hair occurs at the depressed cap centre.

Lentinus velutinus Fr. 1830

Common name: Velvet woodcap
Afrikaans: Fluweelhoutswam

Etymology: LATIN: *lentus* = tough, tenacious, pliant, *-inus* = resembling; *velutinus* = velvety

Synonym(s): *Lentinus natalensis*, *L. pseudociliatus*, *Pocillaria brasiliae*

ECOLOGY: Saprophytic.

DISTRIBUTION: Western Cape, Eastern Cape, Gauteng and KwaZulu-Natal, possibly more widespread. Occurs in the USA, Mexico, Costa Rica, Venezuela, Brazil, Australia and Cameroon.

HABITAT: Grows on dead or rotting buried wood of broadleaved trees; fruit bodies single or grouped.

DESCRIPTION: This mushroom is identified by the velvety, uniformly coloured upper surface of the cap and the velvety surface of the slender stipe. **Cap:** 2–8cm in diameter; thin, tough, leathery; depressed to funnel-shaped; margin thin, inrolled, later turning outward, wavy, covered with hairs; surface velvety uniformly velvety; pale grey-cinnamon to tawny brown or dark brown. **Gills:** decurrent, crowded, full and intermediate lengths, not fusing; pale buff to grey-brown. **Stipe:** 2–10cm long, 0.2–1cm thick; central, sometimes excentric; cylindrical, slender, longer than the diameter of the cap, widening toward the base and apex; can arise from a thickened resting body (pseudosclerotium); concolorous with cap or darker, uniformly velvety; tough, solid. **Ring:** absent. **Flesh:** thin, fibrous; white. **Smell:** no distinctive odour. **Spore print:** cream to pale buff.

SIMILAR SPECIES: Other *Lentinus* species, *Polyporus* species, *Paxillus involutus*.

EDIBILITY: Inedible.

NOTES: This mushroom forms a pseudosclerotium – a mixture of mycelium and substrate tissue hardened into a more or less egg-shaped resting body. The pseudosclerotium survives long after the wood substrate has rotted away, and new fruit bodies may develop from it at a later stage.

Hairs cover the surface, giving the cap a velvety appearance.

A depression forms at the centre of the funnel-shaped cap.

In older specimens, the cap margin becomes wavy and turns outward.

The decurrent gills are densely spaced with full-length and shorter plates.

The cap can expand up to 8cm in diameter.

Neolentinus lepideus (Fr.) Redhead & Ginns 1985

Common names: Scaly woodcap, train wrecker, scaly lentinus
Afrikaans: Skubbige houtswam

Etymology: LATIN: *neo-* = new, *lentus* = tough, tenacious, pliant, *-inus* = resembling; *lepideus* = scaly

Synonym(s): *Lentinus lepideus, L. spretus, Lentodium squamousum, Panus lepideus*

Edible

ECOLOGY: Saprophytic.

DISTRIBUTION: Western Cape, Gauteng and KwaZulu-Natal, possibly more widespread. Occurs in Europe, USA, Mexico, Japan, Russia, Mongolia, Australia and New Zealand.

HABITAT: Emerges from dead and decaying coniferous wood, including old stumps, logs and timber; fruit bodies single or clustered.

DESCRIPTION: This medium-sized to large mushroom is tough, and the coarse, brown scales on the cream-white cap are a recognisable feature. **Cap:** 8–11cm in diameter; hemispherical, flattens with maturity; forms a flattened 'heel' at the base; margin inrolled at first; surface covered with small, brownish scales arranged concentrically, becoming denser toward the central depression; white, bruising yellow. **Gills:** adnate to slightly decurrent, edges uneven; white when young, becoming ochraceous with age. **Stipe:** 3–8cm long, 1–2cm wide; central, sometimes excentric; brown scales mainly on the upper part simulating a ring; white, darker at the base; fibrous. **Ring:** absent. **Flesh:** firm; white. **Smell:** aniseed-like odour when fresh. **Spore print:** white.

EDIBILITY: Edible when young and fresh. The flesh of the fruit bodies has a tough consistency, which increases with maturity, making it inedible when older.

The gills are broadly attached to the short, scaly stipe.

The cap surface is covered with small, brownish scales.

NOTES: This mushroom is one of a small number of fungi that can grow on creosote-treated railway sleepers, causing the wood to rot. However, these days the 'train wrecker' is unlikely to wreak serious damage, as railroad sleepers are treated with chemical preservatives to prevent this mushroom from decomposing the wood.

The fruit bodies grow on dead and decaying coniferous wood.

The young caps are hemispherical, later flattening out with age.

Lactarius deliciosus mushrooms grow under pine trees where they form a symbiotic association with the roots of the trees.

Lactarius deliciosus (L.) Gray 1821

Common names: Pine ring, saffron milk cap
Afrikaans: Oranjemelkswam

Etymology: LATIN: *lactarius* = pertaining to milk, giving milk; *deliciosus* = delicious
Synonym(s): None

Edible

The cap is orange-red to orange, with tan to greenish concentric zones.

ECOLOGY: Mycorrhizal.

DISTRIBUTION: Widespread in South Africa. Occurs in the UK, Europe, Canada, USA, Mexico, Brazil, Chile, Russia, Japan, India, China, Australia and New Zealand.

HABITAT: Grows under pine trees, often covered with pine needles; sometimes on sandy, alkaline soil; fruit bodies single or grouped.

DESCRIPTION: This mushroom is easily recognised by its characteristic shape and colours and the production of orange-coloured sap when damaged or cut. **Cap:** 5–12cm in diameter; fleshy, fragile; dome-shaped, becoming flat to funnel-shaped, with a depressed centre; margin smooth, incurved; surface smooth, matt, slightly sticky when wet; bright orange-red to orange, sometimes with tan or greenish concentric zones, turning dull grey-green with age or when it rains hard. **Gills:** decurrent, crowded, unequal lengths, forked, thick; orange to orange-red, turning greenish. **Stipe:** 3–6cm long, 1–2cm thick; central; smooth, stiff, brittle; marked by fine orange depressions; concolorous with cap, bright orange-red zone underlying the outer layer, turns green when damaged; solid at first, turning spongy to hollow. **Ring:** absent. **Flesh:** thick, firm, brittle; pale yellow to orange; when squeezed; exudes a saffron-coloured 'milk'. **Smell:** no distinctive odour. **Spore print:** off-white to pale ochre.

SIMILAR SPECIES: *Gymnopilus junonius* and *Omphalotus olearius* are also orange in colour; *Paxillus involutus* has an ochre to tawny yellow cap.

EDIBILITY: Edible; has a mild flavour and an almost 'meaty' texture. It is good to eat when young and fresh, with the cap still heavily curved downward; older specimens are tougher.

NOTES: When the stipe is sliced through, a distinct orange ring and a pale centre (reminiscent of a pineapple ring) become visible.

The mushroom exudes a saffron-coloured 'milk'. Occasionally, small green specimens grow at the base of the stipe.

Freshly foraged pine rings.

The cap becomes funnel-shaped with age, exposing the gills, which extend down the stipe below the point of attachment.

Gary B Goldman

Lactarius hepaticus Plowr. 1905

Common names: Liver milk cap, hepatic milk cap
Afrikaans: Oranjemelkswam

Etymology: LATIN: *lactarius* = pertaining to milk, giving milk; *hepaticus* = pertaining to the liver

Synonym(s): None

ECOLOGY: Mycorrhizal.

DISTRIBUTION: Widespread in South Africa. Occurs in the UK, Europe, Canada, USA, Russia and New Zealand.

HABITAT: Grows beneath pines on very acidic soil; fruit bodies scattered or grouped.

DESCRIPTION: The brownish funnel-shaped fruit body, the liver-coloured cap and stipe surface, and the white milky sap that readily oozes from the brownish gills when damaged are key identifying features. **Cap:** 2–5cm in diameter; convex, later flattened, finally funnel-shaped; margin undulate, downturned, slightly striate, finally lobate; surface dry, matt; liver-coloured to dull chestnut. **Gills:** decurrent, close, full and intermediate lengths, thin; buff to deep buff, later powdery white with spores; milky sap exuded when damaged. **Stipe:** 2.5–5cm long, 0.3–0.6cm thick; central; cylindrical, straight or curved; smooth; concolorous with cap; brittle, solid at first, turning hollow. **Ring:** absent. **Flesh:** pink-buff, reddish in stipe, not changing when cut. **Smell:** no distinctive odour. **Spore print:** pale cream.

SIMILAR SPECIES: *Laccaria laccata* looks similar and grows in the same habitat, but does not release a white milky sap.

EDIBILITY: Inedible, due to the bitter flavour of its sap.

The margin of the cap is often crinkled with tiny lobes.

> **NOTES:** This is the only known mushroom in South Africa to ooze a white latex milk from the gills when damaged. The sap appears white at first, then slowly changes to yellow.

A milky sap appears on the surface of damaged gills.

Initially buff, the gills turn powdery white with spores.

Russula capensis grows in association with pines, subsisting on the roots of these trees.

Russula capensis A. Pearson 1950

Common name: Cape russula
Afrikaans: Kaapse rooimus

Etymology: LATIN: *russulus* = reddish; *capensis* = from the Cape
Synonym(s): None

ECOLOGY: Mycorrhizal.

DISTRIBUTION: To date, found only in South Africa.

HABITAT: Grows in coniferous (especially pine) forests; fruit bodies single or grouped.

DESCRIPTION: The fruit body is mostly medium-sized and is often recognised by the pine needles and soil adhering to the sticky reddish cap. **Cap:** 4–10cm in diameter; fleshy; convex at first, expanding with a central depression; margin smooth, even, finally upturned; surface viscid, often with adhering pine needles and other debris; colour varying from pinky purple to deep purplish red, darker at the centre. **Gills:** adnexed, protruding slightly beyond the margin, crowded, fairly deep, brittle; pale cream to primrose yellow to deep buttery or scrambled-egg yellow. **Stipe:** 3–6cm long, 1–2cm thick; central; occasionally excentric; tapering toward the apex; white; solid, becoming almost spongy with age. **Ring:** absent. **Flesh:** firm, thin; white. **Smell:** no distinctive odour. **Spore print:** deep ochre to deep cream.

SIMILAR SPECIES: Most *Russula* species found in South Africa have a reddish cap.

EDIBILITY: Suspect. Eating older specimens with a soft spongy stipe could induce a feeling of inebriation; this is due to the presence of *Mycogone*, a mould-like fungus known to attack this species. Although this is usually regarded as an edible mushroom, it should be cooked only when fresh and young. The taste varies from slightly peppery to bitter.

The gills protrude slightly beyond the margin of the cap.

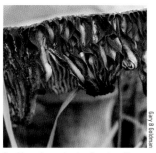

An old specimen, showing decaying gills.

This species has a pronounced depression at the centre of the cap, here filled with rainwater and trapped insects.

The reddish cap and solid stipe of this species are distinctive.

This russula is one of the most common mushrooms in pine forests.

Gary B Goldman

Russula sardonia Fr. 1838

Common names: Purple-stemmed russula, primrose brittlegill, sardonyx russula
Afrikaans: Perssteelrooimus

Etymology: LATIN: *russulus* = reddish; GREEK: *sardonius* = very acrid, bitter

Synonym(s): *Russula chrysodacryon, R. confertissima, R. drimeia, R. drimeja, R. expallens*

Poisonous

ECOLOGY: Mycorrhizal.

DISTRIBUTION: Western Cape and Eastern Cape, possibly more widespread. Occurs in the UK, Europe, Canada, Mexico and Russia.

HABITAT: Grows under coniferous and occasionally broadleaved trees; fruit bodies single or in large colonies.

DESCRIPTION: This mushroom may be recognised by the purplish colours of the stipe and by the deep greyish-purple tones of the cap. **Cap:** 4–10cm in diameter; fleshy, thick; convex; margin wavy, inrolled at first, becoming flat, slightly depressed, then upturned and splitting with age; surface smooth, dry to slightly sticky when wet; deep rose-pink, grey-magenta to grey-ruby or black-purple, colours wash out with the rain. **Gills:** adnexed to slightly decurrent, crowded; lemon to lemon-ochre. **Stipe:** 3–8cm long, 1–2cm thick; central; widening at the apex, rounded base, flattened, elliptical when cut horizontally; surface smooth, can be slightly powdery; white, flushed with pale purple-magenta or entirely pale lilac to grey-rose or pale red-purple; firm, brittle, solid. **Ring:** absent. **Flesh:** thick, firm; creamy white with a green hue. **Smell:** fairly faint, pungent in older specimens. **Spore print:** pale ochre to pale cream.

SIMILAR SPECIES: *Russula xerampelina* has a pinkish tinge on the stipe, but *R. sardonia* can be distinguished by the darker purple colour of its stipe.

EDIBILITY: Poisonous; symptoms include diarrhoea, vomiting and abdominal cramps.

The colour of the cap ranges from deep rose to grey-ruby to black-purple.

The stipe is tinged with hues of purple and lilac.

The gills are crowded and narrowly attached to the stipe.

The dull, smoky colour of the cap, the furrows toward the margin, and the almost funnel-shaped depression at the centre distinguish this species.

Liz Popich

Russula sororia (Fr.) Romell 1891

Common names: Sepia brittlegill, comb russula
Afrikaans: Kam-russula

Etymology: LATIN: *russulus* = reddish; *soror* = sister

Synonym(s): *Russula consobrina* var. *sororia*, *R. livescens* var. *sororia*, *Russula pectinata* var. *sororia*, *R. sororia* f. *pseudoaffinis*

The gills are pale creamy to dirty whitish to brown at the edges.

ECOLOGY: Mycorrhizal.

DISTRIBUTION: Western Cape and Gauteng, possibly more widespread. Occurs in the UK, Europe, Canada, USA, Japan, Australia and New Zealand.

HABITAT: Grows on more or less acidic loamy soil under coniferous and broadleaved trees; fruit bodies single or scattered.

DESCRIPTION: An inconspicuous mushroom, but the smoky brownish-yellow colour of the cap, the short stipe and the strongly downturned margin aid identification. **Cap:** 4–6cm in diameter; convex, later flattened with an almost funnel-shaped depression; margin even, downturned, striate; surface smooth, cuticle slightly sticky when wet; dull smoky brown, becoming paler toward the margin. **Gills:** adnexed, close, edges entire, brittle; pale creamy to dirty whitish to brown at the edges. **Stipe:** 3–4cm long, 1.5–1.9cm thick; central; more or less cylindrical, tapering downward; whitish, but tends to be smoky brown at the apex; smooth, hollow pockets or cavities. **Ring:** absent. **Flesh:** firm, with a texture of mealy apples; white, discolours red-brown with age. **Smell:** rancid odour. **Spore print:** pale cream to pale yellow.

SIMILAR SPECIES: Unlike some other *Russula* species, this mushroom does not have a red or reddish cap. Members of the *Lactarius* genus have similar characteristics, but emit a milky latex when cut.

EDIBILITY: Inedible.

NOTES: Around 750 species of ectomycorrhizal mushrooms found worldwide make up the genus *Russula*. They are common, fairly large, and normally brightly coloured, making them one of the most recognisable genera.

The cap of the young fruit body is convex.

Russula sororia grows under coniferous and broadleaved trees.

Initially convex, the cap flattens out with age.

The colour of the cap is variable, but the stipe is characterised by a rosy to reddish flush from the apex toward the base.

Gary B Goldman

Russula xerampelina (Schaeff.) Fr. 1838

Common names: Shrimp russula, crabmeat russula, shellfish russula, crab brittlegill, crab-scented brittlegill
Afrikaans: Garnaal-russula

Etymology: LATIN: *russulus* = reddish; *xerampelinae* = colour of dried vine leaves

Synonym(s): *Russula atrorosea, R. atrosanguinea, R. borealis*

Edible

ECOLOGY: Mycorrhizal.

DISTRIBUTION: Western Cape, possibly more widespread. Occurs in the UK, Europe, Canada, USA, Costa Rica and Russia.

HABITAT: Grows under coniferous and occasionally broadleaved trees; fruit bodies single, scattered or grouped.

DESCRIPTION: The unmistakable seafood smell of this mushroom distinguishes it from other *Russula* species found in South Africa. **Cap:** 5–11cm in diameter; smooth; convex, then flattening, sometimes becoming depressed at the centre; margin smooth; surface viscid when wet; colours very varied (often mixed), ranging from dull purple, red, wine-coloured and cinnamon to straw, fawn or dull brown. **Gills:** adnexed, fairly broad and thick, brittle, very fragile; white, becoming yellow with age. **Stipe:** 3–9cm long, 1–3cm thick, often shorter than the diameter of the cap; central; swollen or cylindrical, narrowing from the base to the top; white with pink or reddish to rosy blemishes; firm to hard. **Ring:** absent. **Flesh:** thick, soft; whitish, tending to darken yellowish to brown when exposed to air. **Smell:** seafood-like, especially with age. **Spore print:** yellowish to pale ochre.

SIMILAR SPECIES: *Russula sardonia*, but *R. xerampelina* is easily distinguished from other species found in South Africa by the pink coloration of the stipe and a distinctive seafood odour.

EDIBILITY: Edible; excellent for cooking; tastes like crab meat. The taste and smell are accentuated by cooking or drying.

NOTES: A greenish form of this species grows under oak trees in other parts of the world.

In the wild, small animals such as squirrels feed on *Russula xerampelina*.

The flesh stains yellow to brown when damaged or cut.

The cap and stipe of young specimens of *Clitocybe nuda* exhibit violet to violet-brown hues.

Lenita du Plessis

Clitocybe nuda (Fr.) H.E. Bigelow & A.H. Sm. 1969

Common names: Wood blewit, blewit, blue cap, blue foot, true blewit
Afrikaans: Persridderswam

Etymology: ANCIENT GREEK: *klitos* = slope, angle, GREEK: *kybe* = head, cap; LATIN: *nuda* = naked

Synonym(s): *Gyrophila nuda, Lepista nuda, Rhodopaxillus nudus, Tricholoma nudum*

ECOLOGY: Saprophytic.

DISTRIBUTION: Western Cape and Gauteng, possibly more widespread. Occurs in the UK, Europe, Lebanon, Syria, USA, Costa Rica, Brazil, Peru, Russia, Japan, Australia, New Zealand and Tenerife.

HABITAT: Grows in nutrient-rich humus habitats such as compost and thick forest litter; fruit bodies single or grouped, sometimes clustered.

The gills of young specimens are tinged with a bluish-lilac colour.

DESCRIPTION: When young, the entire mushroom has a bluish-lilac colour, but the surface of the cap quickly fades to tan. **Cap:** 4–20cm in diameter; convex, flattening, becoming depressed; margin wavy; surface smooth, almost waxy; violet, purple, lavender or bluish, developing grey to tan or brownish tones, often watery tan with age. **Gills:** adnate to slightly decurrent, crowded; bluish lilac, fading to almost buff with age. **Stipe:** 4–10cm long, 1.5–3cm thick; stout, often slightly bulbous at the base; fibrillose; bluish lilac; fleshy. **Ring:** absent. **Flesh:** thick; bluish lilac. **Smell:** pleasant, sweet, distinct aniseed or orange juice odour. **Spore print:** faintly pinkish.

SIMILAR SPECIES: *Cortinarius violaceus* (not described here), *Lepista sordida, Tricholosporum laeteviolaceum.*

EDIBILITY: Edible; excellent flavour. Slightly poisonous if eaten raw, so parboiling is recommended. Cultivated commercially in the UK, France and the Netherlands.

NOTES: In Cape Town, this species starts to appear when temperatures drop below 8°C, normally around the end of July.

A fleshy mushroom, the edible *Clitocybe nuda* has an excellent flavour.

Clitocybe nuda thrives in nutrient-rich humus.

The young fruit body has a convex cap.

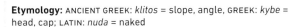

Lepista caffrorum (Kalchbr. & MacOwan) Singer 1951

Common name: Deceptive mushroom
Afrikaans: Skelmsampioen

Etymology: LATIN: *lepista* = wine pitcher, goblet; *caffrorum* = pertaining to the inhabitants of the Cape colony

Synonym(s): *Rhodopaxillus caffrorum, Tricholoma caffrorum*

The cap is initially hemispherical.

ECOLOGY: Saprophytic.

DISTRIBUTION: Western Cape, Eastern Cape and Gauteng, possibly more widespread. Occurs in Lesotho; could be native to southern Africa.

HABITAT: Grows on lawns and in other grassy places; fruit bodies grouped, sometimes in fairy rings.

DESCRIPTION: This very white mushroom typically has white gills that gradually turn pale tan or fawn. **Cap:** 5–20cm in diameter; thick, fleshy; initially hemispherical but expanding to shallow convex; margin strongly inrolled, eventually turning outward and becoming undulate or somewhat lobate; surface smooth, silky, cuticle cracking irregularly; pure white, tinges of pale tan in older specimens. **Gills:** adnate, crowded, notched, thin, edges entire, 0.5–1cm broad, easily breaking away from the cap; white, gradually turning pale tan to pale fawn. **Stipe:** 5–10cm long, 2–4cm thick; central; cylindrical or slightly swollen toward the base; smooth or slightly ridged; white, turning yellowish when bruised; solid, firm, cheesy. **Ring:** absent. **Flesh:** firm, unchanging when cut; white. **Smell:** slight pleasant odour, later turning acrid. **Spore print:** pale pinkish.

SIMILAR SPECIES: *Agaricus, Macrolepiota* and *Amanita* species.

EDIBILITY: Poisonous. Some people have reported eating this mushroom with impunity, whereas others have suffered symptoms such as headaches, giddiness and colic about 24 hours after eating, indicating poisoning.

> **NOTES:** This species is frequently mistaken for the similar-looking *Agaricus campestris*, giving rise to its common name 'deceptive mushroom'. It is, however, distinguishable from *A. campestris* by the absence of a ring on the stipe, its strongly inrolled margin and its white gills.

A fleshy cap typifies the growing mushroom.

The densely arranged gills are white, turning pale tan to pale fawn as the mushroom matures.

The cap margin is strongly inrolled.

Lepista sordida <small>(Schumach.) Singer 1951</small>

Common names: Sordid blewit, lilac blewit, lesser blue foot
Afrikaans: Vuilsampioen

Etymology: LATIN: *lepista* = wine pitcher, goblet; *sordida* = dirty, filthy, soiled

Synonym(s): *Lepista domestica*, *L. nuda* var. *sordida*, *Melanoleuca sordida*, *Rhodopaxillus sordidus*

ECOLOGY: Saprophytic.

DISTRIBUTION: Gauteng and Mpumalanga, possibly more widespread. Occurs in the UK, Europe, USA, Mexico, Costa Rica, Brazil, Japan and Australia.

HABITAT: Grows in coniferous forests, on lawns, in well-composted flower beds and around piles of rotting vegetation; fruit bodies single or grouped, sometimes in fairy rings.

DESCRIPTION: The lilac colours of this attractive mushroom, especially when young, make it easy to identify. **Cap:** 1.5–5.5cm in diameter; fleshy; convex, becoming flattened to depressed or slightly umbonate; margin often wavy, smooth, slightly viscid; surface smooth, matt, hygrophanous; lilac to lilac-brown, fading with age. **Gills:** notched with decurrent tooth, close, tearing free with age, full and intermediate lengths, thin, edges entire, up to 0.6cm broad; lilac, fading to lilac-brown with age. **Stipe:** 2–5cm long, 0.3–0.6cm thick; central; cylindrical, often slightly thickened at the base, occasionally bent; surface smooth, silky; pale toward the apex, concolorous with cap; fleshy-tough, fibrous, stuffed in the centre. **Ring:** absent. **Flesh:** soft cheesy; greyish tinged with lilac, changing to brownish. **Smell:** scented. **Spore print:** pale greyish lilac.

SIMILAR SPECIES: At half the size but more brightly coloured, it looks like a miniature version of *Clitocybe nuda*.

EDIBILITY: Edible; fairly good to eat.

NOTES: This mushroom was described in 1803 by the Danish mycologist, Heinrich C.F. Schumacher, who gave it the scientific name *Agaricus sordidus*. This mushroom was given its current name in 1951, when German-born mycologist Rolf Singer redescribed it as *Lepista sordida*.

The lilac colour of the cap fades with age.

The gills are notched, but may break free from the stipe when older.

The stipe, sometimes bent, is slightly thickened at the base.

Lepista sordida can be seen growing in groups on lawns.

Macrocybe lobayensis (R. Heim) Pegler & Lodge 1998

Common names: None
Afrikaans: None

Etymology: ANCIENT GREEK: *macros* = large, GREEK: *kybe* = head, cap; LATIN: *lobayensis* = pertaining to Lobaye, an area in the Central African Republic
Synonym(s): *Tricholoma lobayense*

Edible

ECOLOGY: Saprophytic.

DISTRIBUTION: Gauteng and KwaZulu-Natal, possibly more widespread. Occurs in Côte d'Ivoire, Ghana, Benin, Nigeria, Central African Republic and the Democratic Republic of the Congo; also reported from India.

HABITAT: Grows in grasslands; fruit bodies single or clustered.

DESCRIPTION: The large, fleshy fruit body and the odour of bitter almonds are distinctive. **Cap:** 8–21cm in diameter; fleshy; convex to flattened; margin lobate, inrolled becoming out-turned, nonstriated; surface smooth, glabrous, dry, finally cracking; dull white to cream, often becoming pale buff with age, occasionally spotted. **Gills:** adnexed to adnate to sinuate, crowded, intermediate lengths, edges entire; white with a pinkish tinge, turning light brown. **Stipe:** 7–13cm long, 2–6cm thick; central, rarely excentric; cylindrical or with a swollen base; white cottony mycelium at the base; smooth or sometimes disrupting into small, reflex scales in dry weather; concolorous with cap, discolouring brownish grey when handled; solid, thick. **Ring:** absent. **Flesh:** thick, firm, fleshy; white. **Smell:** odour of coumarin or of bitter almonds. **Spore print:** glassy appearance.

Cottony mycelial threads are attached to the swollen base.

SIMILAR SPECIES: *Agaricus*, *Termitomyces* and *Lepista* species.

EDIBILITY: Edible; has a starchy taste.

Macrocybe lobayensis is found in grasslands.

The gills are narrowly to broadly attached to the stipe, and are spaced close together.

Tricholoma albobrunneum (Pers.) P. Kumm. 1871

Common name: Brown knightly mushroom
Afrikaans: Denneridderswam

Etymology: GREEK: *trich-* = relating to hair, *lōma* = fringe, border; LATIN: *albus* = white, *brunneus* = brown

Synonym(s): *Gyrophila albobrunneus*

ECOLOGY: Mycorrhizal.

DISTRIBUTION: Western Cape, possibly more widespread. Occurs in the UK, Europe, USA and New Zealand.

HABITAT: Grows on poorer sandy soils beneath coniferous trees, usually pines; fruit bodies grouped or clustered, sometimes in fairy rings.

DESCRIPTION: A tall stipe with a ring-like zone separating the stipe into two differently coloured parts is diagnostic of this species. **Cap:** 4–10cm in diameter; fleshy; conical-convex, becoming depressed, with a low umbo; margin wavy, smooth, inrolled but later striate and turning upward; surface smooth, viscid, shiny when wet, covered with fine innate, radiating fibrils; rust-brown to reddish brown, darker toward the centre. **Gills:** adnexed, crowded, full and intermediate lengths, sinuate, broad, thin, edges entire; white at first, becoming pinkish buff and rust-brown at the edges. **Stipe:** 4–8cm long, 1–2cm thick; central; cylindrical but tapering near the base; smooth, upper part creamy white with a finely scaly surface and separated from the reddish-brown lower part by a ring-like zone; firm, fleshy-fibrous, solid at first, becoming hollow. **Ring:** absent. **Flesh:** firm; white, tinged with reddish brown below the cap cuticle and at the base of the stipe. **Smell:** faintly earthy and mealy odour. **Spore print:** white.

SIMILAR SPECIES: *Tricholoma ustale* (not described here), which many seem to think is the same mushroom, grows under deciduous trees, is smaller and becomes very dark brown with age.

EDIBILITY: Inedible; indigestible and acrid.

NOTES: The similar *Tricholoma ustale* is one of three species most commonly implicated in mushroom poisoning in Japan. Consumption of that mushroom causes gastrointestinal distress, the main symptoms of which are vomiting and diarrhoea.

The cap margin is wavy.

The cap is rust-brown to reddish brown, the colour becoming darker toward the centre.

The stipe is cylindrical but tapering toward the base. The gills are crowded and narrowly attached to the stipe.

The stipe of *Tricholoma saponaceum* is thick at the apex and tapers toward the base.

Gary B Goldman

Tricholoma saponaceum (Fr.) P. Kumm. 1871

Common names: Soapy toadstool, soapy knight, soapy tricholoma, soap-scented knight cap, soap-scented tricholoma
Afrikaans: Seepswam

Etymology: GREEK: *trich-* = relating to hair, *lōma* = fringe, border; LATIN: *saponis* = soap, *-aceum* = resembling

Synonym(s): *Gyrophila saponacea, G. saponaceum*

Inedible

ECOLOGY: Mycorrhizal.

DISTRIBUTION: Western Cape, possibly more widespread. Occurs in the UK, Europe, Canada, USA, Mexico, Costa Rica, China, Japan, Australia and New Zealand.

HABITAT: Grows under pine trees; fruit bodies single or grouped.

DESCRIPTION: Although extremely variable in form and colour, this mushroom is easily identifiable by the soapy odour emitted when crushed. **Cap:** 5–8cm in diameter; fleshy; convex to flattened, later with an umbo; margin even, inrolled at first, becoming wavy, smooth; surface smooth or cracking into scales, wet in moist weather; wide variation in colouring, ranging from fawn to smoky brown or blackish grey, with reddish or olive tints, darkening toward the centre. **Gills:** adnate or notched, sinuate, somewhat distant, full and intermediate lengths, edges entire; waxy yellow-grey, discolouring brown along the edges, sometimes showing a greenish tinge. **Stipe:** 4–8cm long, 1.5–2cm thick at the apex; central; cylindrical or tapering toward the base; smoky brown, rust-brown or olive-tinted; tough, solid. **Ring:** absent. **Flesh:** fairly thick; off-white, staining pinkish. **Smell:** distinctly soapy odour when gills are crushed. **Spore print:** white.

EDIBILITY: Inedible; the soapy smell and flavour, reminiscent of old-fashioned kitchen soap, makes it rather unpalatable.

NOTES: This is a very variable mushroom, with specimens differing mainly in the colour of the stipe or cap and the presence or absence of scales.

The fruit bodies are variable in coloration and form, making it risky to use either of these features for identification purposes.

Tricholoma saponaceum grows on a bed of pine needles.

The gills, consisting of both full and intermediate-length plates, are slightly spaced apart.

The cap margin is inrolled before becoming wavy.

Tricholomopsis rutilans (Schaeff.) Singer 1939

Common names: Plums and custard, strawberry mushroom
Afrikaans: Pruime en vla

Etymology: GREEK: *trich-* = relating to hair, *lōma* = fringe, border,
LATIN: *-opsis* = resembling; LATIN: *rutilans* = reddening

Synonym(s): *Cortinellus rutilans, Flammula squamulosa,
Gyrophila rutilans, Pleurotus rutilans, Tricholoma rutilans*

Edible

ECOLOGY: Saprophytic.

DISTRIBUTION: Gauteng (Pretoria), possibly more widespread.
Occurs in the UK, Europe, USA, Mexico, Russia, Japan, Australia and
New Zealand.

HABITAT: Grows on dead coniferous stumps and logs or from dead
roots close to tree stumps, sometimes on woodchips; fruit bodies
single or clustered.

DESCRIPTION: A mushroom with unusual colouring: the yellow
colour of the cap is almost invisible under a layer of plum-coloured
scales. **Cap:** 5–8cm in diameter; convex, becoming broadly bell-
shaped to nearly flattened; margin inrolled; surface dry, densely
covered with plum-coloured fibres that mature into small scales;
yellow colour just visible. **Gills:** adnate to notched, crowded, close;
pale to bright egg-yellow. **Stipe:** 4–8cm long, 1–2.5cm thick; central;
smooth, dry, fibrillose, more or less powdery; plum to plum-
yellow. **Ring:** absent. **Flesh:** fibrous, hollow in centre; deep yellow.
Smell: odour of rotten pinewood. **Spore print:** white.

EDIBILITY: Edible. Owing to its mediocre flavour, it is not considered
to be of culinary interest.

The cap is convex in young specimens,
and densely covered with plum-coloured
fibres that mature into small scales.

NOTES: This species was assigned to the genus *Tricholoma* by
Paul Kummer in 1871, but was reassigned to its present genus
Tricholomopsis in 1939 by the German-born mycologist, Rolf Singer.

In mature specimens, the scaly cap is
nearly flattened.

The pale to bright egg-yellow gills are
spaced close together.

Tricholosporum laeteviolaceum D.A Reid, A. Eicker, H. Clémençon & C. Roux 1998

Common name: Spotted violet dome cap
Afrikaans: Gespikkelde violet-mus

Etymology: GREEK: *trich-* = relating to hair, *lōma* = fringe, border, *spora* = seeds, spores; LATIN: *laetus-* = abundant, *violaceum* = violet-coloured

Synonym(s): None; described as new to science in 1998

ECOLOGY: Saprophytic.

DISTRIBUTION: To date, found only in South Africa (Gauteng), suggesting it is native to the country.

HABITAT: Grows in moist nutrient-rich humus under indigenous vegetation; fruit bodies single or grouped.

DESCRIPTION: An entirely violet cap and stipe, with ochre-coloured patches showing later on the cap, aid identification of this mushroom. **Cap:** 6–13cm in diameter; convex or hemispherical at first, expanding to plane, becoming somewhat depressed at the centre; margin slightly inrolled, wavy; surface smooth, almost shiny in mature specimens; initially entirely violet, fading to very pale beige or whitish, with the margin remaining bright violet; the colour at the centre of older specimens turns ochraceous. **Gills:** attachment uncertain, probably sinuate, up to 0.6cm deep; lilac to violet. **Stipe:** 5–8cm long, 1.1–2cm thick; more or less cylindrical; smooth, sometimes appearing powdery at the apex due to trapped spores. **Flesh:** soft in the cap, fibrillose in the stipe; white. **Smell:** mushroomy odour. **Spore print:** white.

SIMILAR SPECIES: *Clitocybe nuda* and *Lepista sordida* display a similar lilac, violet or purple colouring.

EDIBILITY: Unknown.

NOTES: This species was first noticed in Hammanskraal, on the banks of the Pienaars River, north of Pretoria, by Cecilia Roux on 7 February 1996. It was described as new to science in 1998. At the time it also represented the first report of the genus *Tricholosporum* from sub-Saharan Africa.

Tricholosporum laeteviolaceum is found only in South Africa.

Initially entirely violet, the cap fades to pale beige or whitish over time.

Young specimens grow in a group in moist humus.

An inrolled margin and lilac to violet gills are diagnostic.

Termitomyces clypeatus R. Heim 1951

Common names: None
Afrikaans: None

Etymology: LATIN: *termes* = woodworm termite, *myces* = mushroom; *clypeus* = round shield
Synonym(s): *Sinotermitomyces taiwanensis*

Edible

ECOLOGY: Farmed by termites.

DISTRIBUTION: Gauteng, possibly more widespread. Occurs in Taiwan, China, Australia, Ghana, Togo, Benin, Nigeria, Democratic Republic of the Congo, Kenya and Zambia.

HABITAT: Grows on termite nests, typically on low mounds, so is often overlooked; fruit bodies closely grouped, occasionally clustered.

DESCRIPTION: The brownish cap with a conspicuously pointed umbo, the cylindrical stipe, and the densely clustered growth habit are key features of this species. **Cap:** 4–8.5cm in diameter; fleshy, thin; narrow conical at first, expanding to broadly bell-shaped, prominent with a strongly pointed umbo; margin incurved, irregularly lobed, splitting at the edges with age; upper surface fibrillose-silky, dry, smooth; dark brown at first, then ochreous brown, finally greyish at maturity with the umbo remaining dark brown. **Gills:** free, crowded, full and intermediate lengths, thin, broad, edges entire; creamy white to pale pinkish brown. **Stipe:** 8–18cm long, 0.7–1.5cm thick above the ground; central; cylindrical, longitudinally striate, slightly thickened below ground level, then tapering downward, single or occasionally with two or three stipes united to form a single, tapering pseudorhiza attached to a fungus comb in the termite nest; tough, solid. **Ring:** absent. **Flesh:** firm, unchanging, thin over the gills; white. **Smell:** no distinctive odour. **Spore print:** pinkish cream.

SIMILAR SPECIES: Other *Termitomyces* species, *Agaricus* species.

EDIBILITY: Edible; delicate flavour, but the tough stipes are best removed before cooking.

The colour of the gills range from creamy white to pale pinkish brown.

The stipe is marked with fine grooves, and is slightly thickened below ground level.

Mature specimens with brown umbos.

Young specimens at the budding stage.

Pseudorhiza attached to an old fungus comb.

Termitomyces microcarpus (Berk. & Broome) R. Heim 1942

Common names: None
Afrikaans: None

Etymology: LATIN: *termes* = woodworm termite, *myces* = mushroom; GREEK: *mikros* = small, *karpos* = fruit

Synonym(s): *Collybia microcarpa, Gymnopus microcarpus, Mycena microcarpa, Podabrella microcarpa*

ECOLOGY: Farmed by termites.

DISTRIBUTION: Gauteng, KwaZulu-Natal, Limpopo and Free State, possibly more widespread. Occurs in India, Malaysia, China, Indonesia, Nigeria, Tanzania and Zambia.

HABITAT: Grows on soil brought to the surface by termites; associated with three species of wood-destroying termites: *Odontotermes badius, O. transvaalensis* and *O. vulgaris*; fruit bodies densely grouped or clustered.

DESCRIPTION: This species is easily identified by the small, whitish fruit body and prominent, pointed umbo. **Cap:** 0.6–1.8cm in diameter; fleshy; convex to bell-shaped, then flattening, with a prominent, pointed umbo; margin inrolled at first, regular to lobate, later upturned, splitting; surface smooth, dry; bright white. **Gills:** adnexed to free, crowded, full and intermediate lengths; white turning light pink with age. **Stipe:** 3–8cm long, 0.5–4cm thick; central; cylindrical; smooth; white; fibrous, solid. **Ring:** absent. **Flesh:** firm; white. **Smell:** no distinctive odour. **Spore print:** light pink.

The gills are narrowly attached to the stipe.

SIMILAR SPECIES: *Coprinellus disseminates*.

EDIBILITY: Edible; very tasty, but a large number are needed to make a meal.

Convex and flattened caps, two with prominent umbos, are clearly visible.

NOTES: Most *Termitomyces* species grow from subterranean termite nests by means of a long, root-like extension of the stipe called a pseudorhiza. However, *T. microcarpus*, which lacks this structure, fruits on the surface in old comb fragments deposited mainly by wood-destroying termites.

The fruit bodies of *Termitomyces microcarpus* are usually densely grouped.

Termitomyces microcarpus grows in old comb fragments deposited by termites.

Termitomyces reticulatus has a low, rounded, brown umbo and concentric rings of brown scales on the cap surface.

A ring is present as a white ridge on the stipe just below the gills, here showing the brown-pink colour associated with mature specimens.

Termitomyces reticulatus Van der Westh. & Eicker 1990

Common names: None
Afrikaans: None

Etymology: LATIN: *termes* = woodworm termite, *myces* = mushroom; *reticulatus* = made of a net, reticulated

Synonym(s): None

ECOLOGY: Farmed by termites.

DISTRIBUTION: To date, found only in South Africa (Gauteng, Mpumalanga, Limpopo, North West Province and Free State), suggesting it is native to the country.

HABITAT: Associated with two species of wood-destroying termites: *Odontotermes badius* and *O. transvaalensis*; fruit bodies grouped.

DESCRIPTION: This large, striking mushroom has concentric rings of brown scales on the cap surface and a long, tough, whitish pseudorhiza, making it easy to recognise. **Cap:** 6–18cm in diameter; egg-shaped at first, expanding to convex or flat with a low, rounded umbo; margin even, smooth, downturned; surface smooth, with concentric brown wart-like patches and soil adhering to them; white, umbo covered with a brown membrane. **Gills:** free or slightly adnexed, crowded, full and intermediate lengths; cream when young, maturing into brown-pink. **Stipe:** 3–8cm long, 1.5–4cm thick; central; cylindrical, could have veil remnants suspended from the apex, arising from a white pseudorhiza, attached to the termite nest by a narrow, branching base; white; tough, solid, then hollowed out by termites. **Ring:** present as a fixed white ridge with a grey to brown margin. **Flesh:** firm; white. **Smell:** faint mushroomy odour. **Spore print:** brownish pink.

SIMILAR SPECIES: Other *Termitomyces* species, *Agaricus* species, *Chlorophyllum molybdites*.

EDIBILITY: Edible; tasty, flavourful and excellent for cooking.

Edible

The young specimen has an egg-shaped cap.

The gills are cream-coloured when young.

Termitomyces reticulatus, showing cream-coloured gills, egg-shaped to flat and upturned caps, and a cylindrical stipe with veil-like remnants.

Mature fruit bodies, here with soil adhering to the caps.

Termitomyces sagittiformis (Kalchbr. & Cooke) D.A. Reid 1975

Common names: None
Afrikaans: None

Etymology: LATIN: *termes* = woodworm termite, *myces* = mushroom; *sagitta* = arrow, *-formis* = shape

Synonym(s): *Termitomyces sagittaeformis*

ECOLOGY: Farmed by termites.

DISTRIBUTION: Gauteng and KwaZulu-Natal, possibly more widespread. Occurs in India and Tanzania.

HABITAT: Grows in soil over termite nests; associated with the wood-destroying termite *Odontotermes latericius*; fruit bodies grouped.

DESCRIPTION: This mushroom is distinguished from other termite mushrooms by having a less pointed umbo, a stout stipe with a swollen base, and a blackish pseudorhiza. **Cap:** 2.5–6.5cm in diameter; conical to bell-shaped, umbo acute, conical, almost spine-like; margin incurved, uneven to lobate, splitting when old; surface smooth, slightly shiny, dry, cracking radially and concentrically, the cuticle sometimes curling into large scales exposing the pale-cream flesh; grey-brown to greyish umber. **Gills:** free or slightly adnexed, crowded, full and intermediate lengths, thin, edges entire at first, later somewhat crenate to irregularly and narrowly segmented; creamy, ageing to ochre-pink to pink-buff. **Stipe:** 2.5–6cm long, 0.6–1.2cm thick, widening downward to 1–3cm thick; central; long, spindle-shaped, but can be thick; striate, widening downward until just below the soil surface, then narrowing into a black-brown pseudorhiza; white; tough, fibrous, solid. **Ring:** absent. **Flesh:** firm; creamy white. **Smell:** mushroomy odour. **Spore print:** ochraceous pink to pinkish buff.

SIMILAR SPECIES: *Termitomyces clypeatus.*

EDIBILITY: Edible; tasty.

The cap is conical to bell-shaped.

Caps with conical umbos and split margins.

Stipe, showing the underground swelling and narrowing black-brown pseudorhiza.

Termitomyces schimperi (Pat.) R. Heim 1942

Common name: Omajowa
Afrikaans: Schimper se termietsampioen

Etymology: LATIN: *termes* = woodworm termite, *myces* = mushroom; *schimperi* = after German botanist Andreas Franz Wilhelm Schimper (1856–1901)

Synonym(s): *Lepiota schimperi*

Edible

Large, thick scales cover the stipe surface.

ECOLOGY: Farmed by termites.

DISTRIBUTION: Gauteng and Limpopo, but is widespread throughout Africa, suggesting it may be native to the continent. Occurs in Côte d'Ivoire, Ghana, Togo, Benin, Cameroon, Equatorial Guinea, Rwanda, Burundi, Central African Republic, Democratic Republic of the Congo, Ethiopia, Tanzania, Kenya, Zambia, Malawi, Mozambique, Namibia and Zimbabwe.

HABITAT: Grows only on or around tall termite mounds, which normally reach 4–5m in height, with the apex always inclined toward north; usually found at the mounds of the termite *Macrotermes michaelseni*; fruit bodies grouped.

DESCRIPTION: The thick, brownish, irregularly cracked scales (resembling sun-dried mud) that cover most of the upper surface of the cap and the long, narrow pseudorhiza are characteristic of this species. **Cap:** 6–25cm in diameter; fleshy; large, initially conical expanding to shallow convex, without a conspicuous umbo; margin even, smooth, straight; surface smooth, covered by a persistent, thick, light- to dark-brown layer that is continuous over the centre but breaks up into thick, flat, irregular, ochraceous-brown to rust-brown scales which are arranged in concentric circles toward the margin, scales sticky when moist; white. **Gills:** free, crowded, full and intermediate lengths, thin, up to 1.4cm broad, edges entire; creamy white at first, changing to pinkish cream. **Stipe:** 8–12.5cm long and 1–2.5cm thick; swollen at the base to 4cm thick, tapering abruptly into a narrow pseudorhiza up to 40cm long below soil level, covered with large, thick scales (the remains of the veil); white, scales brownish; fibrous, tough, solid. **Ring:** absent. **Flesh:** firm, up to 2cm thick, unchanging; white. **Smell:** unknown. **Spore print:** pinkish cream.

EDIBILITY: Edible.

Dried specimen, showing the cracked, scale-like surface of the cap and stipe, and a portion of the pseudorhiza.

The very long pseudorhiza is the result of the fungus being cultivated deep underground in the termite nest.

The mature *Termitomyces umkowaan* has a large dark-beige cap that splits at the margin.

Liz Popich

Termitomyces umkowaan (Cooke & Massee) D.A. Reid 1975

Common names: l'kowe, beefsteak mushroom, amakhowe
Afrikaans: l'kowa

Etymology: LATIN: *termes* = woodworm termite, *myces* = mushroom; ZULU: *amakhowe* (colloquially 'umkowaan') = wild mushrooms

Synonym(s): *Termitomyces umkowaani*

Edible

ECOLOGY: Farmed by termites.

DISTRIBUTION: Eastern Cape, Gauteng, KwaZulu-Natal and Free State, possibly more widespread. Occurs in India, Cameroon and Tanzania.

HABITAT: Grows in association with the wood-destroying termite *Odontotermes badius*, which is widely distributed throughout southern Africa; fruit bodies single or grouped over termite mounds.

DESCRIPTION: The brown cap, white to pinkish gills, and black pseudorhiza are identifying characters of this large, tough fungus. **Cap:** up to 25cm in diameter; large, fleshy; conical at first, expanding to bell-shaped to shallow convex, with a broad umbo; margin incurved, striate, splitting when older; surface smooth, slimy when wet, cuticle occasionally cracking radially and concentrically to form large, loose scales; dull greyish brown when young, becoming dark beige. **Gills:** free, crowded, full and intermediate lengths; cream when young, becoming pink-brown. **Stipe:** 7–15cm long, 1–2cm thick; central; smooth, widening downward to the bulbous base, narrowing below ground to a blackish, striate pseudorhiza; cream; tough-fibrous, solid; **Ring:** absent. **Flesh:** thick, solid, firm; white. **Smell:** pleasant. **Spore print:** pinkish cream to pinkish buff.

EDIBILITY: Edible; excellent flavour, tastes like steak.

The fruit body with the pseudorhiza.

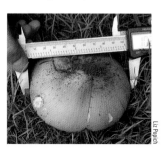

Termitomyces umkowaan is known for its fleshy texture and flavourful taste.

Young specimens have conical caps.

Young buds.

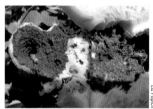

A section of the stipe, with adhering remnants of the fungus comb of *Odontotermes badius* termites.

Campanella capensis, here with the lower surface exposed, appears in groups on living or dead plant material.

Liz Popich

Campanella capensis (Berk.) D.A. Reid 1975

Common names: None
Afrikaans: None

Etymology: LATIN: *campanula* = small bell; *capensis* = from the Cape
Synonym(s): *Cantharellus capensis*, *Merulius capensis*

ECOLOGY: Saprophytic and parasitic.

DISTRIBUTION: To date, found only in South Africa (Western Cape, Eastern Cape, Gauteng and KwaZulu-Natal), suggesting it is native to the country.

HABITAT: Grows on living trees or dead plant material; fruit bodies grouped or scattered.

DESCRIPTION: The small, snow-white, bonnet-shaped fruit body and the pore-like appearance of the gills on the upper surface make this species easy to identify. **Cap:** 0.7–1.2cm in diameter; thin, fleshy; sessile, bonnet-shaped to bell-shaped; margin irregular; surface smooth to slightly depressed over the gills, semi-matt, dry; white to almost translucent. **Gills:** free, distant ridges or folds radiating from the stipe, forked, reticulate toward the furthest parts, with lateral branches giving a coarsely pore-like appearance, full and intermediate lengths; white. **Stipe:** lateral, reduced, continuous with cap; white; fleshy-tough, solid. **Ring:** absent. **Flesh:** thin, membraneous; white. **Smell:** no distinctive odour. **Spore print:** creamy white.

SIMILAR SPECIES: *Crepidotus* species.

EDIBILITY: Unknown.

The caps are laterally attached.

The forked ridges of the gills radiate from the stipe.

The small fruit bodies are bonnet-shaped.

The crowded gills of *Crepidotus mollis* are pallid to white at first, becoming ochre-brown as the mushroom matures.

Crepidotus mollis (Schaeff.) Staude 1857

Common names: Jelly shell fan, peeling oysterling, soft shell, jelly crep, soft crepidotus, flabby crepidotus, soft slipper ear
Afrikaans: Jellieskulpieswam

Etymology: LATIN: *crepid-* = slipper, *-otus* = resembling; *mollis* = soft, supple, tender

Synonym(s): *Crepidopus mollis*

Unknown

ECOLOGY: Saprophytic.

DISTRIBUTION: Western Cape, Eastern Cape, Gauteng and KwaZulu-Natal, possibly more widespread. Occurs in the UK, Europe, Canada, USA, Costa Rica, Brazil, Russia, Japan, Australia, New Zealand and Zambia.

HABITAT: Grows on dead stumps, branches, trunks and sawdust of broadleaved trees, rarely on conifers; fruit bodies single, clustered or grouped, often tiered.

DESCRIPTION: The jelly-like surface and flesh distinguish this mushroom from other, mostly smaller, *Crepidotus* species.
Cap: 1–5cm in diameter; soft, delicate, fleshy; sessile, bracket- or fan-shaped, convex; margin even to somewhat undulate and lobed when mature, striate, downturned; surface covered with fine yellow hairs, occasionally with large, sparse, appressed scales, hygrophanous; initially pale olive-grey at the margin, whitish beyond the water-soaked margin, becoming yellow then ochre-brown with age. **Gills:** decurrent, crowded, radiating from the point of attachment to the substrate, full and intermediate lengths, thin, margin entire; pallid to white at first, becoming ochre-brown. **Stipe:** absent or reduced and lateral; densely covered with white hairs. **Ring:** absent; **Flesh:** soft, brittle, gelatinous beneath the cuticle; whitish. **Smell:** no distinctive odour. **Spore print:** ochre-brown.

SIMILAR SPECIES: Distinguished from other species in the genus by its relatively large size; *Crepidotus variabillis*, for example, is almost three times smaller than *C. mollis*. The small, fragile members of the genus *Pleurotus* are similar in appearance to *Crepidotus* mushrooms.

EDIBILITY: Unknown; best avoided as it is impossible to distinguish this mushroom from other species of *Crepidotus*, some of which may be poisonous.

The fruit bodies grow in tiers on the wood of broadleaved trees.

The stipe is covered with white hairs at the point of attachment to the substrate.

NOTES: The fungus *Hypomyces tremellicola* (not described here) is a parasite that is known to deform the cap of this species.

Fine hairs and, occasionally, scales (seen here) cover the cap surface.

Crepidotus variabilis grows on dead branches and twigs in damp forests.

Liz Popich

Crepidotus variabilis (Pers.) P. Kumm. 1871

Common names: Varied crep, variable oysterling, varied slipper, variable crepidotus, varied slipper ear
Afrikaans: Variërende pantoffel

Etymology: LATIN: *crepid-* = slipper, LATIN: *-otus* = resembling; *variabilis* = variable

Synonym(s): *Claudopus multiformis, C. variabilis, Crepidopus variabilis*

ECOLOGY: Saprophytic.

DISTRIBUTION: Eastern Cape, Gauteng and KwaZulu-Natal, possibly more widespread. Occurs in the UK, Europe, USA, Australia and Tenerife.

HABITAT: Grows on dead twigs and thin branches of broadleaved trees in damp forests; fruit body grouped or clustered, tiered.

DESCRIPTION: This oyster-shaped mushroom is readily identified by its small fruit body and lobed cap margin. **Cap:** 0.5–2cm in diameter; thin, fleshy; sessile, fan-, oyster- to kidney-shaped; margin lobed, inturned; surface dry, felt-like, with some fine fibres; matt white. **Gills:** crowded, radiating from the point of attachment to the substrate, full and intermediate lengths; off-white to pale grey-brown to cinnamon-brown. **Stipe:** absent or rudimentary and lateral. **Ring:** absent. **Flesh:** thin; white. **Smell:** no distinctive odour. **Spore print:** pale pink-brown.

SIMILAR SPECIES: *Campanella capensis*, other *Crepidotus* species, some of which are poisonous.

EDIBILITY: Inedible.

> **NOTES:** Currently, the *Crepidotus* genus encompasses approximately 150 species.

The gills radiate from the stipe.

The caps are distinctly oyster-shaped.

A very rudimentary stipe serves as the point of attachment to the substrate.

The gills roll inward to protect the spore-bearing surface from desiccation.

Liz Popich

Schizophyllum commune Fr. 1815

Common names: Splitgill, common porecrust
Afrikaans: Waaiertjie

Etymology: LATIN: *schizo-* = to split, cleave, part; *-phyllum* = race, tribe, division; *communis* = common, communal

Synonym(s): *Merulius communis*

ECOLOGY: Saprophytic.

DISTRIBUTION: Widespread in South Africa. Occurs on all continents; perhaps the most widespread of all mushroom species.

HABITAT: Grows on dead twigs, branches, logs and stumps of mainly broadleaved trees; fruit bodies grouped or clustered, overlapping on the substrate.

DESCRIPTION: The gills, which split along the edges and curl inward, make this unique species easy to identify. **Cap:** 1–4cm in diameter; leathery; sessile, fan-shaped, sometimes with an elongated base; margin wavy, lobed, split or incised, inturned; surface dry, felt-like, covered with fine fibres; matt white. **Gills:** crowded, radiating from the point of attachment to the substrate, full and intermediate lengths, split longitudinally along the edge, in dry weather rolling inward to protect the hymenium from desiccation; off-white to pale grey-brown to cinnamon-brown. **Stipe:** absent or rudimentary and lateral. **Ring:** absent. **Flesh:** thin, tough; pale grey. **Smell:** no distinctive odour. **Spore print:** white.

EDIBILITY: Edible; muted taste when eaten raw; tough. It is eaten in central and eastern Africa, southeast Asia, Mexico and India, where it is boiled beforehand to tenderise the flesh.

MEDICINAL: This species is known for its antiviral and immune-boosting properties, and for its use in treating certain tumours. It is also a treatment for candida.

Fruit bodies overlap on the substrate.

The cap surface is white and felty.

The gills radiate from the point of attachment.

Fruit bodies with wavy margins.

The deep-orange gills radiate from the point of attachment, as do the ridges on the surface of the caps (visible on the branch in the background).

Anthracophyllum archeri grows in clusters, the fruit bodies sometimes overlapping.

Anthracophyllum archeri (Berk.) Pegler 1965

Common name: Orange fan
Afrikaans: Oranjewaaier

Etymology: GREEK: *anthrac-* = charcoal, *phyll* = leaf; *archeri* = after the Australian architect, naturalist and politician, William Archer (1820–1874)
Synonym(s): *Xerotus archeri*

The fan-shaped cap is distinctive.

ECOLOGY: Saprophytic.

DISTRIBUTION: Mpumalanga (Mashishing), possibly more widespread. Occurs in Australia and New Zealand.

HABITAT: Grows on dead branches and twigs; fruit bodies single or clustered, crowded, sometimes overlapping.

DESCRIPTION: The red to orange coloration and the shell- or fan-shaped cap are key identifying features of this species. **Cap:** 1–2.5cm in diameter; sessile; semicircular to shell- or fan-shaped, shallow convex; margin often lobed; surface smooth and radially ridged; deep red, magenta, tan to light orange, fading to duller tones. **Gills:** adnate, broadly spaced, radiating from the point of attachment to the substrate, full and intermediate lengths; deep red-orange to almost purple or brown. **Stipe:** absent or rudimentary and lateral; if present 0.1cm or shorter; white; **Ring:** absent. **Flesh:** leathery. **Smell:** no distinctive odour. **Spore print:** white.

SIMILAR SPECIES: The unmistakable colour, shape and size of these mushrooms, and their widely spaced fold-like gills, distinguish them from other similar fan-shaped species.

EDIBILITY: Poisonous.

NOTES: The genus *Anthracophyllum* contains 10 known species worldwide, and is widespread in tropical regions. This species, previously known only from Australia and New Zealand, has recently been reported from South Africa.

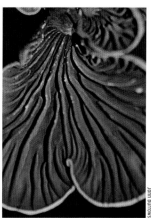

The gills are broadly spaced.

The viscid, orange-brown or pinkish-tan cap and bright yellow pores are distinctive features of this bolete.

Aureoboletus gentilis (Quél.) Pouzar 1957

Common name: Gilded bolete
Afrikaans: Vergulde boleet

Etymology: LATIN: *aureus* = golden, *boletus* = mushroom; *gentilis* = clan, family

Synonym(s): *Boletus gentilis*, *B. sanguineus* var. *gentilis*, *Pulveroboletus gentilis*, *Xerocomus gentilis*

ECOLOGY: Mycorrhizal.

DISTRIBUTION: First reported in South Africa in the Western Cape (Cape Town), but may be more widespread. Occurs in Europe and Russia.

HABITAT: Grows under broadleaved trees, especially oaks; fruit bodies single or grouped.

DESCRIPTION: The reddish-brown to cinnamon-brown or chestnut-brown cap and bright yellow pores are typical features of this mushroom. **Cap:** 2.5–7cm in diameter; rounded convex, becoming broadly convex or nearly flat with age; margin wavy or irregular above pore surface; surface smooth, may not appear sticky in dry weather; debris usually securely attached to the cap surface; reddish brown to cinnamon-brown or chestnut-brown. **Pores:** decurrent, slightly depressed around the stipe; pore mouths small, rounded, enlarging to angular in maturity; light lemon-yellow when young, then golden-yellow, becoming slightly greenish yellow with age; tubes 0.6–1.5cm deep. **Stipe:** 5–9cm long, 0.6–2cm thick; central; narrowing toward the pointed base, with adhering tufts of whitish mycelium, more or less rooting; smooth, dry, viscid when wet, not reticulate (covered in a net-like pattern) or only slightly so at the apex; whitish or pale yellowish white at first, turning pinkish tan or developing ochre-brown discolorations; stout. **Ring:** absent. **Flesh:** firm when young, becoming soft and mushy; whitish to pinkish brown, yellowish in the stipe, sometimes darker at the base. **Smell:** pleasant fruity odour. **Spore print:** dark olive-brown.

SIMILAR SPECIES: *Aureoboletus flaviporus* (not described here).

EDIBILITY: Edible; has a pleasant taste. The cap cuticle should be removed before cooking to avoid the meal becoming slimy.

> **NOTES:** This mushroom was originally described as *Boletus sanguineus* var. *gentilis* by French mycologist Lucien Quélet in 1884. It was reclassified in 1957 as *Aureoboletus gentilis*.

The pores are round at first, expanding with age to become slightly angular.

The tubes extend down the stipe beyond the point of attachment.

The flesh is whitish to pinkish brown, with yellowish tinges in the stipe.

The stipe is usually barrel-shaped but may taper toward the apex.

Clusters of *Boletus aereus* are a lucky find when conditions are perfect.

Boletus aereus Bull. 1789

Common names: Dark cep, queen bolete, black-headed bolete, bronze bolete, tanned cep
Afrikaans: Donker sep

Etymology: LATIN: *boletus* = mushroom; LATIN: *aereus* = of copper or bronze

Synonym(s): *Boletus edulis* f. *aereus, Dictyopus aereus, Suillus aereus, Tubiporus edulis* subsp. *aereus*

ECOLOGY: Mycorrhizal.

DISTRIBUTION: First reported in South Africa in the Western Cape, Eastern Cape and Gauteng, but may be more widespread. Occurs in the UK, Europe, USA and Russia.

HABITAT: Grows under deciduous broadleaved trees, especially oaks; fruit bodies single or scattered, rarely clustered.

DESCRIPTION: This species is easily recognised by its typically dark sepia-coloured cap, which is almost black when young but lightens progressively as it matures. **Cap:** 5–15cm in diameter; thick, fleshy; hemispherical to convex; whitish-yellowish cuticle overhanging at the margin; surface somewhat velvety, slightly curvy; olive-green to brown, almost black. **Pores:** almost free, shortened near the stipe; pore mouths close, small, rounded; white or whitish and pruinose at first, then yellowish, finally olivaceous; tubes 1–2cm deep. **Stipe:** 6–10cm long, 4–8cm thick, usually shorter than the cap diameter; central; thick, may taper toward the apex; cinnamon or saffron, becoming discoloured with age; firm. **Ring:** absent. **Smell:** odour reminiscent of hazelnuts. **Spore print:** dark olive-brown.

SIMILAR SPECIES: Distinguished from *Boletus edulis* and *B. reticulatus* by the darker cap and the cinnamon or saffron colour of the stipe. *Imleria badia* is also similar, but stains bluish green when the pore surface is pressed.

EDIBILITY: Edible; delicious flavour. The flesh softens considerably with age, making young, firm specimens more suitable for cooking.

Edible

The cap is almost black when young.

The cap is hemispherical to convex, and the surface slightly velvety.

A basket full of dark ceps is a chef's delight.

Gary B Goldman

Thick, fleshy and delectable, *Boletus edulis* (porcini) is one of the most sought-after edible mushrooms in the world.

Boletus edulis Bull. 1782

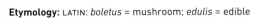

Common names: Porcini, cep, penny bun, squirrel's bread, king bolete
Afrikaans: Eetbare boleet, sep, klipsampioen

Etymology: LATIN: *boletus* = mushroom; *edulis* = edible
Synonym(s): *Ceriomyces crassus, Dictyopus edulis, Leccinum edule, Tubiporus edulis*

Edible

ECOLOGY: Mycorrhizal.

DISTRIBUTION: Widespread in South Africa. Occurs in the UK, Europe, USA, Russia, Australia and New Zealand.

HABITAT: Grows in well-drained soil under broadleaved trees, especially oaks, and sometimes under coniferous trees; fruit bodies single or scattered.

DESCRIPTION: This delicious mushroom, commonly known as porcini, can be identified by the massive appearance of the fruit body, the smooth, tan-coloured cap and the large, barrel-shaped stipe, covered with a network of white threads over the upper half. **Cap:** 5–25cm in diameter; fleshy, thick; hemispherical at first, becoming shallow convex; margin smooth, projecting beyond the tubes; surface smooth, dry, glossy; brown to red-brown or chestnut. **Pores:** almost free, depressed around the stipe; pore mouths small, circular to angular; white at first and stuffed with fungus tissue, resembling a fine sponge, turning creamy yellow to brownish green; tubes 1–4cm deep. **Stipe:** 5–25cm long, 2.5–4cm thick; central; swollen, barrel- to club-shaped or cylindrical, thickened toward the base; upper part covered with a network of raised white threads, meshes rather elongate; base smooth; white to fawn-brown; hard, firm, solid. **Ring:** absent. **Flesh:** thick, firm, spongy when older; white, no discoloration when bruised. **Smell:** distinctive nutty odour. **Spore print:** olive-brown.

SIMILAR SPECIES: *Boletus aereus, B. reticulatus, Imleria badia.*

EDIBILITY: Edible; a mushroom hunter's delight, prized for its excellent flavour and thick, meaty texture. The green tubes should be removed before cooking, as they tend to make the dish slimy. The tubes can be dried and blended into a powder to spice up dishes such as risottos, stews and soups. The dehydration process is said to intensify the nutty flavour of the mushroom. Fresh porcini are available commercially in stores and at food markets.

Ageing porcini are good for drying.

NOTES: In Europe, the USA and other parts of the world the fruit bodies may become infested with maggots soon after they have been picked. South African porcini are free of insect larvae or burrowing worms, making them highly sought after internationally.

The brown to red-brown cap is supported by a swollen stipe, the shape of which can be cylindrical or in the form of a barrel or a club.

The cap surface is matt to finely velvety, with the cuticle tending to extend past the margin. The flesh cracks at the centre as the mushroom matures.

Gary B Goldman

Boletus reticulatus Schaeff. 1774

Common names: Oak bolete, summer bolete
Afrikaans: Eikeboleet

Etymology: LATIN: *boletus* = mushroom; *reticulatus* = reticulated, netted
Synonym(s): *Boletus aestivalis, Ceriporia reticulata, Gloeoporus reticulatus, Polyporus reticulatus*

Edible

ECOLOGY: Mycorrhizal.

DISTRIBUTION: Western Cape, Eastern Cape and Gauteng, possibly more widespread. Occurs in the UK, Europe, Costa Rica, Russia and Japan.

HABITAT: Grows in well-lit areas at the edges of broadleaved (especially oak) forests or sometimes under pines; fruit bodies in small groups or scattered, sometimes clustered.

DESCRIPTION: An exceptionally tasty mushroom, it is easily recognised by its convex, almost round cap and the net-like pattern that extends down most of the bulbous stipe. **Cap:** 5–15cm in diameter; thick, fleshy; almost hemispherical, then convex; margin even, downturned, smooth, slightly overhanging the tubes; surface velvety, dry, dull, often with fine to coarse cracks at the centre; yellowish brown to pale snuff-brown. **Pores:** almost free, depressed around the stipe, notched; pore mouths small, circular; creamy white at first, then yellowish to greenish yellow, olive-brown in mature specimens; tubes 1–2cm deep. **Stipe:** 6–15cm long, 2–5cm thick; central; barrel-shaped, wider toward the base, tapers rapidly to a rounded point; upper three quarters covered with a network of raised threads; whitish at first, then pale brownish; thick, solid, robust. **Ring:** absent. **Flesh:** firm, compact; white throughout, sometimes with slight yellowish tinges. **Smell:** strong but pleasant odour. **Spore print:** olivaceous snuff-brown.

SIMILAR SPECIES: *Boletus edulis, B. aereus, Imleria badia.*

EDIBILITY: Edible; excellent flavour. It is considered by many to be more aromatic than *Boletus edulis* and is arguably the best of all edible mushrooms.

NOTES: The oak bolete was formally described as *Boletus reticulatus* by Jacob Christian Schäffer in 1774 and as *B. aestivalis* by Jean-Jacques Paulet in 1793. Although both names have been used, the current accepted name is *B. reticulatus.*

Boletus reticulatus, commonly known as the oak bolete, grows under oak trees.

The cap is yellowish brown to pale snuff-brown, and is supported by a stout stipe.

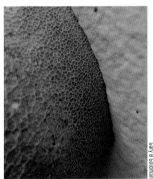

A fine net-like pattern can be seen on the surface of the stipe.

Imleria badia has a sticky surface, which dries to a chestnut or chocolate-brown sheen after picking.

Imleria badia (Fr.) Vizzini 2014

Common names: Bay bolete, bay-brown bolete, bay-capped bolete
Afrikaans: Rooibruinboleet

Etymology: *imleria* = after Belgian mycologist Louis Imler (1900–1993); LATIN: *badius* = chestnut-brown, bay-brown, reddish brown

Synonym(s): *Boletus badius, Ixocomus badius, Suillus badius, Xerocomus badius*

Edible

ECOLOGY: Mycorrhizal.

DISTRIBUTION: Western Cape, Gauteng and Mpumalanga, possibly more widespread. Occurs in the UK, Europe, Canada, USA, Mexico and Russia.

HABITAT: Grows in coniferous and mixed forests, sometimes found under broadleaved trees; fruit bodies single or scattered.

DESCRIPTION: The cylindrical stipe, lined with vertical dark-brown veins on a buffish-yellow background, makes this a distinctive mushroom. **Cap:** 4–14cm in diameter; convex but flattening out with age, eventually turning upward; margin even; surface downy when young, becoming smooth and polished, slightly viscid when wet; brown to dark brick, ochre-brown with age, dries to chestnut or chocolate-brown. **Pores:** slightly depressed around the stipe; pore mouths small, rounded, becoming angular and larger with age; white at first, then olivaceous, blue when bruised; tubes 0.6–1.5cm deep. **Stipe:** 4–12cm long, 0.8–3cm thick; cylindrical, stout; pallid, finely streaked (not forming a net pattern); concolorous with cap, but paler. **Ring:** absent. **Flesh:** firm, then soft, finally flaccid, fibrous in the stipe; whitish, with yellowish tinges, brown just under the cap cuticle. **Smell:** mild mushroomy odour. **Spore print:** olive-brown.

SIMILAR SPECIES: Other bolete species, but the blue bruising of the pores of young *Imleria badia* specimens helps to identify this species.

EDIBILITY: Edible; a delicious mushroom suitable for all meals, especially breakfasts.

> **NOTES:** The blue stains that appear when touching or cutting this mushroom are due to the oxidation of boletol, a harmless substance found in many boletes.

The stipe surface is finely streaked.

The pores turn blue if damaged.

Convex at first, the cap flattens out and eventually turns upward.

The dome-shaped cap and the white stipe covered with greyish vertical striations are clearly noticeable in this young specimen.

Leccinum duriusculum (Schulzer ex Kalchbr.) Singer 1947

Common names: Poplar bolete, slate bolete, leccinum gray
Afrikaans: Populierboleet

Etymology: ITALIAN: *leccinum* = fungus; LATIN: *duriusculum* = hard

Synonym(s): *Boletus duriusculus, Leccinum nigellum, Suillus duriusculus*

Edible

ECOLOGY: Mycorrhizal.

DISTRIBUTION: Widespread in South Africa. Occurs in the UK, Europe, Russia and Japan.

HABITAT: Grows under poplar trees, especially *Populus canescens*; fruit bodies single or scattered.

DESCRIPTION: This medium-sized to large bolete can be found wherever groups of poplar trees occur. **Cap:** 2–15cm in diameter; fleshy, thick; convex; margin regular to almost undulate, slightly overhanging the tubes; surface downy, stippled turning smooth, viscid when wet; sepia-grey to dark brown-grey. **Pores:** free around the stipe, depressed, closely packed, almost solid to the touch; pore mouths small, circular, becoming slightly larger with age; white at first, turning beige, bruising olive-brown; tubes 0.6–1.5cm deep. **Stipe:** 4–12cm long, 1.2–1.9cm thick; widening toward the base, but tapering to the tip; covered with dense vertical striations and black dots in lines coalescing into small scales or a network of lines; white, green to blue hues near the base; firm, solid. **Ring:** absent. **Flesh:** thick, firm; white, tinged blue-green then fading to brownish at the base; in fresh specimens the stipe stains inky blue when cut and exposed to air. **Smell:** mild mushroomy odour. **Spore print:** snuff-brown.

EDIBILITY: Edible; excellent flavour, especially if young, fresh fruit bodies are used. In older specimens, the cap loses texture by becoming too soft and watery and the stipe is woody. The flesh blackens when cooked.

A young fruit body emerges from the soil.

The stipe widens toward the base and tapers toward the apex.

The pores are not attached to the stipe.

Xerocomellus chrysenteron has a convex cap that becomes flattened with age. Beneath the cap, the tubes end in large, angular, yellowish pores.

Despite its fleshy appearance, this edible mushroom has a bland flavour and soft texture. It is found in moist soil, mainly in coniferous woods.

Xerocomellus chrysenteron (Bull.) Šutara 2008

Common names: Red-cracked bolete, red-cracking bolete
Afrikaans: Rooi gekraakte boleet

Etymology: GREEK: *xero* = dry, *come* = hair of the head, *-ellus* = diminutive; *chrysos* = golden, *-enteron* = intestine

Synonym(s): *Boletus chrysenteron, Suillus chrysenteron, Versipellis chrysenteron, Xerocomus chrysenteron*

ECOLOGY: Mycorrhizal.

DISTRIBUTION: Western Cape and Gauteng. Occurs in the UK, Europe, Canada, USA, Mexico, Chile, Japan, Australia and New Zealand.

HABITAT: Grows in moist, humus-rich soil under broadleaved and sometimes coniferous trees; fruit bodies single, grouped or clustered.

DESCRIPTION: The firm stipe streaked coral-red (usually toward the bottom half) and the cracked cap surface with pinkish flesh showing between the cracks are clues to identifying this species. **Cap:** 2–10cm in diameter; shallow convex then flattened; margin uneven; surface covered in white powdery granules, usually cracking; in cold, moist weather the cap appears smooth, not cracked, usually darkish brown; reddish brown, fawn or olive khaki-brown, reddish cerise at the margin. **Pores:** almost free, depressed around the stipe; pore mouths small, angular; pale yellow, later greenish yellow to almost olive, dirty green to bluish when bruised; tubes 0.7–1cm deep. **Stipe:** 4–12cm long, 1.2–1.9cm thick; cylindrical, slightly curved, tapering at the base; upper part covered with red striations, lower part with red dots or striations; yellow, reddish; firm, solid. **Ring:** absent. **Flesh:** soft, spongy; yellowish, tinged with brown or pale red, turning blue then pinkish to purple-pink under the cuticle when cut. **Smell:** mild mushroomy odour. **Spore print:** olivaceous brown.

SIMILAR SPECIES: Young specimens of this mushroom can have a dark, dry surface and downy cap, and may be mistaken for *Imleria badia*.

EDIBILITY: Edible; has a bland flavour and soft texture.

> **NOTES:** Despite its common name 'red-cracked bolete', not all specimens develop a cracked surface.

Sulphur-yellow at first, the stipe later becomes marked with red striations.

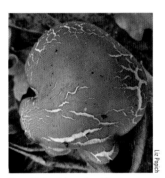

The reddish cuticle cracks with age.

The lemon-cream flesh turns blue when cut.

A rare sight, *Buchwaldoboletus hemichrysus* grows only at ground level on decaying or dead wood, never on tree trunks.

Sulphur-yellow in colour, the tubes are slightly decurrent, very densely arranged and spongy.

Buchwaldoboletus hemichrysus (Berk. & M.A. Curtis) Pilát 1969

Common names: Golden bolete, half-yellow powdery bolete
Afrikaans: Gouboleet

Etymology: *buchwald* = after Danish plant pathologist and mycologist Niels Fabritius Buchwald (1898–1986), LATIN: *boletus* = mushroom; GREEK: *hemi-* = half, *-chrysus* = god of gold

Synonym(s): *Boletus hemichrysus, Ceriomyces hemichrysus, Pulveroboletus hemichrysus, Xerocomus sulphureus*

ECOLOGY: Saprophytic.

DISTRIBUTION: Western Cape (Stellenbosch), possibly more widespread. Occurs in the UK, Europe, USA, Mexico, Brazil, India, Japan, Australia, New Zealand, New Caledonia and Benin.

HABITAT: Grows in association with dead or dying pine trees, always appearing at ground level, never attached to tree trunks; slow-growing, but short-lived; fruit bodies single, grouped or clustered.

DESCRIPTION: Unlike other boletes, this rarely seen mushroom grows only on dead or decaying organic matter, usually at the base of pine trees. **Cap:** 4–10cm in diameter; dome-shaped to convex, irregularly depressed; margin more or less even, initially inrolled; surface powdery at first, later often cracked; sulphur-yellow, rusty orange tones with age. **Pores:** decurrent, slightly depressed around the stipe; hard at first, becoming spongy in older specimens; pore mouths irregular, radially elongated near the stipe but not large; reddish to reddish brown when young, ageing yellow-brown, pores bluing when bruised; tubes up to 1cm deep **Stipe:** 3–7cm long, 1–2cm thick; central or lateral to excentric; short and thick, narrowing toward the base, with adhering tufts of yellowish mycelium; powdery; concolorous with cap. **Ring:** absent. **Flesh:** firm at first, becoming soft with age; yellow with blue tinges. **Smell:** slight mushroomy odour. **Spore print:** brown with olive tones.

EDIBILITY: Edible; a delicious mushroom with a firm, meaty texture, similar in flavour to porcini.

> **NOTES:** The genus *Buchwaldoboletus* contains about a dozen species distributed worldwide, all of which grow on rotting or dead wood.

Edible

When young, the flesh is tinged blue.

The flesh becomes soft and spongy with age.

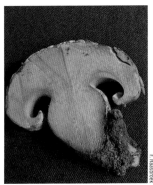

A cross section of the fruit body showing the inrolled margin.

The colour of the cap is variable, ranging from chestnut to cinnamon or pale orange-brown, while the pore surface is creamy white, later becoming pale lemon-yellow.

Gyroporus castaneus (Bull.) Quél. 1886

Common name: Chestnut bolete
Afrikaans: Kastaiingboleet

Etymology: GREEK: *gýros* = round, *porus* = opening; LATIN: *castanea* = chestnut

Edible

Synonym(s): *Boletus castaneus, Leucobolites castaneus*

ECOLOGY: Mycorrhizal.

DISTRIBUTION: Western Cape, Eastern Cape and Gauteng, possibly more widespread. Occurs in the UK, Europe, Canada, USA, Mexico, Honduras, Costa Rica, Brazil, Japan, Australia and New Zealand.

HABITAT: Grows in clearings of coniferous and broadleaved forests, commonly under oaks and chestnuts; fruit bodies single or grouped.

DESCRIPTION: The distinctive colours of the cap and stipe, together with the white pores and the hollow stipe, distinguish this species. **Cap:** 2–7cm in diameter; thick, fleshy; broadly convex to flat, sometimes depressed; margin thin, slightly undulate, incurved at first, finally turning upward; surface velvety, almost plushy, becoming smooth, shiny; chestnut, sometimes tending to cinnamon or pale orange-brown. **Pores:** almost detached from the stipe; pore mouths angular, rounded toward the cap margin and stipe; white to cream to pale lemon-yellow, soon beige, olive-brown when bruised; tubes 0.3–0.6cm deep. **Stipe:** 3–7cm long, 0.6–1.5cm thick; central; more or less cylindrical, sometimes tapering toward the base or bent near the base; smooth, velvety, unmarked; concolorous with cap or slightly lighter; fleshy-tough, stuffed, but soon spongy, becoming hollow. **Ring:** absent. **Flesh:** rather firm, compact, becoming soft; white, light reddish or hazel under cuticle. **Smell:** faint but pleasant odour. **Spore print:** greenish yellow.

EDIBILITY: Edible; has a sweet, nutty taste, similar to hazelnuts.

NOTES: The classic identification test for *Gyroporus castaneus* is to gently squeeze the stipe, which should feel hollow.

The tubes end in small pores and are almost detached from the stipe.

The stipe becomes spongy and hollow with age.

Gyroporus castaneus, showing the stages of development of the cap, from broadly convex to flat, and the margin, from incurved to finally upturned.

The common name refers to the brown colour of the fruit body rather than to any association with the host species.

Suillus bellinii (Inzenga) Watling 1967

Common names: Pine bolete, Bellini's bolete
Afrikaans: Denneboleet

Etymology: LATIN: *suillus* = of pigs; *bellinii* = after the Italian musician, Vicenzo Bellini (1801–1835)

Synonym(s): *Boletus bellinii, Ixocomus bellinii, Rostkovites bellinii*

ECOLOGY: Mycorrhizal.

DISTRIBUTION: Western Cape. Occurs in Portugal, Spain, France, Italy, Bulgaria and Morocco.

HABITAT: Grows under *Pinus halepensis, P. pinaster, P. pinea* – pine species with 'leaves' consisting of paired needles; fruit bodies single or grouped.

DESCRIPTION: This species can be recognised by the colours of the cap, which consist of a darkish-brown central area surrounded by tinges of ivory, and the short downward tapering stipe featuring dark granules on the upper part. **Cap:** 3–10cm in diameter; convex, becoming flattened, eventually bowl-shaped; margin wavy, upturned with maturity; surface viscid when wet, shiny when dry; honey-brown, cream at the margin, finally deep leather-brown. **Pores:** decurrent, slightly depressed around the stipe; pore mouths fine, rounded; cream with an orange tinge at first, changing to greenish yellow, later yellowish olive with orange tints; fresh specimen may exude a reddish latex; tubes up to 1cm deep. **Stipe:** 4–8cm long, 1–1.5cm thick; central; cylindrical, short, tapering downward to a marginally pointed base; whitish, with large brownish or reddish-brown spots along its length; firm, solid. **Ring:** absent. **Flesh:** thick; white with a lemon-yellow tint. **Smell:** pleasant fruity odour. **Spore print:** clay.

SIMILAR SPECIES: Similar in appearance to other *Suillus* species found in South Africa (*S. bovinus, S. granulatus* and *S. luteus*), *S. bellinii* can be identified by its shorter stipe.

EDIBILITY: Edible. Young specimens have a delicious nutty taste when eaten raw – freshly sliced from the stipe, they make a wonderful ingredient in a salad. The sticky skin over the cap and pore surfaces of older specimens should be removed before cooking.

NOTES: In young specimens drops of liquid are present on the pores.

The cap surface is viscid when wet and shiny when dry.

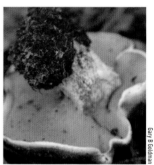

The whitish pores become yellow-green with age.

The tubes are very densely arranged, with the openings measuring less than 0.1cm in diameter.

Suillus bovinus (L.) Roussel 1796

Common names: Cow bolete, bovine bolete, jersey cow bolete, shallow-pored bolete
Afrikaans: Koeiboleet

Etymology: LATIN: *suillus* = of pigs; *bovinus* = pertaining to cattle, oxen, cows

Synonym(s): *Boletus bovinus, Ixocomus bovinus, Mariaella bovina*

ECOLOGY: Mycorrhizal.

DISTRIBUTION: Western Cape and Eastern Cape. Occurs in the UK, Europe, USA, Russia, Japan, Australia and New Zealand.

HABITAT: Grows under coniferous and broadleaved trees; fruit bodies grouped or clustered.

DESCRIPTION: This bolete is notable for its large, compound pore mouths. **Cap:** 3–8cm in diameter; convex and round at first, becoming flattened; margin even or slightly wavy; surface smooth, slimy when wet; dull orange to ochre-brown, sometimes reddening and becoming darker toward the centre. **Pores:** adnate, slightly decurrent on the stipe; large, compound as a result of several tubes converging to form a common opening; pore mouths angular, edges thin, somewhat toothed; ochreous to ochre-orange to clay-buff; tubes up to 1cm deep. **Stipe:** 4–6cm long, 0.5–0.8cm thick; central; cylindrical, short, tapering toward the base; concolorous with cap; solid. **Ring:** absent. **Flesh:** firm; whitish yellow, slowly turning clay pink when cut, yellowish rusty in stipe. **Smell:** fruity odour. **Spore print:** olive-brown.

SIMILAR SPECIES: *Suillus bellinii, S. granulatus, S. luteus.*

EDIBILITY: Edible; has a mild taste. When cooked, it releases excess fluid, which can be reduced or strained to make a sauce. The soft, rubbery consistency of older specimens renders them almost inedible. The flavour is more intense if the flesh is dehydrated.

> **NOTES:** The scientific name of this species is said to have its origins in the Middle Ages. Medieval knights reputedly had a low regard for the culinary value of this bolete, believing it fit only for cattle drovers.

This species has a dull-orange to ochre-brown cap surface.

The short stipe tapers toward the base.

The large compound pores on the undersurface are created when several tubes converge to form a common opening.

Fruit bodies appear in groups under pine trees.

The yellow-orange to rust-brown cap, the small yellow pores, and the stipe that is streaked with dried latex droplets are distinctive features.

Suillus granulatus (L.) Roussel 1806

Common names: Granular stalk bolete, weeping bolete, granulated bolete, dotted-stalk bolete
Afrikaans: Melkboleet

Etymology: LATIN: *suillus* = of pigs; *granulatus* = dotted, granulated, fine grained

Synonym(s): *Boletus granulatus, Ixocomus granulatus, Rostkovites granulatus*

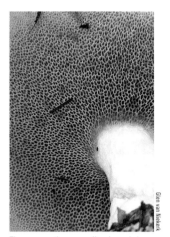

Edible

ECOLOGY: Mycorrhizal.

DISTRIBUTION: Western Cape, Eastern Cape, Gauteng and KwaZulu-Natal. Occurs in the UK, Europe, USA, Russia, Japan, Australia, New Zealand and Cameroon.

HABITAT: Grows under coniferous trees, especially pines; fruit bodies in small groups.

DESCRIPTION: This bolete may be recognised by its dotted upper stipe and the appearance of a milky white latex released from the pores in the young stage. **Cap:** 4–10cm in diameter; fleshy; hemispherical, expanding to convex, finally almost plane; margin regular or slightly wavy; surface smooth, viscid when wet, shiny when dry; yellow-orange to rusty brown. **Pores:** adnexed or also slightly decurrent; pore mouths small, rounded; whitish at first, bruising and spotting cinnamon to brownish, soon pale yellow, finally yellowish olive; tubes 0.6–1.5cm deep. **Stipe** 4–8cm long, 1–1.5cm thick; central; cylindrical or tapering slightly downward to the pointed base, often curved; upper section covered with reddish-brown granules (hardened remnants of latex droplets secreted from the stipe when young); white becoming pale yellow; fleshy-tough, firm. **Ring:** absent. **Flesh:** thick; pale yellow, darker near pores. **Smell:** slight but pleasant odour. **Spore print:** dark brown-yellow.

SIMILAR SPECIES: *Suillus bellinii, S. bovinus, S. luteus.*

EDIBILITY: Edible; fair, suitable for soups, frying and pickling. If, however, the flesh is yellow and drips water when squeezed, it should be discarded. It is advisable to remove the cuticle and pores to avoid the meal becoming slimy.

NOTES: It is recommended to use gloves when handling this mushroom, as touching it may result in an allergic reaction (contact dermatitis). Symptoms include itching, reddening and swelling of the skin at the site of contact.

The pore mouths are small and rounded.

The pore surface is whitish at first, then turning pale yellow and finally yellowish olive.

The cap margin is regular or slightly wavy.

A fairly large bolete, *Suillus luteus* can be identified by the white remains of the veil around the stipe and along the margin. The sticky, smooth cap surface, small, yellow pores and the stipe roughened with dots are also distinctive.

Gary B Goldman

Suillus luteus (L.) Roussel 1806

Common names: Slippery jack, sticky bun, yellow bolete
Afrikaans: Goudgeel-boleet

Etymology: LATIN: *suillus* = of pigs; *luteus* = yellow
Synonym(s): *Boletopsis lutea*, *Boletus luteus*, *Ixocomus luteus*

Edible

ECOLOGY: Mycorrhizal.

DISTRIBUTION: Western Cape, Eastern Cape, Gauteng and Free State, possibly more widespread. Occurs in the UK, Europe, USA, Chile, Russia, Japan, Australia and New Zealand.

HABITAT: Grows under pine trees; fruit bodies single, grouped, sometimes clustered.

DESCRIPTION: This fairly large bolete is easily identified by its tiny yellow pores and the white ring on its stipe. **Cap:** 4–10cm in diameter; fleshy; hemispherical becoming convex, sometimes with a slight umbo; margin even, occasionally with adhering veil remnants; surface smooth, shiny, viscid when wet; brown to sepia, violet hues when wet, light when dry. **Pores:** adnate, briefly decurrent; initially covered by a white membraneous veil; pore mouths small, circular, becoming polygonal with age; sulphur-yellow at first, then pale greenish to pale olivaceous yellow; tubes up to 0.8cm deep. **Stipe:** 4–8cm long, 1–1.5cm thick; granular; yellow above the ring, white or brownish below. **Ring:** large, membraneous, margin glutinous and white at first, becoming dry and brownish violet. **Flesh:** tough, thick; off-white or pale yellow, darkening to orange, then almost black in old specimens, vinaceous in stipe. **Smell:** mushroomy odour. **Spore print:** clay to ochre-brown.

SIMILAR SPECIES: Distinguished from *Suillus bovinus*, *S. bellinii* and *S. granulatus* by the ring on its stipe.

EDIBILITY: Edible; good to eat, considered one of the better edible sticky caps. The slimy, bitter cuticle and any ageing pores are best discarded before cooking. The flesh blackens when cooked.

A basket of slippery jacks can evolve into a good pasta sauce.

Pine forests are the preferred habitat of this species.

A white veil covers the young pores.

Once ruptured, the veil remains as a ring around the stipe.

The slimy, bitter cap cuticle and ageing pores should be removed before cooking.

The large, fleshy, saddle-shaped cap and smooth, dry, irregularly cracked surface are unmistakable features of this species.

Phlebopus sudanicus (Har. & Pat.) Singer 1944

Common name: Bushveld bolete
Afrikaans: Bosveldboleet

Etymology: GREEK: *phlebs-* = open veins, *-bopus* = foot; *sudanicus* = after the former French colony of Sudan, now the independent state of Mali

Synonym(s): *Boletus sudanicus, Phaeogyroporus sudanicus*

ECOLOGY: Mycorrhizal.

DISTRIBUTION: Gauteng, KwaZulu-Natal, Mpumalanga and Limpopo; may be native to South Africa. Occurs in Mali, Guinea, Burkina Faso, Niger, Nigeria, Botswana and Swaziland.

HABITAT: Grows in grasses, often near indigenous broadleaved trees; fruit bodies single.

DESCRIPTION: This mushroom is distinguished by its large fruit body, brownish colours, blue-staining flesh, and short, bulbous stipe. **Cap:** 8–50cm in diameter; fleshy; thick, convex, later becoming plane and centrally depressed, often unequally expanded and saddle-shaped in mature specimens; margin thin, smooth, inrolled until maturity, then wavy; surface dry, smooth, irregularly cracked; olive-brown but ochraceous buff toward the margin. **Pores:** adnexed, later free, shorter toward the margin; pore mouths small, angular, ragged toward the edges; green-yellow turning olive-yellow, ochraceous at the margin; tubes 0.9–3cm deep. **Stipe:** 6–24cm long; 4–9cm thick; mostly excentric; thick, bulbous, inflated at the base (up to 22cm in diameter), with a basal tuft of brown-olive mycelium; smooth, longitudinally grooved over the lower part; dark yellow, concolorous with cap in the upper part; fleshy, tough, solid. **Ring:** absent. **Flesh:** soft to firm; white at first, then yellow to brown-beige, blue-green when cut or bruised. **Smell:** pleasant odour. **Spore print:** olivaceous brown.

SIMILAR SPECIES: May be confused with other large boletes.

EDIBILITY: Suspect. Where it has been eaten (in tropical Africa), it has been reported to cause intoxication.

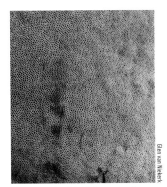
The pore surface is initially green-yellow before turning olive-yellow.

The cap expands unequally, giving the mushroom its saddle shape.

The mushroom cap is supported by a thick, bulbous stipe.

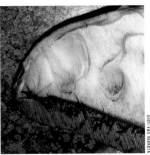
The flesh is white to brown-beige, but turns blue-green when bruised.

The pore surface is white to silvery, containing approximately 30 minute pore mouths per centimetre.

The upper surface of *Amauroderma rude* has concentric zones of varying shades of brown.

Amauroderma rude (Berk.) Torrend 1920

Common names: Brown stalked polypore, dusky-skinned mushroom, red-staining stalked polypore
Afrikaans: Bruinsteelporieswam

Etymology: LATIN: *amauro* = dusky, dark, *-derma* = skin; *rudis* = rough, raw

Synonym(s): *Amauderma rudis, Phellinus rudis, Polyporus rugatus, P. rugiceps*

ECOLOGY: Saprophytic.

DISTRIBUTION: Western Cape, Eastern Cape, Gauteng and KwaZulu-Natal. Occurs in Costa Rica, Brazil and Australia.

HABITAT: Grows in association with dead or dying wattle trees; fruit bodies single or grouped.

DESCRIPTION: This fungus is easily recognised by its brown, woody fruit body, winding stipe and white hymenial surface. **Cap:** 2–8cm in diameter; hard, corky to woody; circular, convex to flat to broadly inverted conical, depressed; margin thick, rounded, even; upper surface finely velvety, smooth or more frequently radially and concentrically grooved and ridged; chestnut brown to umber concentric zones. **Hymenophore:** depressed, free or attached to stipe; mouths small, circular, 30 per cm; white to silvery white, turning red when bruised, later dark blackish brown; tubes up to 0.4cm deep. **Stipe:** 5–12cm long, 0.5–1.5cm thick; central or excentric; more or less cylindrical, straight or winding, occasionally branched; surface smooth or irregularly knobbly; dull umber or snuff-brown, matt; tough, fibrous, solid; occasionally attached to roots. **Ring:** absent. **Flesh:** thick, fibrous; creamy brown, turning red when cut or bruised then darkening blackish. **Smell:** no distinctive odour. **Spore print:** dark brown.

SIMILAR SPECIES: *Lignosus sacer*, but unlike *Amauroderma rude* it does not bruise red.

EDIBILITY: Inedible.

MEDICINAL: *Amauroderma rude* is among a class of fungi that have anticancer properties. Recent research shows that *A. rude* can help to regulate the immune system and potentially inhibit tumour growth.

The stipe is slender and knobbly.

The pores bruise red before turning black.

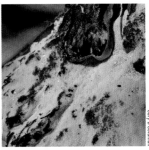

Black bruised pores.

The leathery, slightly corrugated red to brown cap of *Amauroderma sprucei* appears as if lacquered, making it a very distinctive mushroom.

Amauroderma sprucei (Pat.) Torrend 1920

Common names: None
Afrikaans: None

Etymology: GREEK: *amauros* = dark, dusky, *derma* = skin; *sprucei* = after British doctor and naturalist Richard Spruce (1817–1893)

Synonym(s): *Amauroderma avellaneum, A. dubiopansus, Ganoderma sprucei, Porotheleum rugosum*

ECOLOGY: Saprophytic.

DISTRIBUTION: First reported in South Africa in KwaZulu-Natal (New Germany Nature Reserve). Occurs in Nicaragua, Costa Rica, Cuba, Jamaica, Dominican Republic, Puerto Rico, Venezuela, Colombia, Guyana, French Guiana, Brazil and Peru.

HABITAT: Grows under broadleaved trees; fruit bodies single or scattered.

DESCRIPTION: A medium-sized mushroom, this species is easily recognised by the cap, which has a reddish-brown leathery or woody appearance, and the dark, shiny stipe. **Cap:** up to 10cm in diameter; horizontally expanded; margin sometimes inrolled after drying; surface leathery, soft to woody, hairy at first, becoming glabrous, wrinkled with parallel grooves, characteristically with concentric zones; dark reddish brown, greyish brown to blackish brown, margin orangish cream. **Hymenophore:** almost detached from the stipe; mouths rounded to angular, edges entire and a little thickened, 40–70 per cm; white, cream to pale yellowish brown when young, darkening to nearly cinnamon with age, usually darkening to greyish when touched; tubes 0.5–1cm deep. **Stipe:** 4–9cm long, 0.5–1cm thick; central to excentric; cylindrical, sinuous, short or long, broad at the apex, tapering to the base, single or branched; woody, solid. **Ring:** absent. **Flesh:** soft to firm; concolorous with the pore surface. **Smell:** unknown. **Spore print:** translucent to faintly yellowish.

SIMILAR SPECIES: Other *Amauroderma* species. Owing to its lacquered appearance, it may also be confused with species in the *Ganoderma lucidum* complex – bracket mushrooms which grow from roots in the soil, not on tree trunks.

EDIBILITY: Inedible.

Inedible

The cap is typically dark reddish brown, often with concentric zones.

The dark stipe is cylindrical, woody and solid, usually tapering toward the base.

The pore surface is white, darkening to greyish when touched.

The cap surface, marked with a mosaic design, becomes powdery in older specimens.

Favolaschia thwaitesii (Berk. & Broome) Kuntze 1898

Common name: Ping-pong bats
Afrikaans: Tafeltennisrakette

Etymology: LATIN: *favus* = honeycomb, *laschia* = after German pharmacist, botanist and mycologist Wilhelm Gottfried Lasch (1787–1863); *thwaitesii* = after British botanist and mycologist George Henry Kendrick Thwaites (1812–1882)

Synonym(s): *Laschia thwaitesii*

The pore mouths are large and shallow.

ECOLOGY: Saprophytic.

DISTRIBUTION: Western Cape, Gauteng and KwaZulu-Natal. Occurs in Brazil, Australia, New Zealand and Zambia.

HABITAT: Grows on dead and decaying woody material; fruit bodies in large groups.

DESCRIPTION: Occurring mainly at the very beginning of the rainy season, this attractive fungus is easily identified by its delicate, orange, fan-shaped fruit bodies and large, shallow pores. **Cap:** 0.5–1.5cm in diameter; small, delicate, gelatinous-fleshy; fan-shaped to circular; margin entire, wavy and crenulate; surface smooth, marked with a mosaic design; yellow-orange turning orange, translucent, finally powdered. **Hymenophore:** mouths large, shallow, circular to angular, usually larger at the centre; concolorous with cap; tubes about 0.5mm deep. **Stipe:** 0.2–0.8cm long, 0.1–0.2cm thick; absent or short and lateral, attached to the cap obliquely from below; cylindrical or tapering slightly toward the apex, thin; surface slightly granulated, with darker orange patches; concolorous with cap. **Ring:** absent. **Flesh:** gelatinous, tough; paler colour than cap. **Smell:** no distinctive odour. **Spore print:** white.

SIMILAR SPECIES: *Favolaschia calocera* (not described here), first observed in Madagascar, is very similar in appearance.

EDIBILITY: Unknown.

Favolaschia thwaitesii grows on dead wood.

NOTES: Many other species of the genus *Favolaschia* have been described from the tropics, and several colour variants have been named as subspecies of *F. thwaitesii*.

When appearing in large groups, the orange fruit bodies make for a dramatic sight.

The fruit bodies are small and delicate.

Liz Popich

Lentinus arcularius grows on dead wood, to which it is attached by means of a hairy to somewhat scaly stipe. The pores on the lower surface are slightly elongated.

Glen van Niekerk

The cap surface is dry and covered with small, dark scales that increase in number toward the margin.

Lentinus arcularius (Batsch) Zmitr. 2010

Common names: Large-pored funnel cap, spring polypore
Afrikaans: Grootporie-tregterswam

Etymology: LATIN: *lentus* = tough, *-inus* = resembles; *arcularius* = maker of small chests (referring to the pores)

Synonym(s): *Favolus arcularius, Heteroporus arcularius, Polyporus arcularius*

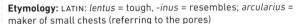
Inedible

ECOLOGY: Saprophytic.

DISTRIBUTION: Western Cape, Eastern Cape, Gauteng, KwaZulu-Natal and Mpumalanga, possibly more widespread. Occurs in Europe, Canada, USA, Mexico, Costa Rica, Brazil, Japan, Australia and New Zealand.

HABITAT: Grows on dead wood of broadleaved trees in contact with the soil; fruit bodies grouped.

DESCRIPTION: The small golden-brown to dark-brown cap fringed with fine hairs and the fairly large, elongated pores distinguish this species. **Cap:** 2–8cm in diameter; fleshy, tough; convex to funnel-shaped, centrally depressed, circular; margin even, thin, with fine short hairs, inrolled when dry; surface dry, scaly, concentrically grooved; golden-brown to buff. **Hymenophore:** sometimes decurrent; mouths hexagonal to angular, slightly radially elongated; white then yellowish light-brown; tubes 0.05–0.3cm deep. **Stipe:** 1.5–6cm long, 0.05–0.3cm thick; central; cylindrical; hairy to somewhat scaly; yellow-brown to dark brown; tough, solid. **Ring:** absent; **Flesh:** thin, leathery; white. **Smell:** slight mushroomy odour. **Spore print:** white to cream.

SIMILAR SPECIES: Other *Lentinus* species.

EDIBILITY: Inedible.

NOTES: This species causes a white rot in wood.

The cap is initially convex.

Fine hairs fringe the margin.

The stipe is hairy and somewhat scaly.

A young specimen.

The cap of *Lentinus arcularius* expands to about 8cm in diameter.

The fruit body of *Lignosus sacer* has a circular cap with white pores on the hymenial surface. The tubes are free from the woody stipe, which grows from an underground sclerotium.

Lignosus sacer (Afzel. ex Fr.) Ryvarden 1972

Common name: Olive-brown funnel cap
Afrikaans: Olyfbruintregterswam

Etymology: LATIN: *lignosus* = woody, *-osus* = indicates abundance; GREEK: *sakos* = shield

Synonym(s): *Leucoporus sacer, Microporus sacer, Polyporus sacer*

ECOLOGY: Saprophytic.

DISTRIBUTION: Eastern Cape, KwaZulu-Natal and Mpumalanga, possibly more widespread. Occurs in Australia, Cameroon, Tanzania, Kenya and Zambia.

HABITAT: Grows in rich humus soil; fruit bodies single or scattered.

DESCRIPTION: An unusual combination of characteristics – a dark, thin, tough, circular cap; a whitish pore surface; and a central, woody stipe that arises from a tuber-like sclerotium – makes this fungus almost immediately recognisable. **Cap:** 3–8cm in diameter; tough-leathery to woody; fan- to kidney-shaped to circular, depressed; margin thin, acute, entire or wavy; surface slightly furrowed, smooth, velvety, glabrous with age, concentrically or radially grooved; white turning cream. **Hymenophore:** free from the stipe; mouths rounded or angular to occasionally elongate; partitions thin, tough, leathery, branch and fuse (like a labyrinth), becoming radially raised in older parts, 0.2 per cm; white turning cream when dry; tubes up to 0.3cm deep. **Stipe:** 2–6cm long, 0.15–0.45cm thick; central; long, cylindrical, tapering upward, straight or bent, arising from a potato-like underground sclerotium (compact mass of hardened mycelium); smooth, velvety; pale brown-buff; woody, hollow; sclerotium oval to irregular, up to 5cm in diameter, horny, hard, usually wrinkled, dirty brown. **Ring:** absent. **Flesh:** thin, membraneous, tough, fibrous, dense; white to cream. **Smell:** strong, sweet, spicy odour. **Spore print:** white.

SIMILAR SPECIES: *Amauroderma rude*, which bruises red.

EDIBILITY: Inedible.

NOTES: The sclerotium of a close cousin, *Lignosus rhinoceros*, is regarded as a medicinal mushroom, as it is said to contain properties that can be used to cure numerous ailments.

The cap surface is concentrically zoned.

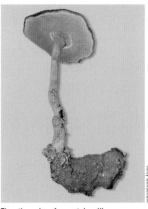

The stipe arises from a tuber-like sclerotium, or mass of hardened mycelium.

The white pore surface turns cream when dry.

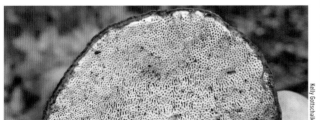

The arrangement of the pore mouths on the surface resembles a labyrinth.

A striking fungus, the concentric rings on the cap surface alternate between shades of orange, brown and chestnut.

Microporus xanthopus (Fr.) Kuntze 1898

Common name: Yellow-footed tiny pore
Afrikaans: None

Etymology: GREEK: *micro-* = small, tiny, *poros* = pore; *xanthopus* = yellow-footed

Synonym(s): *Coriolus xanthopus, Polyporus xanthopus, Polystictus xanthopus, Trametes xanthopus*

Inedible

ECOLOGY: Saprophytic.

DISTRIBUTION: KwaZulu-Natal. Occurs in Brazil, Thailand, Malaysia, the Philippines, Australia, Côte d'Ivoire, Cameroon and Zambia.

HABITAT: Grows on dead or rotting wood, often in open and sunny localities; fruit bodies grouped.

DESCRIPTION: The funnel-shaped cap, with distinct concentric bands in different shades of brown and cream, makes this attractive fungus easily identifiable. **Cap:** 5–10cm in diameter; flexible, tough when wet, hard when dry; funnel-shaped, circular to cap-like with a central depression; margin thin, wavy, lobed; surface smooth, often radially furrowed, concentrically zoned; coloration variable, orange to purple-brown, turning darker to chestnut when dry, often becoming blackish with age, margin usually pale. **Hymenophore:** decurrent; shallow, minute mouths, 80–100 per cm; cream to pale buff, almost pure white at the margin; tubes up to 0.01cm deep. **Stipe:** 5–10cm long, 0.3–0.9cm thick; adnate to somewhat decurrent; central or excentric, distinct, with an expanded disc-like base; smooth, glabrous; yellowish. **Ring:** absent. **Flesh:** thin; white. **Smell:** unknown. **Spore print:** white.

SIMILAR SPECIES: *Stereum ostrea.*

EDIBILITY: Inedible.

NOTES: This species causes a white rot in wood.

The funnel-shaped fruit bodies occur in groups. Water and organic debris collect in the central depressions.

Microporus xanthopus grows on dead or rotting wood, usually in open and sunny localities.

Picipes badius (Pers.) Zmitr. & Kovalenko 2016

Common names: Black-footed polypore, bay polypore, liver-brown polypore, black-footed funnel cap, black leg
Afrikaans: Groot swartvoettregter

Etymology: LATIN: *piceus* = pitch-black, *pes* = foot; *badius* = chestnut-brown, bay-brown, reddish brown

Synonym(s): *Polyporellus badius, Polyporus badius, P. dibaphus, P. durus, P. picipes, Royoporus badius*

ECOLOGY: Parasitic and saprophytic.

DISTRIBUTION: Western Cape, Eastern Cape, Gauteng and Mpumalanga, possibly more widespread. Occurs in the UK, Europe, USA, Mexico, Brazil, Russia, Japan, Australia and New Zealand.

HABITAT: Grows on dead and living broadleaved trees, occasionally on conifers; fruit bodies single or grouped.

DESCRIPTION: The smooth, reddish-brown caps, almost white pore surface and short, black stipe give this mushroom its distinctive appearance. **Cap:** 4–20cm in diameter; irregular, fan-shaped to broadly convex, centrally depressed; margin thin, incurved, wavy, often lobed; surface viscid when wet, shiny when dry; coloration variable, tan to chestnut-brown to dark reddish brown, often blackening slowly from the centre with old age, margin usually paler. **Hymenophore:** adnate to somewhat decurrent; pore mouths small, shallow, round to angular, 40–70 per cm; white to pale ochre near the margin when fresh, yellowish brown with age; tubes numerous, short, separate, 1–2mm deep. **Stipe:** 1–6cm long, 0.3–1.5cm thick; excentric; short, cylindrical, tapering to the base; frequently black or blackish below the pores; sometimes two or more fruit bodies may arise from the same stipe. **Ring:** absent. **Flesh:** firm, pliable, almost cartilaginous in texture; white. **Smell:** no distinctive odour. **Spore print:** white.

EDIBILITY: Inedible; too bitter and tough to use for cooking.

NOTES: Some fruit bodies can live for years.

The cap is viscid when wet, shiny when dry.

The cap is fan-shaped to broadly convex with a depressed centre.

The lower surface is white, becoming pale ochre near the wavy margin.

The fruit body has a short, off-centre stipe.

Fistulina africana Van der Byl 1928

Common names: None
Afrikaans: None

Etymology: LATIN: *fistula* = pipe, tubes, *-ina* = similar to; *africana* = pertaining to Africa

Synonym(s): None

Unknown

ECOLOGY: Parasitic and saprophytic.

DISTRIBUTION: To date, found only in South Africa (Western Cape, Eastern Cape, Gauteng and Mpumalanga), suggesting it is native to the country.

HABITAT: Grows on trunks of living and dead broadleaved trees; fruit bodies single.

DESCRIPTION: This unmistakable fungus occurs very rarely. It is identifiable by the reddish-brown surface colour, reddish lateral stipe and fleshy texture. **Cap:** 5–12cm in diameter; fleshy; bracket- to fan-shaped, convex; margin slightly incurved, uneven; crust horny and rough, owing to dark, raised pustule-like protuberances; dark brown-red to maroon. **Hymenophore:** pore mouths circular; surface deep ochraceous at first, darkening to brown; tubes numerous, short, separate, 1–2mm deep. **Stipe:** lateral; cylindrical, short; longitudinal grooves, rough because of raised pustules, many with brownish tips; dark pink to vermillion; solid, fleshy. **Ring:** absent. **Flesh:** soft, gelatinous; colourless to grey, turning brown with age. **Smell:** no distinctive odour. **Spore print:** yellow-brown.

Fistulina africana occurs very rarely.

SIMILAR SPECIES: *Fistulina hepatica* (not described here) has reddish flesh and blood-red sap, both of which are absent in *F. africana*.

EDIBILITY: Unknown.

> **NOTES:** *Fistulina africana* was first reported from Knysna on the trunk of a living white alder (*Platylophus trifoliatus*). Fungi in the genus *Fistulina* are distinguished by having separate tubes, whereas most other polypores have securely fused tubes.

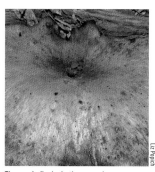

The cap is fleshy in the upper layer.

The spores are distinct and free from each other.

The margin of this young specimen is slightly incurved.

Phellinus gilvus occurs in small groups or in overlapping tiers on the dead wood of broadleaved trees.

Liz Popich

Phellinus gilvus (Schwein.) Pat. 1900

Common name: Golden bracket
Afrikaans: Geelbruinrakswam

Etymology: GREEK: *phellos* = cork, *-inus* = resembling;
LATIN: *gilvus* = yellowish

Synonym(s): *Fuscoporia gilva, Polyporus gilvus, Polystictus pallidus, Trametes keetii*

ECOLOGY: Saprophytic.

DISTRIBUTION: Widespread in South Africa. Occurs in the USA, Guatemala, Honduras, Costa Rica, Brazil, Peru, Nepal, Malaysia, Japan, Australia, New Zealand, Tanzania, Zambia and Zimbabwe.

HABITAT: Grows on dead wood of broadleaved trees; fruit bodies grouped, often in overlapping tiers.

DESCRIPTION: This species is variable in form and appearance, with the surface ranging from smooth to very rough, although the reddish colour is relatively constant. Identification should be verified microscopically. **Cap:** 2.5–10cm in diameter, 2–6cm radius, 0.2–2cm thick; hard, corky, tough; sessile, fan-shaped to semicircular, convex; margin entire, thin, rounded; upper surface velvety or rough with stiff hairs, turning hairless, usually zoned; yellow-brown to red-brown, eventually blackish. **Lower surface:** pore mouths very small, circular, 6–8 per cm; velvety, red-brown or darker; tubes 0.1–0.5cm deep. **Flesh:** tough, corky to woody; yellow-brown, darker in lower parts. **Smell:** no distinctive odour. **Spore print:** white.

EDIBILITY: Inedible; far too tough for eating.

NOTES: The fruit bodies of this species may survive for several years under favourable conditions.

Inedible

The upper surface is red-brown, but darkens with age.

The margin is yellowish and velvety.

Fan-shaped with a convex surface, the cap is usually zoned.

Small, circular pore mouths line the lower, spore-bearing surface.

Distinctly wood-like in appearance, *Phellinus rimosus* develops a pronounced cracked surface, hence its common name 'cracked bracket'.

Phellinus rimosus (Berk.) Pilát 1940

Common names: Cracked bracket, medicinal cracked-cap polypore, cracked-cap polypore
Afrikaans: Barsrakswam

Etymology: GREEK: *phellus* = cork, *-inus* = resembling; LATIN: *rima* = fissure

Synonym(s): *Fomes rimosus, Fulvifomes rimosus, Polyporus rimosus, Pyropolyporus rimosus*

ECOLOGY: Parasitic and saprophytic.

DISTRIBUTION: Western Cape, Eastern Cape, Gauteng and KwaZulu-Natal. Occurs in Europe, Canada, USA, Mexico, Costa Rica, Brazil, Australia, Kenya, Zambia and Zimbabwe.

HABITAT: Grows on dead and living trees; fruit bodies single; perennial.

DESCRIPTION: This is one of a number of species with hard, cracking fruit bodies, giving the appearance of a cow's hoof. **Cap:** 3–36cm in diameter, 3–37cm radius, 1.5–28cm thick; very hard, woody; sessile, bracket- to hoof-shaped, slanted or almost vertical; margin velvety, thick, rounded, even, merging into the upper surface; surface smooth, hairless at first, marked with parallel and concentric grooves, becoming black and cracking as if burned; red-brown to grey, then black, margin yellowish brown. **Lower surface:** pore mouths minute, circular; velvety, yellow-brown to dark brown; tubes 0.2–0.6cm deep. **Flesh:** hard, woody; yellowish brown to reddish brown. **Smell:** no distinctive odour. **Spore print:** brown.

SIMILAR SPECIES: *Phellinus linteus* (not described here).

EDIBILITY: Inedible; too tough to eat.

MEDICINAL: *Phellinus rimosus* has antibacterial, anti-inflammatory, antitumour and antiviral properties. It may play a role in preventing ailments as diverse as gastroenteric dysfunction, diarrhoea, haemorrhage and some cancers. Australia's Aboriginal people have used *Phellinus* fruit bodies medicinally for centuries.

NOTES: *Phellinus rimosus* is associated with heart rot in a variety of tree species.

The yellowish margin is velvety at first.

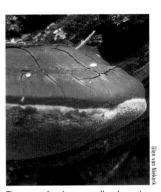

The pore surface becomes yellow-brown to red-brown.

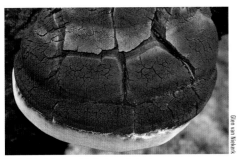

The fruit body is shaped in the form of a hoof.

The green colour is caused by algae growing on the fruit body.

The large fruit bodies of *Daedalea quercina* are easily identified by the maze-like spore surface, formed by the large, irregularly shaped pore openings.

Glen van Niekerk

Daedalea quercina (L.) Pers. 1801

Common names: Oak maze gill, thick maze gill, thick-walled maze polypore, maze gill mushroom, oak polypore
Afrikaans: Eikedoolhofswam, roskamswam

Etymology: GREEK: *daedalos* = after Daedalus (in Greek mythology, the builder of the Labyrinth in Crete); LATIN: *quercinus* = pertaining to oak

Synonym(s): *Daedaleites quercinus, Lenzites quercina, Striglia quercina, Trametes quercina*

ECOLOGY: Saprophytic.

DISTRIBUTION: Western Cape and Eastern Cape, possibly more widespread. Occurs in the UK, Europe, USA, Mexico, Costa Rica, Brazil, Russia and Australia.

HABITAT: Grows on dead oak stumps and logs; fruit bodies single or occasionally in shelved groups.

DESCRIPTION: While most bracket fungi have fairly small pore openings, those of Daedalea quercina are large, elongate and maze-like. **Cap:** 4–20cm in diameter, 3–15cm radius, 3–8cm thick; hard, corky; sessile, more or less fan-shaped, convex to flat; margin thick, rounded, entire; upper surface uneven, knobbed, with ill-defined concentric growth zones; beige to creamy at first, becoming ochraceous and tinged with grey, often darker in specimens that are several years old. **Lower surface:** ochraceous-cream or straw-yellow; pores large, elongate, forming an irregular maze, 0.1cm or wider; white at first, then beige to light fawn; tubes 0.5–3cm deep. **Flesh:** tough, corky; whitish to pale brown. **Smell:** faint but pleasant mushroomy odour. **Spore print:** whitish.

EDIBILITY: Inedible; too tough to eat.

The colour of the lower surface changes from white to beige and, later, to light fawn.

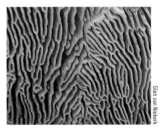

The pore surface resembles a labyrinth.

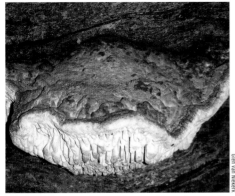

Specimens that are several years old, such as this one, have a darker cap coloration.

Dead oak stumps and logs are this bracket's preferred habitat.

The large fruit body of *Laetiporus baudonii* is variously coloured, sometimes in concentric zones. The young specimen is bright orange-yellow, but darkens to brownish with age.

The lower surface of the spongy fruit body consists of small, angular pore mouths, with up to 40 pores occurring per centimetre.

Laetiporus baudonii (Pat.) Ryvarden 1991

Common name: Orange-yellow rough top
Afrikaans: Bloekomvoetswam

Etymology: GREEK: *laetus* = bright, gay, abundant, *poros* = pore; *baudonii* = after M. Baudon, who collected this species from the Congo (modern-day Democratic Republic of the Congo) in 1914

Synonym(s): *Cladoporus baudonii, Polyporus baudonii, Psuedophaeolus baudonii*

ECOLOGY: Parasitic and saprophytic.

DISTRIBUTION: Western Cape, Eastern Cape, Gauteng and KwaZulu-Natal, possibly more widespread. Occurs in Australia, Democratic Republic of the Congo, Zambia, Malawi, Angola, Zimbabwe, Mozambique and Madagascar; may occur naturally throughout Africa.

HABITAT: Grows on or close to buried roots and dead stumps of broadleaved trees, including eucalyptus; fruit bodies single or scattered, sometimes clustered.

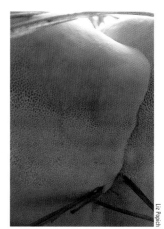

The pore surface is yellowish orange to apricot in fresh specimens.

DESCRIPTION: The large, brightly coloured, spongy fruit body makes for easy identification of this species. **Cap:** up to 48cm in diameter, 12–40cm radius, up to 3.5cm thick; large, spongy, soft, fragile; either attached by a narrow pad or by a compound stipe; circular, mostly cone-shaped but broadly inverted, or bracket-shaped to more or less kidney-shaped; margin rounded, thick, wavy or lobed; upper surface flat, finely downy to hairless, uneven with rounded lumps, grooved or with short ridges, sometimes concentrically zoned; bright orange-yellow, darkening to brownish with ageing and drying. **Lower surface:** pore mouths angular, 10–40 per cm, labyrinth-like, partitions even, thin; yellowish orange to lemon-yellow to apricot when fresh, drying to brown; tubes 0.1–0.4cm deep. **Stipe:** up to 6cm long, 6cm thick; distinct to almost absent, expanding upward; concolorous with cap. **Flesh:** soft, felty; pale orange-yellow to orange-buff when fresh, brownish when dry. **Smell:** mushroomy to slightly unpleasant odour. **Spores:** white.

SIMILAR SPECIES: *Laetiporus sulphureus, Phaeolus schweinitzii.*

EDIBILITY: Inedible.

NOTES: *Laetiporus baudonii* is found in miombo woodland in tropical Africa, where it is a root-rotting parasite, fruiting on the ground from buried roots, often close to dead stems or stumps. It has also been recorded as having caused root infections in tea plants in southern Malawi and in eucalyptus forests in Australia.

Laetiporus baudonii often engulfs grasses and twigs that lie in its growth path.

Patrick Madon

Laetiporus sulphureus is a conspicuous tiered bracket. It occurs parasitically on living trees, such as the specimen shown here growing on an oak tree, or saprophytically on dead wood, seen in the example below.

Gary B Goldman

Individual brackets have a wavy margin and are up to 40cm wide.

Laetiporus sulphureus (Bull.) Murrill 1920

Common names: Chicken-of-the-woods, sulphur polypore, crab-of-the-woods, sulphur shelf
Afrikaans: Swaelswam, swawelrakswam

Etymology: GREEK: *laetus* = bright, gay, abundant, *poros* = pore; LATIN: *sulphureus* = sulphur-yellow

Synonym(s): *Cladoporus sulphureus*, *Grifola sulphurea*, *Polyporus sulphureus*, *Tryometes sulphureus*

ECOLOGY: Parasitic and saprophytic.

DISTRIBUTION: Widespread in South Africa. Occurs in the UK, Europe, Canada, USA, Russia, Japan and Australia.

HABITAT: Occurs on dead and living broadleaved trees; fruit bodies clustered, in overlapping tiers.

DESCRIPTION: This large, fan-shaped bracket, identifiable by its luminous yellow to yellow-orange colours, is very conspicuous. **Cap:** size variable, 10–40cm in diameter, 10–20cm radius, 1–5cm thick; fleshy, thick, turning rigid and brittle in older specimens; sessile, fan-shaped to semicircular; margin fairly thick, rounded, wavy; upper surface uneven, lumpy, wrinkled, suede-like, with indistinct zones; sulphur-yellow to yellow-orange, almost luminous, dulls to white with age. **Lower surface:** pore mouths angular, 30–50 per cm; bright sulphur-yellow turning white; tubes up to 0.5cm deep. **Flesh:** thick; white to pale yellow or pale salmon; young fruit bodies succulent and exuding a clear to yellowish liquid when squeezed, older fruit bodies become cheese-like, crumbly and white. **Smell:** strong mushroomy odour. **Spore print:** white.

SIMILAR SPECIES: *Laetiporus baudonii* is bright yellowish orange when fresh; *L. conifericola* (not described here), also commonly known as 'chicken-of-the-woods' or 'sulphur shelf', occurs only on coniferous trees.

EDIBILITY: Edible. The young fruit bodies taste like chicken. Specimens harvested from certain host trees, such as eucalyptus, can cause digestive problems in some people.

MEDICINAL: Has antibacterial properties.

> **NOTES:** *Laetiporus sulphureus* is a pathogen of living oak, eucalyptus and occasionally poplar trees, in which it causes a brown, cubical heart-rot. The spores gain entry through cut or broken branches. The fruit bodies can survive saprophytically on the wood of their host tree long after it has died.

A sulphur-yellow fruit body.

Gary B Goldman

The upper surface is lumpy and wrinkled.

Glen van Niekerk

Fruit bodies become crumbly with age.

Liz Popich

The bracket arises from a short, almost central stipe. The greenish-yellow pores on the lower surface are clearly distinguishable.

The upper surface is velvety in parts and somewhat depressed.

Phaeolus schweinitzii (Fr.) Pat. 1900

Common names: Dye polypore, dyer's polypore, velvet-top fungus, Norway chicken, dyer's maze gill
Afrikaans: Dennevoetswam

Etymology: GREEK: *phae* = dusky, dark, *-olus* = somewhat; *schweinitzii* = after American botanist and mycologist Lewis David von Schweinitz (1780–1834), founder of North American mycological science

Synonym(s): *Coltricia schweinitzii, Hapalopilus schweinitzii, Phaeolus schweinitzii, Polyporus schweinitzii*

ECOLOGY: Parasitic and saprophytic.

DISTRIBUTION: Western Cape, Eastern Cape and Gauteng, possibly more widespread. Occurs in the UK, Europe, Canada, USA, Mexico, Russia, Japan, Australia, New Zealand and Tenerife.

HABITAT: Grows on buried roots and stumps, and at the base of living conifers (rarely reported on deciduous trees); fruit bodies single, clustered or in rosettes, appear in overlapping tiers in compound structures.

DESCRIPTION: Arising from a very short, almost central stipe, this bracket has a brilliant sulphur-yellow margin and dark-greenish pores on the lower surface. **Cap:** up to 30cm in diameter, 4–25cm radius, up to 3.5cm thick; some clusters up to 60cm in diameter; soft, corky or spongy; stipe absent or present, central or excentric; bracket- to fan- to kidney-shaped, somewhat depressed, growing laterally in compound structures, may also be inverted cone-shaped; margin even or wavy, rounded, sterile below; upper surface downy, older parts becoming more velvety or covered with coarse hairs, wrinkled and roughened; yellow to lemon-yellow, ochre-yellow, yellow-brown to deep red-brown, yellow to lemon-yellow at the margin, dark brown and brittle with age (resembling cow dung). **Lower surface:** pore mouths angular, 10–20 per cm at the margin, larger and irregular in oldest parts; creamy yellow to greenish yellow when fresh, becoming dark reddish brown to maroon-brown on bruising or dying; tubes 3–6cm deep. **Stipe:** 1–6cm long, 1–4cm thick; absent or central or excentric, branched or unbranched, occasionally fused with others and expanding upward; sometimes rooting. **Flesh:** soft, corky to spongy when fresh, brittle when dry; yellowish brown to rust-brown. **Smell:** no distinctive odour. **Spores:** white to pale ochre-yellow.

SIMILAR SPECIES: Could be confused with *Laetiporus sulphureus* and *L. baudonii*.

EDIBILITY: Unknown.

NOTES: *Phaeolus schweinitzii* is a pathogen of pine trees, causing a brown, cubical rot in the roots and lower trunks. The young fruit bodies contain fluids from which dyes of different colours can be extracted.

Glen van Niekerk

An ochre-yellow specimen.

Gary B Goldman

As it decays, the bracket turns dark red-brown and becomes brittle.

Gary B Goldman

The pore surface is creamy to greenish yellow when fresh.

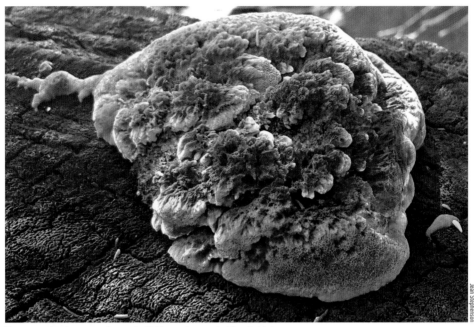

The upper surface is uneven and grooved, with the margin covered with matted hairs.

The upper surface is rose to mauve in the young parts and grey-fawn, brown or dark grey in the older sections.

Rhodofomitopsis lilacinogilva (Berk.) B.K. Cui, M.L. Han & Y.C. Dai 2016

Common name: Lilac shelf fungus
Afrikaans: Persrakswam

Etymology: GREEK: *rhodon* = rose, rosy, LATIN: *foma* = form, *-opsis* = resembling; LATIN: *lilaceus*, *lilacinus* = lilac, *-gilvus* = yellow

Synonym(s): *Fomitopsis lilacinogilva*, *Microporus lilacinogilvus*, *Polyporus lilacinogilvus*, *Trametes lilacinogilva*

ECOLOGY: Saprophytic.

DISTRIBUTION: Western Cape, Gauteng and KwaZulu-Natal, possibly more widespread. Occurs in Costa Rica, Brazil, Peru, Argentina, India, Indonesia, Papua New Guinea (including New Britain Island), Australia and New Zealand.

HABITAT: Grows on dead wood of broadleaved trees, notably *Eucalyptus* and *Quercus* species; fruit bodies grouped or compound, in tiers.

DESCRIPTION: The pink to mauve coloration, especially along the margin, makes this a most recognisable fungus. **Cap:** 3–10cm in diameter, 2–4cm radius, 0.4–0.8cm thick; leathery to corky; sessile, bracket-shaped, flat; margin acute, even, soft, matted hairs, often in pointed bundles; upper surface uneven, grooved; rose to mauve in young parts, turning grey-fawn, brown or dark grey in older parts. **Lower surface:** pore mouths circular, partitions thick; bright rose to lilac-mauve; tubes 0.05–0.25mm deep. **Flesh:** firm, corky, fibrous; dark rose-pink to lilac-mauve. **Smell:** faint mushroomy odour. **Spore print:** white.

EDIBILITY: Inedible; too tough to be considered edible.

The pore surface is bright rose to mauve.

Fruit bodies fuse together, creating the impression of a single, large fungus.

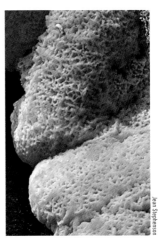

Thick partitions separate the circular pores.

The fungus is broadly attached to the substrate, usually a tree trunk.

A thick, woody fungus, *Ganoderma applanatum* is bracket-shaped to semicircular, with an uneven, concentrically grooved upper surface.

Ganoderma applanatum (Pers.) Pat. 1887

Common names: Artist's palette, artist's conk, artist's fungus, bear bread, giant shelf fungus
Afrikaans: Paletswam

Etymology: GREEK: *ganos* = beauty, lustre, *derma* = skin; LATIN: *applanatum* = flattened

Synonym(s): *Fomes applanatus, F. longiporus, Friesia applanata, Polyporus applanatus*

ECOLOGY: Parasitic and saprophytic.

DISTRIBUTION: Widespread in South Africa. Occurs worldwide; large global distribution.

HABITAT: Grows on the trunks of broadleaved trees, rarely on coniferous trees; fruit bodies single, scattered or compound.

DESCRIPTION: The mushroom may be recognised by the large, dull-brown, horny upper surface of the bracket. **Cap:** 10–75cm in diameter, 10–40cm radius, 5–10cm thick; hard, thick, woody; sessile, widely attached; bracket-shaped to semicircular; margin acute; upper surface flat, uneven, sometimes knobbly or corrugated, covered with a hard crust, concentrically grooved, not shiny, but opaque; dull brown, typically with pockets of white tissue. **Lower surface:** pore mouths small, circular, 40–60 per cm; white, bruises brown; tubes 0.5–4cm deep. **Flesh:** felt-like; cinnamon-brown. **Smell:** mushroomy odour. **Spore print:** brown.

Tiers of fruit bodies grow parasitically on a living tree.

SIMILAR SPECIES: *Ganoderma lucidum* and other brown-coloured brackets, which may be distinguished only by means of microscopic identification.

EDIBILITY: Inedible; too tough and with a bitter taste. Based on her research, primatologist and conservationist Dian Fossey noted that the fruit bodies are a favourite food of mountain gorillas.

MEDICINAL: This species has antibacterial, anti-inflammatory and antitumour properties, and is used in the treatment of lung and respiratory infections.

NOTES: This bracket releases millions of spores at a time, causing the surrounding area to be covered with a dense brown dust. This tough bracket lives for many years and develops noticeable annual growth ridges on the upper surface. Cutting through the bracket will reveal layers of tubes, the number of layers providing a clue as to the age of the fruit body.

The released spores form a dense brown dust around the fungus.

The cap can grow up to 75cm in width.

The lower surface, consisting of densely arranged tubes, is white to cream.

The cap is occasionally fused with others to form a very large bracket, measuring up to 30cm or more in width.

Jean Stephenson

Ganoderma lucidum (Curtis) P. Karst. 1881

Common names: Reishi, orange-brown lacquered bracket, varnished polypore
Afrikaans: Oranjebruinvernisswam, gesteelde lakswam

Etymology: GREEK: *ganos* = beauty, lustre, *-derma* = skin;
LATIN: *lucidum* = shining, lucid

Synonym(s): *Fomes lucidus, Phaeoporus lucidus, Placodes lucidus, Polyporus lucidus*

Inedible

ECOLOGY: Parasitic and saprophytic.

DISTRIBUTION: Widespread in South Africa. Occurs worldwide.

HABITAT: Grows on or near the trunks of broadleaved trees; stipitate forms attached to buried roots appear to emerge from the soil; fruit bodies single or grouped, often in overlapping tiers.

DESCRIPTION: The shiny upper surface is the most distinctive characteristic of this bracket fungus, although a number of similar species share this feature. **Cap:** 10–30cm in diameter, 10–20cm radius, up to 3cm thick; corky turning woody; sessile or stipitate, often laterally fused with others or in overlapping tiers; cylindrical, large, bracket- or kidney-shaped; margin thin; upper surface flat, velvety when young, sometimes concentrically grooved, covered with a thin, shiny, varnished crust, usually extending downward and covering the stipe; pale cream to red to chestnut, resembling varnished wood. **Stipe:** absent or lateral to excentric, up to 0.8cm long; cylindrical; varnished appearance. **Lower surface:** pore mouths small, circular to angular, 30–40 per cm; white, turning brown when bruised or aged; tubes 0.3–1.5cm deep. **Flesh:** soft, fibrous to corky; white to brown. **Smell:** no distinctive odour. **Spore print:** rust-brown.

SIMILAR SPECIES: *Amauroderma sprucei, Ganoderma applanatum.* The caps of *G. tsugae* and *G. curtisii* (neither of which is described here) also resemble varnished wood.

EDIBILITY: Inedible.

MEDICINAL: Known as the 'King of Herbs' in ancient China, *Ganoderma lucidum* has antibacterial, antiviral, antioxidant, anti-candida, anti-inflammatory and antitumour properties. This fungus may also be used to treat health problems relating to blood pressure, blood sugar, cardiovascular disease, lung and respiratory infections and the kidneys, and is known to help to lower cholesterol levels, boost the immune system and reduce the impact of stress.

NOTES: The *Ganoderma lucidum* species complex is a large group of closely related species, many of which are relatively newly discovered and whose identification and classification have not yet been verified. Species discovered in South Africa include *G. austroafricanum, G. cupreum, G. destructans, G. enigmaticum* and *G. resinaceum.*

The upper surface is relatively flat, concentrically grooved, and covered with a shiny crust.

The fruit body has a whitish margin.

The upper surface is concentrically zoned with bands that are initially buff to cinnamon-brown; these later darken to red-brown.

In older specimens, the concentric zones and wrinkled surface are conspicuous.

Daedaleopsis confragosa (Bolton) J. Schröt. 1888

Common names: Blushing bracket, thin maze gill, red-pored bracket
Afrikaans: Rooiporierakswam

Etymology: GREEK: *daedalos* = after Daedalus (in Greek mythology, the builder of the Labyrinth in Crete), LATIN: *-opsis* = resembling; LATIN: *confragosa* = rough, uneven

Synonym(s): *Icshnoderma confragosum, Lenzites confragosa, Trametes rubescens*

ECOLOGY: Saprophytic.

DISTRIBUTION: Western Cape, possibly more widespread. Occurs in the UK, Europe, Canada, USA, Mexico, Guatemala, Nicaragua, Brazil, Russia, Japan, Australia, Cameroon and Equatorial Guinea.

HABITAT: Grows on the trunks of dead or dying deciduous trees; fruit bodies single or clustered, sometimes in tiers.

DESCRIPTION: This semicircular bracket can be recognised by the large size of the fruit body and the thick, maze-like pore surface consisting of elongated pores radiating from the attachment point. **Cap:** 5–20cm in diameter, 4–10cm radius, 1.5–5cm thick; sessile, sometimes with a thickened basal hump at the point of attachment; shell-shaped, flattened; margin acute; upper surface velvety, concentrically grooved, often irregularly radially wrinkled; zoned in lighter and darker shades of red-brown, more often yellowish, reddish or brownish, margin often white; older brackets are woody with concentric tan and brown ridges, hairy tufts and thinner margins. **Lower surface:** pore mouths delicate, radially elongate, slot-like, variable, maze-like in pattern; white to faintly grey, bruises pink to red, in older fruit bodies pores become uniformly reddish brown; tubes up to 0.3cm deep. **Flesh:** rubbery to cork-like; zoned, whitish then reddish or pale brown; when fruit body is in active growth, it stains violet when in contact with ammonia. **Smell:** pleasantly fruity odour. **Spore print:** white.

SIMILAR SPECIES: *Daedaleopsis tricolor* (not described here) is considered by some as the same species as *D. confragosa*.

EDIBILITY: Inedible; too tough for consumption.

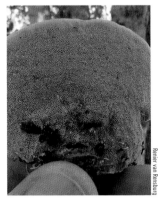

The pore surface bruises pink to red.

In older brackets, the upper surface becomes woody and the margin thinner.

The fruit bodies sometimes grow in tiers on dead wood.

The pore surface of older specimens is reddish brown.

Hexagonia tenuis grows singly or in groups, usually on dead wood of broadleaved trees.

The large, angular pore openings form a honeycomb-like pattern on the lower surface.

Hexagonia tenuis (Hook.) Fr. 1838

Common name: Thin-cap honeycomb bracket
Afrikaans: Dunhoedheuningkoekswam

Etymology: GREEK: *hexagonoides* = appearing hexagonal;
LATIN: *tenuis* = thin, fine, slender, narrow

Synonym(s): *Daedaleopsis tenuis*, *Hexagonia caliginosa*, *Pseudofavolus tenuis*, *Trametes tenuis*

ECOLOGY: Saprophytic.

DISTRIBUTION: Western Cape, Eastern Cape, Gauteng and KwaZulu-Natal, possibly more widespread. Occurs in the USA, Mexico, Costa Rica, Cuba, Venezuela, Brazil, South Korea, Myanmar, Thailand, Malaysia, Papua New Guinea, Australia, Togo, Benin, Nigeria, Zambia, Zimbabwe and Mauritius.

HABITAT: Grows on dead wood of broadleaved trees, often in open and sunny localities; fruit bodies single or grouped; can revive and grow after dry conditions, but not between seasons.

DESCRIPTION: The honeycomb pattern formed by the large pores on the lower surface is a key identifying feature of this species.
Cap: 3–7cm in diameter, 2–4.5cm radius, 0.05–0.20cm thick; thin, leathery, flexible, stiff when dry; sessile, semicircular to shell- to fan-shaped, flat or slightly depressed; margin thin, acute, entire to lobed or wavy; upper surface hairless, shiny, smooth or grooved; concentrically zoned in bands of colour from brown to cinnamon to hazel to chestnut. **Lower surface:** pore mouths very large, angular, thin partitions; brown; tubes 0.05–0.10cm deep **Flesh:** tough, fibrous; rust-brown. **Smell:** no distinctive odour. **Spore print:** white.

EDIBILITY: Inedible; too tough for consumption.

The upper surface is concentrically zoned in several shades of brown.

The fruit body measures up to 7cm across.

The pore surface of fruit bodies that have grown together.

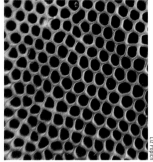

Thin partitions divide the pores.

Liz Popich

The distinct gill-like appearance of the pore surface distinguishes *Lenzites betulina* from other brackets.

Liz Popich

A tough, leathery and furry bracket, *Lenzites betulina* has a furrowed and grooved appearance.

Lenzites betulina (L.) Fr. 1838

Common names: Gilled polypore, gill polypore, birch maze gill, multicolour gill polypore, birch lenzite
Afrikaans: Lamelporieswam

Etymology: LATIN: *lenzites* = after German mycologist Harald Othmar Lenz (1798–1870); *betulinus* = pertaining to birch (the preferred host tree of this species)

Synonym(s): *Lenzites betulinus*, *L. hispida*, *L. isabellina*, *L. ochracea*, *L. pertenuis*, *Trametes betulina*

Inedible

ECOLOGY: Saprophytic.

DISTRIBUTION: Western Cape, Eastern Cape and Gauteng, possibly more widespread. Occurs in the UK, Europe, USA, Mexico, Brazil, Russia, Nepal, Mongolia, Japan, Australia, New Zealand and Tenerife.

HABITAT: Grows on branches and stumps of dead or dying deciduous trees, also on cut timber and telegraph poles; it has been reported on *Podocarpus* (yellowwood) species in Knysna, and is occasionally seen on dead branches of living trees; fruit bodies single, grouped or compound, often in tiers.

DESCRIPTION: This semicircular bracket can be identified by a leathery upper surface that is covered with fine hairs and zoned in shades of brown. The gill-like undersurface distinguishes it from most other brackets. **Cap:** 1.5–7cm in diameter, up to 6cm radius, 0.3–1.5cm thick; tough, leathery; sessile, occasionally grow together laterally, often in overlapping tiers; semicircular, bracket- to fan-shaped; margin thin, acute, entire, sometimes wavy; velvety; upper surface flat, thickish, furry, slightly furrowed and grooved, concentric zones; when young, whitish grey becoming pale green with yellowish and golden-brown bands, dark rust when old. **Lower surface:** thick, firm, forking pore depressions, gill-like partitions, elongate, branching, edges entire; white to cream, slightly darker on drying; tubes up to 0.5cm deep. **Flesh:** tough, fibrous; white. **Smell:** no distinctive odour. **Spore print:** white.

EDIBILITY: Inedible. Mature specimens are too tough to consume but some reports indicate that the young mushrooms are edible, and have a nutty flavour.

MEDICINAL: *Lenzites betulina* has antioxidant, antimicrobial, antitumour and immunosuppressive properties.

NOTES: This species is very variable, both in thickness and in zoning of the cap, which is sometimes not unlike that of *Trametes versicolor*. The gill-like lower surface is characteristic.

When young, the upper surface is concentrically zoned in shades of white, grey, yellow and green.

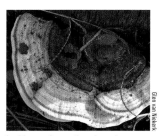

In older specimens, the colours deepen to shades of cream, greyish brown and dark rust.

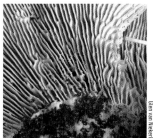

The pores radiate from the attachment point.

The bright reddish-orange fruit body is velvety at first, becoming smooth and shiny with age.

The fruit body is narrowly attached to the substrate, appearing to have a stipe.

Pycnoporus sanguineus (L.) Murrill 1904

Common names: Tropical cinnabar bracket, orange polypore, blood-red bracket
Afrikaans: Dunhoedrooirakswam

Etymology: ANCIENT GREEK: *pyknos-* = thick, dense, *-porus* = pores; LATIN: *sanguinea* = blood red

Synonym(s): *Coriolus sanguineus, Fabisporus sanguineus, Polyporus sanguineus, Trametes sanguinea*

ECOLOGY: Parasitic and saprophytic.

DISTRIBUTION: Widespread in South Africa. Occurs in the USA, Mexico, Costa Rica, Colombia, Brazil, Argentina, Peru, Malaysia, Singapore, Japan, Indonesia, Papua New Guinea, Australia, Lord Howe Island, Fiji, New Zealand, Nigeria, Democratic Republic of the Congo, Tanzania, Kenya, Zambia and Réunion Island.

HABITAT: Occurs on dead wood of broadleaved and coniferous trees, often in exposed positions; fruit bodies single, grouped or clustered, often in tiers.

DESCRIPTION: The bright, reddish-orange coloration of the fruit bodies makes this species easy to identify. **Cap:** 2–8cm in diameter, 1–5cm radius, 0.1–0.5cm thick; tough, corky to leathery to rigid; can appear to have a short stipe, narrowly attached, can be fused laterally or grow in overlapping tiers; fan- to bracket- to kidney-shaped; margin thin, acute, even, velvety with fine hairs; upper surface velvety turning smooth, shiny; vivid orange to bright orange-red or blood red, with lighter concentric zones, fading with age to grey or dirty white. **Lower surface:** pore mouths minute, circular to angular, 50–60 per cm; concolorous with the upper surface but darker, velvety; tubes 0.05–0.20cm deep. **Flesh:** thin, tough, velvety; concolorous with cap. **Smell:** no distinctive odour. **Spore print:** white.

SIMILAR SPECIES: *Pycnoporus cinnabarina* (not described here), more common in temperate areas of the northern hemisphere, is a closely related brilliant red to orange-red species, but is much thicker and fades less readily. The fruit bodies of *P. coccineus* (not described here) are thicker, yellow-orange, shelf-like and broadly attached.

EDIBILITY: Inedible; too leathery to consider edible.

Pycnoporus sanguineus occurs on dead wood of broadleaved and pine trees.

The pore mouths are rounded to elongated.

The colourful dried brackets are used in flower arranging.

Trametes cingulata can be distinguished by the black upper surface and distinctive creamy white margin.

This bracket fungus occurs singly or grouped on the dead wood of broadleaved trees.

Trametes cingulata Berk. 1854

Common name: Black cork polypore
Afrikaans: Witrandkurkporieswam

Etymology: LATIN: *trametes* = thin, skinny; *cingul* = to gird, to surround, *-ata* = similar to

Synonym(s): *Coriolus cingulatus, Polyporus decorsei, P. granulatus, Trametes jalapensis*

ECOLOGY: Saprophytic.

DISTRIBUTION: Eastern Cape, Gauteng and KwaZulu-Natal, possibly more widespread. Occurs in Europe, Canada, USA, Costa Rica, Brazil, Japan, China, the Philippines, Australia, Sierra Leone, Nigeria, Cameroon, Equatorial Guinea, Uganda, Sudan, Kenya, Zambia, Malawi and Madagascar.

HABITAT: Grows on dead wood of broadleaved trees, often in dry, exposed positions; fruit bodies single or grouped, occasionally in overlapping tiers; annual, but occasionally survives to the following season.

The fungus is attached to the substrate by means of a reduced base.

DESCRIPTION: The black surface, which contrasts strongly with the creamy white margin and pore surface, is characteristic of this common wood-rotting fungus. **Cap:** 3–9cm in diameter, 1.6–5cm radius, 0.3–1cm thick; leathery to woody; sessile, broadly attached or with a reduced base, sometimes fused laterally with other caps, occasionally in overlapping tiers; fan- to kidney-shaped or shelf-like, convex to flat; margin even, acute, thin or thick, rounded, velvety in young actively growing specimens; upper surface concentrically grooved, smooth or rough; black, becoming grey with age, margin creamy white, darkening to yellowish brown on drying. **Lower surface:** pore mouths circular, 30–40 per cm; white turning yellow or brown with age, glistening; tubes up to 0.3cm deep. **Flesh:** fibrous, corky; white to cream. **Smell:** pleasant mushroomy odour. **Spore print:** white.

SIMILAR SPECIES: *Laxitextum bicolor.*

EDIBILITY: Inedible; too tough and leathery.

Trametes cingulata is irregularly fan- to kidney-shaped.

> **NOTES:** *Trametes cingulata* causes an extensive white rot of the sapwood of trees, especially wattle and eucalyptus trees.

Initially white, the spore surface turns yellow or brown with age.

The green colour on the surface of these specimens is due to the presence of algae.

The pores radiate from the point of attachment to the margin, the partitions branching and fusing to create a gill-like pore surface.

Trametes elegans (Spreng.) Fr. 1838

Common name: Elegant bracket
Afrikaans: Bruidsrakswam

Etymology: LATIN: *trametes* = thin, skinny; *elegans* = elegant

Synonym(s): *Artolenzites elegans, Daedalea elegans, Daedaleopsis elegans, Whitfordia elegans*

Inedible

ECOLOGY: Saprophytic.

DISTRIBUTION: Eastern Cape, Gauteng and KwaZulu-Natal, possibly more widespread. Occurs in the USA, Mexico, Costa Rica, Brazil, Peru, India, Bangladesh, Thailand, Malaysia, Japan, Papua New Guinea, Pitcairn Islands, Australia, Equatorial Guinea, Zambia, Zimbabwe

HABITAT: Grows on dead logs of broadleaved trees; fruit bodies single or grouped; annual, but can survive to the following season.

DESCRIPTION: This large, strikingly beautiful bracket can be distinguished by its pure white coloration, smooth upper surface and radiating elongated pores. **Cap:** 5–25cm in diameter, 2–15cm radius, up to 3cm thick; leathery to woody; sessile, narrowly attached laterally or with a short, indistinct stipe; fan- to kidney-shaped to circular, depressed; margin thin, acute, entire or wavy; upper surface hairless, smooth, sometimes concentrically or radially grooved; white turning cream, later dirty brown. **Lower surface:** pore mouths elongated, radiating, somewhat maze-like, the partitions branching and anastomosing, 10–20 per cm; white turning cream or ochraceous; tubes 0.1–0.4cm deep. **Flesh:** dense, tough, fibrous; white to cream. **Smell:** strong, sweetly fragrant, spicy odour. **Spore print:** white.

SIMILAR SPECIES: *Lenzites betulina* also has white to cream fruit bodies with gill-like pores.

EDIBILITY: Inedible; too tough to eat.

> **NOTES:** *Trametes elegans* causes a severe white rot; infected wood has a sweet, spicy odour.

The brackets often overlap on decaying logs of broadleaved trees.

The pore surface is whitish.

The colour of the upper surface turns cream to dirty brown with age.

The upper surface is concentrically grooved.

Although initially as white as the margin, the upper surface can rapidly become green as a result of being colonised by algae.

The fruit body is roughly semicircular and the upper surface is distinctly lumpy and downy.

Trametes gibbosa (Pers.) Fr. 1838

Common names: Lumpy bracket, bulbous polypore, beech bracket, gibbous polypore
Afrikaans: Klonterige rakswam

Etymology: LATIN: *trametes* = thin, skinny; *gibbosus* = with humps, lumpy, humpback

Synonym(s): *Lenzites gibbosa*, *Polyporus gibbosus*, *Pseudotrametes gibbosa*

ECOLOGY: Saprophytic.

DISTRIBUTION: First reported in South Africa in the Western Cape and Gauteng. Occurs in the UK, Europe, Canada, USA, Mexico, Japan, Australia, Togo and Benin.

HABITAT: Grows on dead branches, trunks and stumps of deciduous trees; fruit bodies single or grouped in tiers.

DESCRIPTION: This species is easy to recognise by the white cottony zones on the upper and lower surfaces and the radially elongated pores. **Cap:** 10–30cm in diameter, 5–20cm radius, 1–4cm thick; corky turning woody; sessile, with a characteristic hump where fruit bodies attach to the substrate; semicircular or fan-shaped; margin obtuse; upper surface lumpy, concentrically grooved; young specimens chalk-white, becoming greyish, centre green due to the presence of microscopic algae, margin often brownish. **Lower surface:** pore mouths radially elongated, sometimes rounded, sometimes fused together, slot-like, almost maze-like; whitish to cream; tubes up to 0.4cm deep. **Flesh:** compact, thick, very firm, corky or rubbery; whitish. **Smell:** no distinctive odour. **Spore print:** white.

SIMILAR SPECIES: When viewed from above, it could be mistaken for *Daedalea quercina*, which has a cap surface that is slightly velvety and paler than that of *Trametes gibbosa*.

EDIBILITY: Inedible; too tough to eat.

> **NOTES:** Groups of these fungi can grow to impressive sizes, reaching more than 1m in diameter.

Inedible

The fruit bodies appear in tiered groups.

The lower surface is whitish to cream.

A large bracket, *Trametes gibbosa* may reach up to 30cm across.

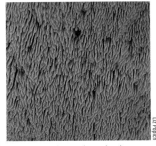

The pores are elongated, creating the impression of a maze on the lower surface. The tubes are up to 0.4cm deep.

Trametes versicolor is admired for the variety of its zoned, velvety fans, the colours ranging from cream, orange and brown to blue, black, grey and green. The margin is white to cream.

Trametes versicolor (L.) Lloyd 1920

Common names: Turkey tail, many-zoned polypore, multicoloured bracket, varicoloured bracket, rainbow bracket
Afrikaans: Elwebankie, reënboograkswam

Etymology: LATIN: *trametes* = thin, skinny; *versicolor* = multicoloured, various colours

Synonym(s): *Bjerkandera versicolor*, *Coriolus versicolor*, *Polyporus versicolor*, *Polystictus castanicola*

ECOLOGY: Saprophytic.

DISTRIBUTION: Widespread in South Africa. Occurs worldwide; large global distribution.

HABITAT: Grows on dead or decaying trunks, stumps or branches of broadleaved trees; fruit bodies grouped, compound, sometimes in rosette formation.

DESCRIPTION: This species can be recognised by the silky cap, lobed margin edge and multicoloured concentric zones on the upper surface. **Cap:** 2–7cm in diameter, 2–5cm radius, 0.1–0.2cm thick; tough, fibrous, thin; sessile or narrowly attached with a reduced base, often growing together laterally or arranged in overlapping tiers or forming rosettes; semicircular, fan- to kidney- to bracket-shaped; margin wavy; upper surface velvety; concentric zones of cream, orange and brown, sometimes also blue, black, grey and green, margin usually white to cream. **Lower surface:** pore mouths fine but visible, 30–60 per cm; white to cream; tubes 0.05–0.10cm deep. **Flesh:** tough, cottony, leathery; white to pale cream. **Smell:** faint, pleasant, mushroomy to slightly fishy odour. **Spore print:** white to straw-yellow.

EDIBILITY: Inedible; too tough to eat.

MEDICINAL: *Trametes versicolor* has antibacterial, antioxidant and antiviral properties, and is known to reduce cholesterol levels. It is also well known for its use in treating breast cancer. A tea made of dried *T. versicolor* is believed to have a beneficial impact on the immune system.

NOTES: The porous lower surface of this mushroom is very rich in a compound called ergosterol. When exposed to ultraviolet light, it is converted to vitamin D_2.

The fruit bodies appear in dense rows and tiers on dead or decaying wood.

The colours of *Trametes versicolor* are diverse.

This species is widespread in South Africa.

The fans are semicircular and narrowly attached to the substrate.

The fruit bodies of *Chondrostereum purpureum* grow flat on the bark substrate.

When fertile, the fruit bodies of *Chondrostereum purpureum* are purple.

Chondrostereum purpureum (Pers.) Pouzar 1959

Common names: Silverleaf fungus, violet crust fungus
Afrikaans: Loodglansswam

Etymology: ANCIENT GREEK: *khondro-* = grain, cartilage, *stereós* = hard, tough, solid; LATIN: *purpureus* = purple, dark red

Synonym(s): *Stereum ardoisiacum, S. argentinum, S. nipponicum, S. purpureum, Thelephora purpurea*

ECOLOGY: Parasitic and saprophytic.

DISTRIBUTION: Western Cape, Gauteng and KwaZulu-Natal. Occurs in the UK, Europe, Canada, USA, Guatemala, Costa Rica, Argentina, Russia, Mongolia, Japan, Australia and New Zealand.

HABITAT: Grows on bark of living deciduous trees, rarely on conifers; fruit bodies scattered, in tiered rows of linked brackets.

DESCRIPTION: This species is easily identified by its lilac to purple colour when young, velvety texture and wavy margin. **Fruit body:** 0.5–3cm wide, 2–6cm radius, 0.2–0.5cm thick; leathery, horn-like when dry; resupinate, sheet-like, could have overlapping caps, fused with others and tiered; margin undulate; upper surface hairy, velvety to hairless, wrinkled when fertile; purple to brown when fertile, then ochre to buff, margin white. **Lower surface:** purple to brown; smooth, waxy. **Flesh:** gelatinous; white, becoming discoloured and relatively rigid. **Smell:** no distinctive odour. **Spore print:** white.

SIMILAR SPECIES: *Terana caerulea, Hymenochaete rubiginosa* and *Amylostereum areolatum*, which appears only on conifer wood (none of these species is described here).

EDIBILITY: Inedible; too thin and leathery to be of culinary value.

> **NOTES:** *Chondrostereum purpureum* is a pathogen of fruit trees, including apple, plum, apricot and cherry trees, as well as maple, poplar, hornbeam, plane, oak and several other tree species. It causes the leaves to turn silver, hence the common name 'silverleaf fungus'. In South Africa it has also been observed on wattle trees. Although affected trees may not show any symptoms at first, the fungus causes spots in the wood and a white rot, and can kill off branches and trees.

The upper surface of the fruit body is hairy and velvety when young.

With age, the fruit bodies become wrinkled and leathery.

This resupinate crust grows on the bark of living deciduous trees.

Serpula himantioides (Fr.) P. Karst. 1884

Common names: None
Afrikaans: None

Etymology: LATIN: *serpis* = serpent, *-ula* = resembling;
GREEK: *himant* = leather strap, thong, *-oides* = similar to, likeness

Synonym(s): *Coniophora dimitiella, Gyrophana himantioides, Merulius himantioides, Sesia himantioides*

ECOLOGY: Saprophytic.

DISTRIBUTION: Western Cape, Gauteng and Mpumalanga. Occurs on all continents except Antarctica.

HABITAT: Grows on the underside of dead logs, mainly those of conifers; fruit bodies single or scattered.

DESCRIPTION: The presence of irregular ridges, which form a pore-like pattern over the hymenial surface, is characteristic of the genus, while the colour of the ridges distinguishes the species. **Fruit body:** resupinate, spreading over substrate surface; older parts have irregular ridges that form a net-like to pore-like pattern over the hymenial surface; margin thin; lilac turning brown to dark brown, margin white. **Flesh:** soft, thin; pale, brown-yellow. **Smell:** no distinctive odour. **Spore print:** yellow-brown.

SIMILAR SPECIES: This fungus, mainly found in the wild, is the lesser-known relative of the dry-rot fungus *Serpula lacrymans*, which is notorious for destroying wood in poorly ventilated buildings. *S. lacrymans* is hardly ever found in the wild, preferring timber in buildings and on construction sites.

EDIBILITY: Inedible.

NOTES: This species causes a brown rot.

The irregular ridges on the hymenial (spore-bearing) surface form a net-like or pore-like pattern. Initially lilac, the fruit body turns brown to dark brown with age.

The fruit body can be identified by the brown pore-like hymenial surface and thin, white margin.

Cymatoderma elegans Jungh. 1840

Common names: Ridged bracket, leathery goblet, wine glass fungus
Afrikaans: Leerbeker

Etymology: GREEK: *cymatos* = wave, *derma* = skin; LATIN: *elegans* = refined, elegant

Synonym(s): *Cladoderris australica, C. roccati, C. scrupulosa, Stereum lamellatum*

ECOLOGY: Saprophytic.

DISTRIBUTION: Western Cape, Gauteng and KwaZulu-Natal. Occurs in the USA, Mexico, Costa Rica, French Guiana, Brazil, Thailand, Malaysia, Singapore, Taiwan, Indonesia, Papua New Guinea, Australia, Lord Howe Island, Norfolk Island and Nigeria.

HABITAT: Grows on dead stumps and trunks or fallen branches of broadleaved trees; fruit bodies mostly grouped.

DESCRIPTION: The tough fruit body is quite striking and is readily recognised by its distinctive shape and warty, ribbed lower surface. **Cap:** Up to 15cm across the widest part; thin, leathery to woody; short, lateral to excentric stipe, bracket-shaped, fan-shaped or circular, somewhat depressed or almost funnel-shaped, adjacent caps frequently grow together; margin thin, acute, wavy, unevenly bayed, at times appearing almost frayed from ridges projecting beyond the intervening tissue; upper surface usually completely covered with a dense, felt-like layer that overlies the sharp, knife-edged ridges, which radiate from the central area over the stipe; pale fawn to tawny to almost snuff-brown in the oldest parts, margin pale. **Lower surface:** white to pale beige or pinkish brown with age; prominent branching folds radiating from the stipe, scantily to densely covered by short, wart-like spines. **Stipe:** up to 5cm long, 0.5–1.5cm thick; short or rudimentary in fan-shaped forms, cylindrical in funnel-shaped forms; covered with thick, felt-like hairs, matt; fawn to brown. **Ring:** absent. **Flesh:** thin, tough-leathery, fibrous; pale wood-colour. **Smell:** unknown. **Spore print:** white to pale fawn.

EDIBILITY: Inedible.

MEDICINAL: Has anticancer properties.

The warty, ribbed lower surface is distinctive.

The upper surface is covered with a felt-like layer.

The spore-bearing surface is smooth.

The upper surface of *Laxitextum bicolor* is marked by concentric zones of brown to lighter brown colours.

Liz Popich

Laxitextum bicolor (Pers.) Lentz 1956

Common name: Light-rimmed crust cap
Afrikaans: Ligbruin gerande kruiphoed

Etymology: LATIN: *laxus* = loose, *textus* = tissue, woven, braided; *bicolor* = two colours

Synonym(s): *Lloydella bicolor*, *Stereum bicolor*, *S. laxum*, *Thelephora bicolor*

ECOLOGY: Parasitic and saprophytic.

DISTRIBUTION: Eastern Cape, Gauteng and KwaZulu-Natal. Occurs in Europe, Canada, USA, Brazil and Australia.

HABITAT: Grows on dead wood of broadleaved trees, preferring wattle, eucalyptus and oak, rarely on conifers; fruit bodies clustered.

DESCRIPTION: Although this species is variable in appearance, the unique and contrasting colour combination of the hymenium and the reflexed part of the fruit body make it readily recognisable. **Cap:** around 5cm wide, up to 15cm radius, 0.2–0.3cm thick; soft, spongy; mostly resupinate-reflexed, sometimes laterally attached, overlapping and laterally fused together; margin thin, rounded, even to wavy; surface smooth, concentrically furrowed or zoned; snuff-brown, margin white. **Lower surface:** white to creamy white; smooth, velvety, smooth, cracking on drying. **Flesh:** thin, spongy; brownish. **Smell:** faint mushroomy odour when fresh. **Spore print:** white.

SIMILAR SPECIES: *Stereum ostrea*, *Trametes cingulata*.

EDIBILITY: Inedible; too tough to be considered edible.

NOTES: The variation in size and shape of the fruit bodies is mostly determined by the position in which they form on the substrate.

The margin is rounded to wavy.

The upper surface has a spongy texture.

Laxitextum bicolor grows on dead wood of broadleaved trees.

The lower surface is smooth and velvety.

Fruit bodies appear in densely clustered tiers and overlapping shelves on dead wood.

Stereum hirsutum (Willd.) Pers. 1800

Common names: Hairy crust cap, hairy curtain crust, hairy stereum, hairy bracket, hairy leather-bracket, hairy parchment, white-rot fungus, false turkey tail
Afrikaans: Harige kruiphoed

Etymology: ANCIENT GREEK: *stereós* = hard, tough, solid;
LATIN: *hirsutus* = shaggy, bristly, hirsute

Synonym(s): *Stereum bombycinum*, *S. leoninum*, *S. necator*, *S. ochraceum*, *S. variicolor*

Inedible

ECOLOGY: Parasitic and saprophytic.

DISTRIBUTION: Widespread in South Africa. Occurs worldwide.

HABITAT: Grows on dead stumps and branches of broadleaved trees, occasionally on conifers; fruit bodies densely clustered, in tiers and overlapping shelves.

DESCRIPTION: Commonly appearing in densely tiered clusters, this crust fungus can be identified by its small, wavy margin and smooth hymenial surface. The colour is variable, although the yellow to tan forms are most common. **Cap:** 1–3.5cm wide, 0.7–5cm radius, 0.05–0.20cm thick; clusters may be up to a few metres long; leathery; sessile, bracket-shaped or flat but curling at the edges to almost flat; resupinate when young, often grow together laterally in overlapping shelves; margin thin, wavy to lobed; pliant when young, tough in mature specimens; upper surface hairy, grooved and concentrically zoned; orange-brown to yellow-brown, older tissue grey to greyish brown. **Lower surface:** orange-buff to pale buff; smooth; if zoned, the bands are less conspicuous than those on the upper surface. **Flesh:** leathery, tough, insubstantial; pale yellow-brown. **Smell:** no distinctive odour. **Spore print:** white.

SIMILAR SPECIES: *Trametes hirsuta* has a pored hymenial surface (not described here).

EDIBILITY: Inedible; too tough and thin to be of culinary use.

NOTES: *Stereum hirsutum* is parasitised by certain jelly fungi.

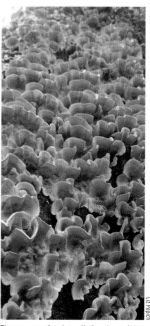

The caps are often laterally fused together.

Orange-brown to yellow-brown bands are visible on the upper surface.

The upper surface is covered with fine hairs.

Stereum ostrea occurs on dead wood of broadleaved trees, often in indigenous forests.

Stereum ostrea (Blume & T. Nees) Fr. 1838

Common names: False turkey tail, golden curtain crust
Afrikaans: Vals elwebankie

Etymology: ANCIENT GREEK: *stereós* = hard, tough, solid;
LATIN: *ostrea* = oyster

Synonym(s): *Stereum australe, S. concolor, S. liechkardtianum,
S. pictum, S. sprucei, S. transvaalium, S. zebra*

ECOLOGY: Saprophytic.

DISTRIBUTION: Widespread in South Africa. Occurs in Europe,
Canada, USA, Mexico, Costa Rica, Panama, Dominican Republic,
Brazil, Singapore, Japan, South Korea, Papua New Guinea, New
Caledonia, Australia, New Zealand, Seychelles and Madagascar.

HABITAT: Grows on dead wood of broadleaved trees, usually in
humid places such as moist forests or along streams and rivers;
fruit bodies grouped.

DESCRIPTION: At first sight, this fungus may be confused with the
multicoloured *Trametes versicolor*. However, unlike *T. versicolor*, this
mushroom does not have pore openings on the hymenial surface.
Cap: 2–6cm wide, 4–10cm radius, 0.1–0.3cm thick; leathery; wedge-
to fan- to funnel-shaped; attached by a reduced base, usually not
resupinate, can fuse with others; margin thin, wavy, entire to lobed or
splitting; upper surface thin, finely hairy, velvety layer of matted hair
rubs off in old specimens, concentrically furrowed and zoned, some
zones hairless; grey to green-grey with light yellow-brown to red-
brown, hazel or chestnut zones, but can be quite variable.
Lower surface: cream to pale buff; smooth. **Flesh:** thin, tough,
pliable; yellow. **Smell:** no distinctive odour. **Spore print:** white.

The upper surface is furrowed.

SIMILAR SPECIES: *Stereum hirsutum* and *Laxitextum bicolor*; closely
resembles the bracket fungus *Trametes versicolor*.

EDIBILITY: Inedible; too tough and thin to be considered edible.

NOTES: All *Stereum* species lack a pore surface. Instead, they have
a smooth undersurface, which classifies them as crust fungi rather
than polypore fungi.

The lower surface is cream to buff.

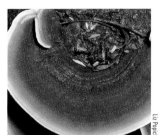

The fruit body has a leathery surface.

A funnel-shaped specimen.

Fruit bodies are narrowly attached.

The fruit bodies are faintly zoned, with colours ranging from rust-brown to dark brown.

The fruit bodies of older specimens are almost black.

Thelephora terrestris Ehrh. 1787

Common names: Earth fan, common earth fan, earthfan fungus, common fibre vase
Afrikaans: Fraiingswam

Etymology: ANCIENT GREEK: *thele-* = nipple, GREEK: *phora* = motion, movement; LATIN: *terrestris* = of the earth

Synonym(s): *Thelephora crustose, T. minor, T. rhipidium, T. tristis*

Inedible

ECOLOGY: Mycorrhizal and saprophytic.

DISTRIBUTION: Widespread in South Africa. Occurs in the UK, Europe, Canada, USA, Mexico, Venezuela, Brazil, Russia, China, Mongolia, Japan, South Korea, Australia, New Zealand and Tenerife.

HABITAT: Grows on the soil surface or just beneath it in coniferous forests, preferring soil that is acrid and dry; fruit bodies clustered.

DESCRIPTION: Similar in appearance to some lichens, the fringed, fan-shaped fruit body is well camouflaged by the earth-like colours. **Cap:** 1–5cm wide, up to 7cm radius, 0.15–0.30cm thick; sessile or stipitate; rosette-like, fan-shaped to flat; margin fringed; upper surface radially fibrous, faintly concentrically zoned; rusty brown to dark brown, almost black with age, margin white to pale brown. **Lower surface:** clay-brown to chocolate-brown, powdery appearance; irregularly warty, wrinkled to dented, or radially ridged, or with small projections, less fibrous than the upper surface. **Flesh:** thin, fibrous, leathery; brown. **Smell:** sweet, earthy odour. **Spore print:** purplish brown to dark brown.

EDIBILITY: Inedible. There are more than 50 *Thelephora* species worldwide; most are considered inedible.

NOTES: Although thought to benefit trees by forming a mycorrhizal association with them, this fungus has been known to kill conifer seedlings in nurseries.

Liz Popich
Younger specimen with an irregularly fringed margin.

Gary B Goldman
Fruit bodies are rosette-like.

Liz Popich
The upper surface is covered with fibres.

Gary B Goldman
Fruit bodies grow on dry, sandy soil.

Liz Popich
Spore-bearing lower surface.

Cyathus olla (Batsch) Pers. 1801

Common names: Grey-egg bird's nest fungus, grey bird's nest
Afrikaans: Gladde voëlnesswam

Etymology: GREEK: *kyathos* = cup; LATIN: *olla* = pot, jar

Synonym(s): *Crucibulum albosaccum, Cyathus ollaris, C. similis, C. umbrinus, Nidularia heribaudi*

Inedible

ECOLOGY: Saprophytic.

DISTRIBUTION: Widespread in South Africa. Occurs in the UK, Europe, Canada, USA, Mexico, Costa Rica, Puerto Rica, Colombia, Brazil, Peru, Argentina, Iran, Russia, Japan, Australia, New Zealand and Tenerife.

HABITAT: Grows on soil containing decaying plant material or on half-buried dead wood, usually in the open; fruit bodies grouped.

DESCRIPTION: This species is one of a group of similar species that resemble birds' nests. It has grey 'eggs' (peridioles containing the spores) that turn black with age. **Fruit body:** 0.5–1.5cm tall, 0.6–1cm in diameter; inversely conical or bell-shaped, tapering downward to the base; mouth incurved at first, turning straight or flaring, often wavy along the edge; outer surface covered with woolly, appressed hairs, light brown turning grey-brown; inner surface smooth, shining, lead-grey, grey-brown or silver-brown; contains 5–10 peridioles. **Peridioles:** 0.20–0.35cm in diameter; lens-shaped, attached to the fruit body by a thin, white, detachable thread; pale grey, covered with a thin, white membrane, turning dull olive-brown to black when mature.

EDIBILITY: Inedible; too small and hard.

Woolly hairs cover the outer surface.

> **NOTES:** The fruit bodies of bird's nest fungi are referred to as 'splash cups' in certain parts of the world. This is because when drops of rain hit the interior of the 'cup' at the appropriate angle and velocity, the peridioles are dislodged and dispersed.

Fruit bodies grouped on dead wood.

The cup-shaped fruit body may contain up to 10 'eggs', or peridioles.

The peridioles of mature specimens turn dull olive-brown to black.

Cyathus stercoreus (Schwein.) De Toni 1888

Common names: Dung-loving bird's nest, black-egg bird's nest, dung splash cup, dung nest fungus
Afrikaans: Donker voëlnesswam

Etymology: GREEK: *kyathos* = cup; LATIN: *stercorarius* = of dung

Synonym(s): *Cyathia stercorea, Cyathodes stercoreum, Cyathus boninensis, C. brazlaviensis, C. elegans*

Inedible

ECOLOGY: Saprophytic.

DISTRIBUTION: Gauteng (Pretoria), possibly more widespread. Occurs in the UK, Europe, USA, Mexico, Guatemala, Costa Rica, Puerto Rico, Brazil, Russia, Japan, Australia and New Zealand.

HABITAT: Grows on dung and organic debris; fruit bodies grouped.

DESCRIPTION: Mostly associated with herbivore dung, this fungus is easily identified by its shaggy outer surface, smooth, unlined inner surface and dark-grey to black eggs. **Fruit body:** 0.6–1.5cm tall, 0.4–0.8cm in diameter; funnel- or barrel-shaped; outer surface resembling shaggy, untidy hair, in older specimens the outer hairy layer may wear off, golden brown to blackish brown at maturity; inner surface smooth, grey to bluish black; contains 15–20 peridioles. **Peridioles:** 0.1–0.2cm in diameter; flattened or lentil-like, hard, smooth; attached to the fruit body by a short, white thread; dark grey to blackish.

SIMILAR SPECIES: *Cyathus olla, C. striatus.*

EDIBILITY: Inedible; too small.

MEDICINAL: In traditional Chinese medicine, a decoction of this fungus is used to help relieve the symptoms of gastralgia, a type of stomach ache.

The fruit body contains 15–20 peridioles.

Fruit bodies are funnel-shaped.

The fruit bodies are grouped in large numbers on herbivore dung.

Immature fruit bodies showing incurved mouths.

Cyathus striatus tapers downward to a stipe-like base at the point of attachment.

Liz Popich

Cyathus striatus (Huds.) Willd. 1787

Common names: Fluted bird's nest fungus, splash cup
Afrikaans: Geriffelde voëlnesswam

Etymology: GREEK: *kyathos* = cup; LATIN: *striatus* = striated, furrowed, striped

Synonym(s): *Cyathella striata, Cyathia hirsuta, C. lentifera, Cyathus hirsutus*

ECOLOGY: Saprophytic.

DISTRIBUTION: Western Cape and Gauteng, possibly more widespread. Occurs in the UK, Europe, Canada, USA, Mexico, Costa Rica, Brazil, Russia, India, Thailand, China, Japan, Australia and New Zealand.

HABITAT: Grows on dead woody material, fence posts, stumps, twigs, cones and dead leaves beneath trees; fruit bodies single, grouped or clustered.

DESCRIPTION: The grooved striations on the inner surface of the nest-like fruit body distinguish this species from other bird's nest fungi. **Fruit body:** 0.6–1.2cm tall, 0.5–1cm in diameter; at first rounded, becoming vase- or cone-shaped, tapering downward to the base; outer surface shaggy or furry to hairy, grey-buff to dark brown; inner surface grooved and lined, distinct striations, shiny, light to dark grey; contains 10–12 peridioles. **Peridioles:** 0.15–0.25cm in diameter; lentil-shaped, sheathed, attached to the fruit body by thin threads; pale grey.

EDIBILITY: Inedible; too small and hard for consumption.

Young specimens have a shaggy surface.

Fruit bodies mature to become vase-shaped.

Single and grouped fruit bodies.

Densely clustered fruit bodies.

Up to 12 peridioles develop in the fruit body.

Sphaerobolus stellatus Tode 1790

Common names: Shooting star, cannonball fungus, shotgun fungus, artillery fungus, ball-bearing, sphere thrower
Afrikaans: Artillerieswam

Etymology: GREEK: *sphaera-* = globe, sphere, *-bolus* = throw; LATIN: *stellatus* = starred

Synonym(s): *Carpobolus stellatus, Sphaerobolus carpobolus*

ECOLOGY: Saprophytic.

DISTRIBUTION: First reported in South Africa in Gauteng (Pretoria), but may be more widespread. Occurs in the UK, Europe, USA, Mexico, Costa Rica, Brazil, Russia, Japan, Australia, New Zealand and Tenerife.

HABITAT: Grows on dead wood, fallen leaves, herbivore dung and other organic debris; fruit bodies grouped or clustered.

DESCRIPTION: The minute size and bright yellow colour distinguish this species from most other cup-shaped fungi. **Fruit body:** 0.1– 0.3cm in diameter; globose or more or less round at first; outer wall splitting in a star-like manner, forming 5–8 rays or 'teeth' and exposing the spore-bearing peridiole; innermost layer turning outward at maturity to forcefully eject the peridiole; remnants of the inner layer translucent, inflated, forming a whitish ball temporarily attached to the ray tips; outer layer white to dull yellow-orange or ochraceous at first, rays bright orange; inner layer tinged yellow to orange. **Peridiole:** about 0.1cm in diameter; more or less round, smooth; spore-bearing mass sticky or slippery; dark brown at maturity. **Spore mass:** glassy, transparent.

SIMILAR SPECIES: May be confused with other yellowish-orange, cup-shaped fungi such as *Anthracobia melaloma* and *Scutellinia scutellata*, but this species is smaller.

EDIBILITY: Inedible; too small for culinary use.

NOTES: The many common names of this species – 'shooting star', 'cannonball fungus', 'shotgun fungus', 'artillery fungus', 'ball-bearing' and 'sphere thrower' – aptly describe the forceful manner in which the spore-bearing mass is propelled outward, sometimes over a distance of up to 2m. The peridiole, which contains the spores, is launched when the innermost peridial layer abruptly and forcefully turns outward. This layer persists as a translucent, white hemisphere atop the star-shaped rays after the peridiole has been 'shot off'.

The fruit bodies appear singly or clustered on decaying wood.

Just a few millimetres wide, this is one of the smallest bird's nest fungi.

The spore dispersal mechanism, illustrated above (from top to bottom), starts when the outer layer splits apart in a star-like manner to expose the single peridiole. The translucent inner layer pops outward to shoot the egg sac into the air, leaving behind a hemispherical membrane.

Battarrea phalloides (Dicks.) Pers. 1801

Common names: Sandy stiltball, scaly stalked puffball, tall stiltball, desert-stalked puffball
Afrikaans: Jelliebeurssteelstuifbal

Etymology: *battarrea* = after Italian mycologist A.C.J. Battarra (1714–1789); GREEK: *phalloides* = phallus-like
Synonym(s): *Battarrea guicciardiniana, B. levispora, B. stevenii, Lycoperdon phalloides*

Inedible

ECOLOGY: Saprophytic.

DISTRIBUTION: Northern Cape, Gauteng and Free State, possibly more widespread. Occurs in the UK, Europe, Canada, USA, Mexico, Brazil, Argentina, Australia, Botswana, Mozambique and Swaziland.

HABITAT: Grows in sandy soil, preferring open spaces; fruit bodies single, sometimes grouped.

DESCRIPTION: This distinctive species can be identified by its tall, shaggy stipe and convex, rust-brown spore mass. **Spore sac:** 1.5–7cm in diameter; bell-shaped to convex; firm at first, then cushion-like; covered with a glossy, white to cream or ochreous membrane attached to a thin, concave, cream to buff base; surface membrane splitting at maturity to fall away in one cap-like piece, exposing the spore mass. **Stipe:** 13–32cm long, 1–4cm thick; central; cylindrical to elongate-ovoid, narrowing to the base; rust-brown volva at the base, often disappearing; surface grooved, shaggy, with elongate, membraneous scales; grey to ochraceous to dull brown; woody, fibrous, leathery, hollow. **Ring:** absent. **Smell:** no distinctive odour.
Spore mass: powdery, disintegrates over the upper surface of the base after the spores have been released, leaving spore base and stipe bare; grey-brown to rust-brown.

The surface membrane, visible at the base of the stipe, is discarded to expose the spores.

SIMILAR SPECIES: *Podaxis pistillaris. Tulostoma* species are smaller, and the spore sac remains intact after the release of the spore mass.

EDIBILITY: Inedible.

> **NOTES:** According to studies conducted in 2000 and 2004, *Battarrea phalloides* is the same species as *B. stevenii*. Since *B. phalloides* was discovered and named in 1785 and *B. stevenii* only in 1814, the species is known by the earlier scientific name.

The spore mass becomes powdery as it disintegrates.

Podaxis pistillaris grows on termite mounds, and is commonly found on those of the harvester termite *Trinervitermes tinervoides.*

Liz Popich

Podaxis pistillaris (L.) Fr. 1829

Common names: False ink cap, desert shaggy mane, stalked puffball
Afrikaans: Slangkop

Etymology: GREEK: *pod* = foot, *axis* = axis; LATIN: *pistillum* = pestle, *-aris* = pertaining to

Synonym(s): *Lycoperdon carcinomale, Podaxis podaxon, Podaxon pistillaris, Scleroderma pistillare*

Inedible

The cylindrical stipe extends to the apex of the cap.

ECOLOGY: Saprophytic.

DISTRIBUTION: Northern Cape, Gauteng and Free State, possibly more widespread. Occurs in the USA, Mexico, Guatemala, Brazil, Argentina, Azerbaijan, Russia, Australia, Cape Verde Islands, Sierra Leone, Burkina Faso and Kenya.

HABITAT: Usually grows on termite mounds or in dry, sandy or gravelly soil; fruit bodies single or grouped.

DESCRIPTION: Although the fruit bodies vary in size, the distinctive form of this species makes it relatively easy to recognise.
Cap: 2–15cm tall, 2–7cm in diameter; elongate-ovoid, surrounding and attached to the stipe; covered with large, brown scales which, when detached, leave a silver-white rind; rind turning grey-brown to umber, becoming brittle, releasing spores by tearing from the stipe at the lower edges and splitting along the margin. **Stipe:** 13–32cm long, 1–4cm thick; cylindrical, straight or curved, extending to the cap apex; base enlarged into a bulbous or tuberous structure of mixed fungal threads and soil; volva absent; longitudinally grooved, covered with scales, but often smooth with age; concolorous with cap; solid or hollow. **Flesh:** white at first, becoming discoloured with age. **Smell:** no distinctive odour. **Spore mass:** white and firm at first, turning greenish brown to dark reddish brown; powdery at maturity.

SIMILAR SPECIES: *Podaxis africana, P. beringamensis* (neither described here), *Battarrea phalloides, Coprinus comatus.*

EDIBILITY: Inedible; said to be edible when very young and still white inside, but tough, dusty and inedible when maturing.

MEDICINAL: The dark-brown spore powder has been used in folk medicine in the treatment of cancer. It has also been used in a mixture with unsalted fat as a salve for the treatment of nappy rash in infants.

Large scales cover the cap and stipe.

NOTES: *Podaxis pistillaris* is part of a group of fungi called sequestrate fungi. These fungi bear spores on gill-like structures that are enclosed by the cap as a protective measure (unlike other mushroom-forming species, which have the gills on the underside of the cap). Once the spores mature, the exterior layer breaks down to release the spores – similar to the spore dispersal mechanism in puffballs. For this reason, and to make identification easier, this species has been included here among the puffballs.

About 50 *Podaxis* species have been described, but it has been argued that many of them most likely represent morphological variations of *Podaxis pistillaris.*

As the fungus disintegrates, the tip of the cap becomes powdery.

Tulostoma albicans grows in sandy soil among leaf litter. The spore sac, ranging from dirty white to beige, is usually encrusted with soil particles.

Tulostoma albicans V.S. White 1901

Common name: Stalked puffball
Afrikaans: Gesteelde snuifbal

Etymology: GREEK: *tylos* = knot, callus, knob, *stoma* = mouth;
LATIN: *albesco* = to become white

Synonym(s): *Tulostoma albicans* var. *nigrostium*

ECOLOGY: Saprophytic.

DISTRIBUTION: Northern Cape, Gauteng and Free State, possibly more widespread. Occurs in the USA, Mexico, Chile and Australia.

HABITAT: Grows in sandy soil, obtaining nutrients by decomposing roots, buried wood and other plant remains; fruit bodies scattered or grouped.

DESCRIPTION: This species can be identified microscopically by the very pale, almost white spore sac of the young fruit body and by the size and surface ornamentation of the spores. **Spore sac:** 0.8–1.5cm in diameter; subglobose, raised above soil level on a dark-coloured stipe partly immersed in the soil; outer wall bay-brown to red-brown, covered with soil, breaking away to expose the inner wall which is attached at the base to a depressed cup-like part of the outer wall; inner wall dirty white to grey or beige, smooth, tough, membraneous; circular, apical pore on a short ridge. **Stipe:** 2–4.5cm long, 0.2–0.5cm thick; cylindrical, widening into a basal bulb; grooved, with adhering soil grains; dark reddish brown. **Flesh:** whitish. **Smell:** no distinctive odour. **Spore mass:** rusty brown; powdery when mature, puffing out through the apical pore when the spore sac is depressed by raindrops or other means.

SIMILAR SPECIES: There are 14 species of *Tulostoma* in South Africa and more than a hundred worldwide, all commonly known as stalked puffballs. They can be distinguished microscopicallly by their spore and spore sac characters.

EDIBILITY: Inedible; too tough.

The spore sac sits atop the grooved stipe.

The reddish-brown stipe is cylindrical.

The pore is supported on a short, tubular ridge at the apex of the spore sac.

Spores are released through the apical pore.

Small conical warts cover the outer surface of *Lycoperdon pratense*, but wear away as the fruit body matures.

The white fruit bodies of young specimens are delicious and should be eaten as soon as possible after being picked.

Lycoperdon pratense Pers. 1794

Common names: Common puffball, little white puffball, meadow puffball, field puffball, puffball
Afrikaans: Oueltjie, wit stuifbal

Etymology: GREEK: *lykos* = wolf, *perdomai* = to break wind; LATIN: *pratensis* = growing in a meadow

Synonym(s): *Lycoperdon hyemale, Utraria pratensis, Vascellum pratense*

ECOLOGY: Saprophytic.

DISTRIBUTION: Widespread in South Africa. Occurs in the UK, Europe, Canada, USA, Mexico, Costa Rica, Brazil, Argentina, Kyrgyzstan, Russia, Mongolia, Japan, Australia and New Zealand.

HABITAT: Grows in open, grassy areas containing plant litter and compost, in pastures and on golf courses during the rainy season; fruit bodies scattered, grouped or clustered; sometimes in fairy rings.

Fruit bodies grow in open, grassy areas.

DESCRIPTION: The small conical warts on the surface of this spherical to pear-shaped fungus make it easy to recognise. **Fruit body:** 2–4cm in diameter; sessile, attached to the substrate by short, root-like threads; spherical to almost spherical to top- or pear-shaped, can be flattened at the apex, tapering toward the base; firm becoming softer; thin membrane within the fruit body separates the gleba (fertile spore mass) in the upper part from the sterile subgleba in the base; outer layer (exoperidium) covered with small conical warts when young, warts larger toward the apex, white to cream-coloured, wearing away to reveal the smooth inner layer; inner layer (endoperidium) white turning grey-brown to brown with age; apical pore tearing open to release the spores. **Flesh:** soft, spongy in young specimens, then mushy; white but soon yellow, eventually becoming a yellow- to olivaceous-brown spore mass. **Smell:** pleasant mushroomy odour. **Spore mass:** firm; white when young, turning into soft, spongy, yellowish tissue when mature; drying into powdery, yellow-brown spore mass.

SIMILAR SPECIES: *Lycoperdon perlatum, Scleroderma citrinum.*

EDIBILITY: Edible; delicious, especially when gently fried in butter. Only the immature white-flesh specimens are edible, and they should be consumed as soon as possible after having been collected. Yellowing or darkening specimens should be discarded.

Short, root-like threads attach the fungus to the soil in which it grows.

Yellow-brown spore mass.

Lycoperdon perlatum turns a buff to brown colour with age.

Liz Popich

Lycoperdon perlatum Pers. 1796

Common names: Gem-studded puffball, warted puffball, devil's snuff-box, devil's tobacco pouch, common puffball
Afrikaans: Pêrelstuifbal

Etymology: GREEK: *lykos* = wolf, *perdomai* = to break wind; LATIN: *perlatus* = to carry through

Synonym(s): *Lycoperdon bonordenii, L. gemmatum* var. *perlatum*

ECOLOGY: Saprophytic.

DISTRIBUTION: Occurs worldwide.

HABITAT: Grows among leaf litter of broadleaved trees, occasionally under conifers; fruit bodies grouped or clustered.

DESCRIPTION: The white to yellowish-brown fruit body, which is covered with short blunt spines, each surrounded by smaller grain-like scales, is distinctive. **Fruit body:** up to 3cm in diameter, up to 5cm tall; pear- to top-shaped, with mycelial threads attached to the base; thickly studded with tiny, persistent, straw-coloured spines and granules over the apex, interspersed with more pointed, umber, erect warts which soon disappear, leaving small, light-coloured depressions in a net-like pattern over the spore sac; spore sac white at first, becoming buff, greyish brown to olive-brown; raised apical pore tearing open to release the spore mass. **Flesh:** white, changing to golden brown, maturing to greyish brown, olive-brown or chestnut-brown; firm at first, powdery when mature. **Smell:** no distinctive odour. **Spore mass:** firm, white when young, turning into soft, spongy, fertile, yellowish tissue; drying into powdery, yellow-brown spore mass.

SIMILAR SPECIES: *Lycoperdon pratense, Scleroderma citrinum.*

EDIBILITY: Edible when the flesh is still white.

Fruit bodies with closed pores at the apex.

The surface is densely studded with tiny straw-coloured spines and granules.

The fruit body is pear- to top-shaped.

As the fruit body matures, the outer layer of the fruit body cracks and darkens to brown before flaking off to expose the spore mass.

Pisolithus tinctorius (Mont.) E. Fisch. 1898

Common names: Dyeball, horse dung fungus, bohemian truffle, dead man's foot
Afrikaans: Kleursnuifbal

Etymology: GREEK: *piso-* = pea, *lith* = stone; LATIN: *tinctorius* = pertaining to dyeing

Synonym(s): *Lycoperdon arhizon, Pisolithus arhizus, P. arrhizus, Scleroderma arrhizum*

ECOLOGY: Mycorrhizal.

DISTRIBUTION: Widespread in South Africa. Occurs in the UK, Europe, Canada, USA, Mexico, Costa Rica, Panama, Argentina, Pakistan, South Korea, Australia, New Zealand and Burkina Faso.

HABITAT: Grows under broadleaved trees, especially eucalyptus, sometimes under conifers, usually in acidic, sandy soil; fruit bodies single, grouped or scattered.

DESCRIPTION: The characteristic outer skin that darkens and cracks before flaking off to reveal the internal spore-bearing structure makes this a readily recognisable species. The young fruit bodies yield a dark, brown-staining liquid when squeezed or cut. **Fruit body:** 5–20cm tall, 5–17cm in diameter; variable in size and form, globose to subglobose or pear-shaped, often irregularly lobed, narrowing into a stout, stipe-like rooting base, up to 6–10cm long, around 3cm thick; base partially buried, attached underground by yellow rhizomorphic strands; outer layer (exoperidium) thin, almost smooth, shiny, ochreous to bright yellow at first, darkening to greyish brown and to dark grey with dark-brown surface markings, flaking to expose the yellow to olive-brown spores in the irregularly polygonal or egg-shaped chambers; chambers initially whitish, turning olive-brown to umber as the spores mature, becoming powdery as the thick, black, dividing walls of the cavities disintegrate.
Peridioles: appear as small pea-sized stones or gravel, rubber-like, becoming brittle and powdery. **Flesh:** firm, solid when young; hard, woody, dark brown at maturity. **Smell:** no distinctive odour.
Spore mass: rust to olive-brown to umber or cinnamon; powdery when mature.

SIMILAR SPECIES: Easily distinguished from other ball-shaped fungi.

EDIBILITY: Inedible.

The fruit body narrows to form a rooting base, commonly buried underground.

Yellow rhizomorphic strands anchor the fungus in the soil.

NOTES: The spore-containing peridioles of this species differ from those in the *Cyathus* genus (p. 258–261) in that they are enclosed in irregular spore chambers inside the fruit body. By contrast, those of *Cyathus*, commonly referred to as 'eggs', are enclosed in a thick casing in a cup-shaped fruit body.
   The viscous gel that covers younger specimens is used as a natural dye for textiles. A purple dye can be extracted from the apex region and a yellow dye is derived from the base. *Pisolithus tinctorius* is also one of the major mycorrhizal fungi used as a root development stimulant in gardening and horticulture – whether in soil mixes or in liquid or powder form.

Dissected fruit body showing the irregularly polygonal array of the spore chambers.

Scleroderma citrinum, showing mature specimens, the compact inner spore mass and the basal column with adhering mycelial strands.

The surface is covered with large, irregular, flattened wart-like protuberances, making it appear rough and scaly.

Scleroderma citrinum Pers. 1801

Common names: Common earthball, pigskin poison puffball
Afrikaans: Vratjiesnuifbal

Etymology: GREEK: *scler* = hard, *derma* = skin; LATIN: *citrinum* = the colour of lemon

Synonym(s): *Lycoperdon aurantium, L. tessellatum, Scleroderma aurantium, S. vulgare*

Poisonous

ECOLOGY: Mycorrhizal.

DISTRIBUTION: Western Cape, Eastern Cape, Gauteng, KwaZulu-Natal and Mpumalanga, possibly more widespread. Occurs in the UK, Europe, Canada, USA, Brazil, Chile, Russia, Pakistan, Japan, South Korea, Papua New Guinea, Australia and Tenerife.

HABITAT: Grows underneath pine and sometimes broadleaved trees; fruit bodies single or grouped, occasionally clustered.

DESCRIPTION: This hard, ball-like fungus has a yellowish, scaly outer surface that cracks to reveal a powdery, purplish to black spore mass inside. **Fruit body:** Up to 8cm in diameter; hard; more or less spherical or flattened at the base, yellow, root-like mycelial threads at the base; surface covered with large, irregular, flattened, wart-like protuberances or small warts, especially over the upper part; does not form a well-defined pore through which spores are released; outer layer (exoperidium) 0.15–0.3cm thick, leathery, woody, white, cracking open at the top to expose the spores; bright lemon-yellow when fresh, turning ochre to brown. **Flesh:** young specimens white (turning pink when cut), becoming a dark purplish-black spore-bearing mass; corky with age. **Smell:** no distinctive odour. **Spore mass:** white when young, chocolate-brown to dark grey and powdery when mature.

SIMILAR SPECIES: *Lycoperdon perlatum, L. pratense.*

EDIBILITY: Poisonous. Although fresh, young fruit bodies are said to be edible, it is best to avoid this species. Mature fruit bodies that are eaten raw may cause gastrointestinal irritation, with the patient experiencing vomiting, sweating, pallor and even unconsciousness. In severe cases, it could cause death. Symptoms may develop within 30–45 minutes of consumption, although there is no definitive time frame for their onset. There is some indication that alcohol may worsen the effect.

NOTES: *Scleroderma citrinum* is sometimes parasitised by the bolete *Pseudoboletus parasiticus* (not described here).

Dark purplish-black spore mass.

Maturing fruit bodies turn ochre to brown.

Root-like mycelial threads form at the base.

The ragged, open pore of this old specimen indicate that the spores have been released.

Geastrum fornicatum (Huds.) Hook. 1821

Common names: Arched earthstar, acrobatic earthstar, star vault
Afrikaans: Vierpuntaardster

Etymology: ANCIENT GREEK: *geo-* = of the earth, *astèr* = star;
LATIN: *fornic* = vault, *-atum* = possessing

Synonym(s): *Geaster fornicatum, G. fornicatus, Geastrum fenestratus, G. fornicatus*

ECOLOGY: Saprophytic.

DISTRIBUTION: Gauteng (Pretoria), possibly more widespread. Occurs in the UK, Europe, Canada, USA, Mexico, Brazil, Japan, Australia and New Zealand.

HABITAT: Grows under coniferous and broadleaved trees; fruit bodies single or scattered.

DESCRIPTION: The elevated spore sac that is supported by rays pushing off the ground (instead of lying flat) and the ray tips that remain attached to the basal cup are identifying features. **Fruit body:** 5–8cm in diameter when expanded; globose, developing from a ball-like structure; outer layer (exoperidium) splitting open into 3–6 rays, typically 4–7.5cm long; rays curving backward to stand upright on tips when mature; rays usually remaining attached to the basal cup, attached to the soil by rhizomorphs at their tips; lower (outer) surface usually smooth, tan to brown; upper (inner) surface chocolate-brown to dark brown, often tinged with blue or purple. **Spore sac:** 1.5–2.5cm in diameter; round or subglobose, mounted on a short stalk (pedicel), often with a compressed collar; raised into the air on rays; surface finely velvety, rough; brown-grey to dark chocolate-brown; apical pore fibrous, opening to release the spores. **Smell:** no distinctive odour. **Spore mass:** firm, white at first, becoming chocolate- to dark brown; powdery at maturity.

SIMILAR SPECIES: Other *Geastrum* species, most of which are of a similar form.

EDIBILITY: Inedible.

NOTES: This species was named *Fungus anthropomorphus* when first described in 1695 because of its uncanny resemblance to a human figure.

The rays curve backward, lifting the spore sac into the air.

The rounded spore sac has a greyish colour.

The outer layer splits open into several rays.

The apical pore is fibrous.

The spore sac rests on a short stalk.

Geastrum hieronymi grows in sandy but humus-rich soil, usually in moist forests.

Liz Popich

Geastrum hieronymi Henn. 1897

Common names: None
Afrikaans: None

Etymology: ANCIENT GREEK: *geo-* = of the earth, *astèr* = star; *hieronymi* = after German botanist George Hans Emmo Wolfgang Hieronymus (1846–1921)
Synonym(s): *Geaster hieronymi*

ECOLOGY: Saprophytic.

DISTRIBUTION: Gauteng (Pretoria), possibly more widespread. Occurs in the USA, Mexico, Brazil, Argentina and Namibia.

HABITAT: Sandy soil mixed with humus in moist forests; fruit bodies single, grouped or clustered.

DESCRIPTION: Readily recognised as an earthstar, this species can be distinguished by the pale to brown outer layer and metallic to dark-brown spore sac when dry. **Fruit body:** 3–7cm in diameter when expanded; globose, developing from a ball-like structure; outer layer (exoperidium) covered with earth or debris, splitting open into 6–8 rays; rays inflexible, inrolled, acute, tips attached to the substrate by rhizomorphs; inner (upper) surface of rays fibrous, fleshy, thick when fresh, often peeling away, chestnut or flesh-coloured when young, darker when dry; outer (lower) surface pale to dark brown. **Spore sac:** 2–3cm in diameter; adnate, subglobose, with a short stalk (pedicel); slightly elevated on rays; metallic to dark brown; apical pore fibrous, delicately fringed or toothed. **Smell:** no distinctive odour. **Spore mass:** sepia-brown; powdery at maturity.

EDIBILITY: Inedible.

The outer layer splits into 6–8 rays.

The slightly elevated apical pore ruptures to release the spores.

When expanded, the fruit body is 3–7cm in diameter.

The spore sac rests on the outcurved rays.

Geastrum kotlabae is hygroscopic, and so responds to moisture levels in the air. When it is dry, the rays are folded around the spore sac to protect it from the heat and from predators. Conversely, when it rains, the rays curve backward to encourage spore dispersal.

Geastrum kotlabae V.J. Stanek 1958

Common name: Kotlaba's earthstar
Afrikaans: Vogabsorberende aardster

Etymology: ANCIENT GREEK: *geo-* = of the earth, *astèr* = star; *kotlabae* = after the Czech botanist, naturalist and mycologist, František Kotlaba (1927–present), known for his contribution to taxonomic mycology

Synonym(s): None

ECOLOGY: Saprophytic.

DISTRIBUTION: First reported in South Africa in Gauteng, possibly more widespread. Occurs in Europe, USA, Mexico, Brazil, Russia, Japan and Kenya.

HABITAT: Grows in humus-rich or calcareous soil; fruit bodies single or grouped.

DESCRIPTION: The ability of this species to open its fleshy rays to expose the spore sac in humid conditions and to close them again in drier conditions aids identification. **Fruit body:** 0.7–1.4cm in diameter when expanded; globose, developing from a ball-like structure; outer layer (exoperidium) splitting open into 8–15 rays, curving around the spore sac; rays hygroscopic, slowly unfolding and flattening out when moistened, not reflexing; inner (upper) surface of rays creamy brown; outer (lower) surface finely cracked, encrusted with soil debris, whitish to greyish. **Spore sac:** 0.7–1.4cm in diameter; sessile, often more or less globose, with a short stalk (pedicel); more or less smooth; grey to purple-brown; apical pore elongate, deeply grooved, beak-like, demarcated from the rest of the sac. **Smell:** No distinctive odour. **Spore mass:** very dark greyish brown; powdery at maturity; almost charcoal black when dry.

SIMILAR SPECIES: *Astraeus hygrometricus*, *Gaestrum arenarium* *G. corollinum* and *G. floriforme* (none described here) are all hygroscopic. An expert may be required to distinguish between the *Gaestrum* species.

EDIBILITY: Inedible.

NOTES: Like most other earthstar fungi, *Geastrum kotlabae* displays the classic star shape resulting from the outer layer splitting open during maturity. However, its hygroscopic (water-absorbing) characteristics differentiate it from most other similar species. Whereas the rays of other earthstars are more or less rigid once opened, *G. kotlabae* can repeatedly open or close its fleshy rays in humid or dry conditions to either expose or protect its spore sac.

The outer layer splits into 8–15 rays.

Minuscule warts appear on the spore sac.

A brownish furrowed fringe surrounds the elevated pore mouth.

The pore mouth is deeply grooved and beak-like at first, making it easy to distinguish from other earthstars.

Geastrum pectinatum Pers. 1801

Common names: Beaked earthstar, beret earthstar, star comb, grooved earthstar
Afrikaans: Gepunte aardster, geriffelde aardster

Etymology: ANCIENT GREEK: *geo-* = of the earth, *astèr* = star; LATIN: *pentines* = comb, *-atum* = resembling

Synonym(s): *Geaster pectinatus, Geastrum plicatum, G. tenuipes*

ECOLOGY: Saprophytic.

DISTRIBUTION: Gauteng (Pretoria), possibly more widespread. Occurs in the UK, Europe, Canada, USA, Mexico, Costa Rica, Brazil, Chile, Russia, Japan, Australia and New Zealand.

HABITAT: Grows in humus-rich soil or on rotting wood in coniferous forests and sometimes under broadleaved trees; fruit bodies single or grouped.

DESCRIPTION: The prominent stalk and 'beaked' mouth of the spore sac distinguish this earthstar from most others. **Fruit body:** 3–7cm in diameter when expanded; globose, developing from a ball-like structure; outer layer (exoperidium) splitting open into 5–12 irregular, pointed star-like rays; rays curving backward to raise the spore sac into the air; outer (lower) surface of the rays encrusted with debris and fungal matter, whitish to greyish; inner (upper) surface fleshy when young, cracking or flaking with age, whitish when young, then purple-brown to grey-brown, remaining unchanged for long periods when dry. **Spore sac:** 0.5–2.5cm in diameter; round to somewhat urn-shaped, borne on a prominent, slender, radially wrinkled stalk (pedicel); surface more or less smooth, grey to purple-brown; apical pore elongate, deeply grooved, beak-like, demarcated from the rest of the sac. **Smell:** no distinctive odour. **Spore mass:** dark brown; powdery in mature specimens.

SIMILAR SPECIES: *Geastrum schmidelii* is similar, but is much smaller and has a shorter 'beak' and a short, thick stipe. *G. striatum* (not described here) has a collar at the base of the spore sac.

EDIBILITY: Inedible.

NOTES: Earthstars are part of a group of fungi known as gasteroids or stomach fungi. This is because the spore-bearing mass is not borne on the surface but in a cavity inside the fruit body where it is entirely enclosed by the peridium (outer layer or skin). Once the fungus matures and the spores have developed, the outer skin tears, allowing the spores to escape and be dispersed by the wind.

Inedible

Young fruit body, showing spherical spore sac.

The short, slender stalk is radially wrinkled.

The inner surface is fleshy in younger fungi.

As *Geastrum schmidelii* matures, the expanded rays become cracked and papery.

Geastrum schmidelii Vittad. 1842

Common name: Dwarf earthstar
Afrikaans: Dwergaardster

Etymology: ANCIENT GREEK: *geo-* = of the earth, *astèr* = star; *schmidelii* = after German physician and botanist Casimir Christoph Schmidel (1718–1791)

Synonym(s): None

ECOLOGY: Saprophytic.

DISTRIBUTION: Gauteng (Pretoria), possibly more widespread. Occurs in the UK, Europe, Canada, USA, Argentina, Russia and the Philippines.

HABITAT: Grows in calcareous soil in fields, on dunes or in open areas in coniferous forests. Fruit bodies clustered or grouped in large numbers.

DESCRIPTION: The small fruit body, dark-brown, beak-like, striated pore mouth, and rays that become papery when mature make this species readily identifiable. **Fruit body:** 0.5–3.5cm in diameter when expanded; egg-shaped to globose, developing from a ball-like structure; outer layer (exoperidium) splitting open into 5–8 pointed rays; rays papery when mature. **Spore sac:** 0.5–1cm in diameter; sessile, supported on a short, slender stalk (pedicel); surface sometimes covered with a fine, whitish bloom, plum-coloured; apical pore fringed by small projections. **Smell:** no distinctive odour. **Spore mass:** dark brown; powdery at maturity.

SIMILAR SPECIES: Several other *Geastrum* species have the same appearance, but this species can be distinguished by its small size. An expert may be needed to make a positive identification.

EDIBILITY: Inedible.

Ranging between 1.5 and 3.5cm, this is one of the smallest members of the genus.

The elongated, deeply grooved appendages surrounding the pore opening create a distinct beak-like appearance.

An old specimen, identified by the absence of the beak-like appendage around the pore mouth.

Liz Popich

This tiny species grows on decaying wood, where it appears in large clusters or groups.

Liz Popich

The outer layer of rays is thick and fleshy, with the split lobes tending to be less curvy than those of other earthstars.

Geastrum schweinitzii (Berk. & M.A. Curtis) Zeller 1948

Common names: None
Afrikaans: None

Etymology: ANCIENT GREEK: *geo-* = of the earth, *astèr* = star; *schweinitzii* = after American botanist and mycologist Lewis David von Schweinitz (1780–1834), founder of North American mycological science
Synonym(s): *Coilomyces schweinitzii*

ECOLOGY: Saprophytic.

DISTRIBUTION: Gauteng and Mpumalanga, possibly more widespread. Occurs in the USA, Mexico, Nicaragua, Costa Rica, Panama, Cuba, Haiti, Dominican Republic, Galápagos Islands, Venezuela, Colombia, French Guiana, Brazil, India, China, Japan, Australia, New Zealand, Nigeria, Cameroon and Zambia.

HABITAT: Grows on decaying logs, wood debris and leaf litter; fruit bodies clustered or grouped in large numbers.

DESCRIPTION: This tiny fungus can be recognised by the yellowish-white, crust-like growth of mycelium by which it is attached to dead wood or other organic debris and by the thin thread-like fibres around the pore mouth. **Fruit body:** 0.5–2cm in diameter when expanded; globose, developing from a ball-like structure; outer layer (exoperidium) splitting open into 5–7 rays; rays not completely rolled outward; inner (upper) surface of rays whitish to pale fawn; outer (lower) surface covered with fine hairs, grey-brown. **Spore sac:** 0.25–0.6cm in diameter; sessile, depressed, globose to subglobose, with a short stalk (pedicel); thin, thread-like fibres surround the pore mouth. **Smell:** no distinctive odour. **Spore mass:** dark chocolate-brown; powdery at maturity.

EDIBILITY: Inedible.

Ball-like structure of the early fruit body.

About 5–7 rays expand outward to expose the spore sac.

The inner layer can be identified by the whitish to fawn surface.

Thread-like fibres surround the pore mouth.

As with other earthstars, the pale grey-brown spore sac is mounted on a star-shaped base, consisting of 4–8 fleshy lobes.

A collar of fleshy tissue develops around the spore sac as the rays of the fruit body bend and crack.

Geastrum triplex Jungh. 1840

Common names: Collared earthstar, saucered earthstar, triple earthstar
Afrikaans: Gekraagde aardster

Etymology: ANCIENT GREEK: *geo-* = of the earth, *astèr* = star;
LATIN: *triplex* = triple, threefold
Synonym(s): None

ECOLOGY: Saprophytic.

DISTRIBUTION: Western Cape, Gauteng and KwaZulu-Natal, possibly more widespread. Occurs in the UK, Europe, Canada, USA, Mexico, Colombia, Argentina, Russia, India, Japan, North Korea, Australia and New Zealand.

HABITAT: Grows among leaf litter of broadleaved trees in well-composted soil; fruit bodies single or grouped.

DESCRIPTION: Readily recognised as an earthstar, it is the thick, fleshy collar around the spore sac and the recurving rays that distinguish this species. **Fruit body:** 5–10cm in diameter when expanded; bulb-shaped at first; in young stages, the outer layer (exoperidium) is smooth, hairless, dirty white to ochraceous, forming a prominent point at the apex; outer layer later splitting open into 4–8 rays; rays rubbery when fresh, curving backward, becoming attached to the substrate by numerous white mycelial threads; inner (upper) surface of rays thick, fleshy, usually cracking to leave a collar of tissue around the spore sac, pale ochraceous, darkening to cinnamon or reddish brown. **Spore sac:** 1.5–3cm in diameter; sessile, subglobose; smooth, pale grey-brown; pale ring around the slightly raised pore mouth; apical pore surrounded by fibrils forming a low, conical ring and arising from a narrow, disc-like area. **Smell:** no distinctive odour. **Spore mass:** firm, white at first, dark brown to umber; powdery at maturity.

SIMILAR SPECIES: Most earthstars have a similar appearance, differing mainly in size and form. *Geastrum triplex* is the largest member of the genus and can be distinguished by its distinct layers.

EDIBILITY: Inedible.

In the young stage, the fruit body is dirty white to ochraceous, forming a prominent point at the apex.

A light-grey ring encloses the slightly raised pore mouth.

The spore sac, littered with fine spores, rests on tapering, pointed rays that are attached to the soil by numerous white mycelial cords.

Liz Popich

Myriostoma coliforme (Dicks.) Corda 1842

Common names: Pepper pot earthstar, pepper pot, salt-shaker earthstar
Afrikaans: Peperbus

Etymology: GREEK: *myrios* = myriad, numerous, *stomatos* = mouth; LATIN: *colum* = strainer, *forma* = form, shape

Synonym(s): *Geastrum coliforme*, *G. coliformis*, *Lycoperdon coliforme*

ECOLOGY: Saprophytic.

DISTRIBUTION: Western Cape, Gauteng and KwaZulu-Natal, possibly more widespread. Occurs in the UK, Europe, USA, Mexico, Guatemala, Brazil, Bolivia, Argentina, Russia and Australia.

HABITAT: Grows on dead wood of broadleaved trees and in soil; fruit bodies single or grouped.

DESCRIPTION: This species is distinguished from other earthstars by the presence of several pore mouths. **Fruit body:** 2–10cm in diameter when expanded; globose, developing from a ball-like structure; outer layer (exoperidium) splitting open into a star-shaped structure consisting of 5–14 tapering, pointed rays; rays curving backward and spreading, becoming attached to the substrate by numerous white mycelial threads; outer (lower) surface smooth, brown; inner (upper) surface fleshy, pale, later darkening to grey-brown. **Spore sac:** 1–5cm in diameter; subglobose, often flattened; usually mounted on several slender, short, sometimes inconspicuous columns (pedicels); surface rough, greyish brown; 4–15 irregular, circular or elliptical pores (peristomes) on the upper surface, resembling a pepper pot; falling raindrops cause spores to be puffed out. **Smell:** no distinctive odour. **Spore mass:** firm, white when young, turning umber; powdery at maturity.

SIMILAR SPECIES: The many pores on the surface of the spore sac differentiate this from similar-looking *Geastrum* species.

EDIBILITY: Inedible.

The spore sac has multiple pores.

Spores form a fine powder on the surface.

Viewed from above, these earthstars, with their perforated spore sacs, resemble salt shakers.

The spore mass becomes powdery with age.

The slimy spore mass is borne on the diaphragm, a disc-like structure at the centre of the fruit body, and at the base of the arms.

The thick spore mass is initially dark green-brown before turning black.

Aseroë rubra Labill. 1800

Common names: Star stinkhorn, anemone stinkhorn, sea anemone fungus, starfish fungus
Afrikaans: Sterstinkhoring

Etymology: ANCIENT GREEK: *asē* = disgusting, *roē* = juice; LATIN: *ruba* = red

Synonym(s): *Aseroë corrugata, A. hookeri, A. lysuroides, A. pallida, A. poculiformis, Lysurus aseroëformis*

Inedible

ECOLOGY: Saprophytic, possibly also mycorrhizal.

DISTRIBUTION: Western Cape, Eastern Cape and KwaZulu-Natal, possibly more widespread. Occurs in the USA, Mexico, Costa Rica, Colombia, Papua New Guinea, Australia, New Zealand, Madagascar and Swaziland.

HABITAT: Grows on soil, rotting wood and humus underneath trees, in organically rich soil, and in newly mulched garden beds; fruit bodies single or scattered.

DESCRIPTION: This fragile, short-lived fungus is readily recognised by the bright colour of the fruit body, the star-like, radiating arms that split toward the ends, and the strong, fetid odour. **Fruit body:** up to 14cm tall; arising as a stipe from a globose, membraneous sac (egg) up to 3cm in diameter; egg attached below ground by thick mycelial strands, inner layer gelatinous, surface scaly, whitish, bruises purple, sac splitting to allow for the emergence of the fruit body; stipe apex covered by a disc-like structure (diaphragm), extending inward to form a central pore and outward into 5–11 radiating arms; arms up to 3.5cm long and 0.6cm in diameter at the base, curved outward, expanding from the stipe like a star, each arm bifurcating, forming two tapering ends, longitudinally grooved, smooth or rough; orange to red. **Stipe:** 3.6–6cm long, 1–2cm thick; cylindrical, erect; white below, pink toward the apex; hollow. **Volva:** persisting as remnants of the egg at the base of the stipe. **Flesh:** fragile, thin; white. **Smell:** fetid odour; smell attracts flies, which disperse the spores. **Spore mass:** mucilaginous; dark green-brown to black; restricted to upper surface of the diaphragm and the basal portions of arms.

Gary B Goldman

Aseroë rubra in the egg stage.

Gary B Goldman

An open egg, showing the inner layers.

SIMILAR SPECIES: *Clathrus archeri, Lysurus corallocephalus.*

EDIBILITY: Inedible, although eggs in the early stage of development are treated as a delicacy in the East.

NOTES: The first *Aseroë rubra* was found by the French botanist, Jacques-Julien Houtou de Labillardière, in 1800 in the south of Tasmania, Australia. Of the four known species currently accepted in the *Aseroë* genus, only *A. rubra* is known to occur in southern Africa. *A. archnoidea* is found in China and the Hawaiian Islands, *A. coccinea* in Jamaica and *A. floriformis* in Brazil.

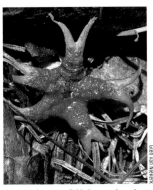

Glen van Niekerk

The radiating arms divide into two branches.

Stinkhorn fruit bodies are short-lived and usually dry out within 24 hours.

The dark olive-green spore mass is borne in patches on the inside of the red arms.

Clathrus archeri (Berk.) Dring 1980

Common names: Red stinkhorn, octopus stinkhorn, devil's fingers, cuttlefish fungus
Afrikaans: Inkvisstinkhoring

Etymology: LATIN: *clathri* = lattice work, cage; *archeri* = after Australian architect, naturalist and politician, William Archer (1820–1874)

Synonym(s): *Anthurus archeri, Lysurus archeri, Pseudocolus archeri, Schizmaturus archeri, S. aseroiformis*

ECOLOGY: Saprophytic.

DISTRIBUTION: Western Cape, Eastern Cape and Gauteng, possibly more widespread. Occurs in the UK, Europe, USA, Colombia, Russia, Japan, Australia and New Zealand.

HABITAT: Grows in cool, moist forests under broadleaved trees; fruit bodies scattered or grouped.

DESCRIPTION: The red radiating arms, slimy, black spore mass borne in patches on the arms and unpleasant odour of rotten meat that the fungus emits make this a conspicuous species. **Fruit body:** 5–12cm tall; emerging as a stipe from a globose, somewhat flattened, membraneous sac (egg) up to 6cm in diameter; egg attached below ground by thick mycelial strands, inner layer gelatinous, surface scaly, furrowed, buff to pinkish, sac splitting irregularly at the apex to allow for the emergence of the fruit body; stipe splitting into 4–8 arms, initially joined at the apex but separating and spreading outward as the fruit body matures; arms 7–15cm long, spreading out sideways, tapering toward the tips, resembling the tentacles of an octopus; surface finely wrinkled, pitted, honeycomb-like; inner (upper) surface vivid red; outer (lower) surface distinctly furrowed, pale pink. **Stipe:** 1–5cm long, 1–2.5cm thick; cylindrical, short, flared; surface rough, with transverse ridges; white at the base, reddish above; hollow, spongy. **Volva:** persisting as remnants of the egg at the base of the stipe. **Flesh:** fragile, thin; whitish to pinkish. **Smell:** unpleasant odour of rotten meat; smell attracts flies, which disperse the spores. **Spore mass:** mucilaginous; dark olive-green; occurring along the entire length of the blood-red inner surfaces of the arms, soon separating into patches.

EDIBILITY: Inedible. The egg is said to be edible, but reports indicate that both the texture and flavour are unpleasant.

> **NOTES:** Stinkhorns resemble puffballs when they first appear, but a cross-section of a stinkhorn egg reveals the characteristic gelatinous spore layer, which is absent in puffballs.

Inedible

The arms are initially fused at the apex.

As the fungus matures, the arms spread out.

The fungus can have up to 8 tapering arms.

The fruit body consists of spongy columns surmounted by a clathroid, or latticed, mesh. The ruptured, white volva persists at the base.

Clathrus transvaalensis A. Eicker & D.A. Reid 1990

Common names: None
Afrikaans: None

Etymology: LATIN: *clathri* = lattice work, cage; *transvaalensis* = after Transvaal, a former province of South Africa (now divided into Gauteng, Mpumalanga, North West Province and Limpopo)

Synonym(s): None.

Inedible

ECOLOGY: Saprophytic.

DISTRIBUTION: Gauteng (Pretoria); indigenous to South Africa.

HABITAT: Grows among grasses or on broadleaved humus; fruit bodies single or grouped.

DESCRIPTION: This fragile and short-lived fungus is characterised by a spongy, multiarch, lattice-like structure. **Fruit body:** 8–10cm tall; emerging from an ellipsoidal to spheroidal membraneous sac (egg) up to 5cm in diameter; egg attached below ground by thick mycelial strands, inner layer gelatinous, surface smooth, whitish, sac splitting irregularly at the apex to allow for the emergence of the fruit body; fruit body consisting of up to 8 fragile, stout, erect columns, each 5–7cm long and 0.6–1cm in diameter, supporting a clathroid mesh; surface transversely grooved; columns white to yellowish or cream-coloured in the lower parts, darkening upward to pale pinkish brown, mesh pinkish-brown or salmon-coloured. **Stipe:** absent. **Volva:** with irregularly lobed margin; persisting as remnants of the egg at the base of the stipe. **Flesh:** fragile, spongy, porose; whitish. **Smell:** fruity odour, similar to granadilla or pineapple; smell attracts flies, which disperse the spores. **Spore mass:** mucilaginous; olivaceous; borne on unique spore-bearing organs mostly located at the junctions of the arms, but also elsewhere.

SIMILAR SPECIES: *Clathrus ruber* (not described here) has a reddish fruit body; *Ileodictyon gracile* becomes detached from the volva remnants.

EDIBILITY: Inedible.

The fruit body arises from a white volva.

The net-like structure consists of circular and elongate openings.

The spores develop on the inner surface.

The fruity odour of this fungus attracts flies, which disperse the spores.

Blumenavia angolensis (Welw. & Curr.) Dring 1980

Common names: None
Afrikaans: None

Etymology: *blumenavia* = after Blumenau, a city in Brazil; *angolensis* = after Angola, from where it was originally described

Synonym(s): *Blumenavia usambarensis, Clathrus angolensis, Colonnaria angolensis, Laternea angolensis*

Inedible

ECOLOGY: Saprophytic.

DISTRIBUTION: First reported in South Africa in Gauteng (Pretoria), but may be more widespread. Occurs in the USA, Brazil, Ghana, Togo, Benin, Nigeria, Cameroon, Equatorial Guinea, Tanzania and Angola.

HABITAT: Grows on mulch or fertile soil; fruit bodies single or grouped.

DESCRIPTION: This fungus is distinguished by the small number of fairly rigid, white columns that join at the apex of the fruit body, and the membraneous glebifers (organs that produce the sticky spore-filled slime) restricted to the upper quarter or upper third of the columns. **Fruit body:** up to 10cm tall, 4–7cm in diameter; emerging from an elongate to ovoid membraneous sac (egg) 3–6cm in diameter; egg attached below ground by thick mycelial strands, inner layer gelatinous, surface scaly, whitish but often darker, sac splitting irregularly at the apex to allow for the emergence of the fruit body; fruit body comprising 3–5 large, irregular lobes, then expanding into unbranched, hollow columns, each up to 1cm in diameter; columns joined at the apex to form a lattice; outer surface fairly smooth, not grooved; inner surface rough; yellowish white. **Stipe:** absent. **Volva:** with irregularly lobed margin; persisting as remnants of the egg at the base of the stipe. **Flesh:** fragile, thin; white to off-white to cream. **Smell:** foul odour; smell attracts flies, which disperse the spores. **Spore mass:** mucilaginous; greyish green to olive at first, dark brown to black when dry; restricted to two rows of ragged, delicate 'teeth' (glebifers) that extend the entire length of the inner angles on each side of each column.

SIMILAR SPECIES: The membraneous organs (glebifers) that are attached to the inner angles of each column and that produce spore-filled slime help distinguish *Blumenavia* species from the similar *Clathrus* species.

EDIBILITY: Inedible.

> **NOTES:** The genus *Blumenavia* contains three other known species, *B. rhacodes, B. toribiotalpaensis* and *B. usambarensis* (none of which is described here), found in Africa and South America.

The young fruit body emerges as short lobes.

A mature specimen, with expanded columns joined at the apex.

Fruit bodies appear singly or grouped on soil or mulch.

Ileodictyon gracile Berk. 1845

Common names: Smooth cage stinkhorn, smooth lattice, white basket fungus
Afrikaans: None

Etymology: LATIN: *ileum* = small intestine, groin, GREEK: *dictyon* = net; LATIN: *gracilis* = slender, thin, simple

Inedible

Synonym(s): *Clathrus cibarium* var. *gracile*, *C. gracilis*, *C. intermedius*, *Ileodictyon cibarium* var. *gracile*

ECOLOGY: Saprophytic.

DISTRIBUTION: Western Cape (Cape Town). Occurs in Europe, Japan, South Korea, Australia, Samoa and New Zealand.

HABITAT: Grows in gardens, along path edges, or where woodchips, compost or humus are present; fruit bodies single or grouped.

DESCRIPTION: This short-lived stinkhorn can be recognised by its delicate latticed, or basket-like, structure. **Fruit body:** 20–30cm in diameter when expanded; emerging from a globose to egg-shaped membraneous sac (egg) up to 4cm in diameter; egg attached below ground by thick mycelial strands, inner layer gelatinous, surface matted, fibrous, off-white, sac rupturing irregularly at the apex to allow for the emergence of the fruit body; fruit body comprising a hollow, spherical to egg-shaped, cage-like structure consisting of 10–30 polygons; arms 0.5cm in diameter, broader where they join, relatively smooth, often flattened, ribbon-like; structure eventually becoming free from the volva, rolling around with no obvious top or bottom; outer surface fairly smooth, not grooved; inner surface rough; yellowish white. **Stipe:** absent. **Volva:** empty volva remains after latticed ball hatches and rolls off. **Flesh:** fragile, thin; whitish. **Smell:** sour milk or camembert cheese odour; smell attracts flies, which disperse the spores. **Spore mass:** mucilaginous; olive-brown to sage-green; borne on the entire inner surface of the arms.

SIMILAR SPECIES: *Ileodictyon cibarium* (not described here) is larger than *I. gracile*. *Clathrus transvaalensis* and *Clathrus ruber* (not described here) appear similar, the latter being more reddish than white.

EDIBILITY: Inedible, although the egg is said to be edible.

The mature fungus detaches itself from the volva to roll around freely. The spore-bearing slime is carried on the inner arms.

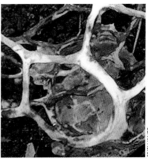

This white, cage-like fungus consists of up to 30 meshes, formed by ribbon-like arms that broaden at the points where they fuse.

The fruit body and stipe rise from the membraneous sac. The spores are borne on intricate appendages at the top of the stipe.

Itajahya galericulata Möller 1895

Common name: Jacaranda stinkhorn
Afrikaans: Jakarandastinkhoring

Etymology: *itajahya* = after the Itajaí-Açu River in Brazil from where this fungus was originally described; LATIN: *galerum* = cap- or helmet-like head covering, wig, *ata* = indicating possession or likeness
Synonym(s): *Phallus galericulatus*

Inedible

ECOLOGY: Saprophytic, possibly also mycorrhizal.

DISTRIBUTION: Gauteng (Pretoria), possibly more widespread. Occurs in the USA, Brazil, Bolivia and Australia.

HABITAT: Generally grows under *Jacaranda mimosifolia*, an invasive tree species introduced to South Africa from Brazil; fruit bodies single, grouped or clustered.

DESCRIPTION: *Itajahya* species are clearly related to the other stinkhorns, but the presence of a cap (calyptra) at the apex of the spore-bearing mass and the intricately branched, white, cauliflower-like structures on which the spores are borne are unique to this genus. **Fruit body:** 7–16cm tall; globose to egg-shaped membranous sac (egg) 3–8cm in diameter; egg attached below ground by thick mycelial strands, inner layer gelatinous, surface matted, fibrous, greyish white, becoming brownish, sac rupturing irregularly at the apex to allow for the emergence of the stipe and spore cap (calyptra); cap solid, smooth at the apex, centrally depressed, margin irregular, white; cap bearing folded and branched structures which form small, cauliflower-like processes containing the dark spore mass. **Stipe:** 7–16cm long, 1.6–4cm thick; cylindrical or tapering slightly toward both the base and apex, straight or curved; white; hollow, spongy, brittle. **Volva:** persisting as remnants of the egg at the base of the stipe. **Flesh:** fragile, porose, spongy; whitish. **Smell:** strong putrid odour; smell attracts flies, which disperse the spores. **Spore mass:** mucilaginous; initially mottled dark grey, turning green-black.

SIMILAR SPECIES: *Itajahya rosea*, which can be distinguished by its pinkish glow; most *Phallus* species.

EDIBILITY: Inedible.

A white calyptra covers the dark spore mass.

The stipe is hollow at the centre.

The spore mass at the apex of the stipe.

A membrane encloses the spore mass.

Cross section of the young fruit body.

The viscous spore mass emits a strong fetid odour that attracts flies and other insects, which assist with spore dispersal.

Glen van Niekerk

Itajahya rosea (Delile) E. Fisch. 1929

Common names: None
Afrikaans: None

Etymology: *itajahya* = after the Itajaí-Açu River in Brazil from where this fungus was originally described; LATIN: *rosa* = rosy, pink

Synonym(s): *Phallus roseus*

ECOLOGY: Saprophytic, possibly also mycorrhizal.

DISTRIBUTION: First reported in South Africa in Gauteng (Pretoria), but may be more widespread. Occurs in Europe, USA, Brazil, Paraguay, Israel, Yemen, Pakistan, India and Namibia.

HABITAT: Generally grows in grassy areas in direct sunlight; fruit bodies single, grouped or clustered.

DESCRIPTION: Like other members of this genus, this fungus has a cap-like structure (calyptra) atop the spore-bearing mass, but the rosy-pink colour of the stipe distinguishes the species. **Fruit body:** 7–10cm tall; at first an egg- to pear-shaped membraneous sac (egg) 2–5cm in diameter; egg attached below ground by thick mycelial strands, inner layer gelatinous, surface matted, fibrous, off-white to yellowish brown, sac splitting at the apex to allow for the emergence of the stipe and spore cap (calyptra); spore cap at the apex of the spore-bearing mass, roughly bell-shaped, rosy pink, cylindrical, smooth. **Stipe:** 7–10cm long, 1.6–4cm thick; cylindrical or tapering slightly, straight or curved; surface smooth; rosy pink; hollow, spongy, brittle. **Volva:** persisting as remnants of the egg at the base of the stipe. **Flesh:** brittle, porose, spongy; rosy pink. **Smell:** rotten meat odour; smell attracts flies, which disperse the spores. **Spore mass:** mucilaginous; initially mottled dark olive, turning greenish black; attached to the cap surface.

SIMILAR SPECIES: *Itajahya galericulata*, which is white and without a pinkish hue; most *Phallus* species.

EDIBILITY: Inedible.

> **NOTES:** *Itajahya rosea*, initially classified in the genus *Phallus*, was transferred to *Itajahya* in 2012 when DNA sequencing showed that it was not closely related to other *Phallus* species.

The stipe is slightly tapered and curved.

The calyptra breaks away from the stipe apex.

The stipe emerges from a membraneous sac.

The species appears singly or in clustered groups.

Cross section of the young fruit body, showing the dark spore mass and developing stipe.

The scarlet head of this species consists of multiple finely wrinkled branches.

Lysurus corallocephalus Welw. & Curr. 1870

Common names: Coralhead stinkhorn, coral-top stinkhorn
Afrikaans: Koraaltopstinkhoring

Etymology: GREEK: *lysis* = loosening, *-urus* = pertaining to; *corall* = red coral, *cephal* = head

Synonym(s): *Kalchbrennera corallocephala, K. tuckii* var. *clathroides, Simblum clathratum*

ECOLOGY: Saprophytic, possibly also mycorrhizal.

DISTRIBUTION: Eastern Cape, KwaZulu-Natal and Mpumalanga, possibly more widespread. May be native to Africa; occurs in Ghana, Togo, Nigeria, Cameroon, Uganda, Democratic Republic of the Congo, Kenya and Angola.

HABITAT: Grows among plant litter in several habitats, on soil in maize fields, in acacia woodlands, and in grassy areas near forests; fruit bodies single or scattered.

DESCRIPTION: The scarlet head, which has multiple forked branches that surround a number of polygonal meshes, and the distinctive stipe make this species instantly recognisable. **Fruit body:** 3–11cm tall; stipe emerging from a subglobose to egg-shaped membraneous sac up to 4cm in diameter; egg attached below ground by thick mycelial strands, inner layer gelatinous, surface matted, fibrous, thin, tough, whitish, sac splitting irregularly at the apex to allow for the emergence of the stipe and fruit body; fruit body distinctly stipitate, consisting of a hollow, dome-shaped, latticed structure composed of transversely finely wrinkled arms; arms bearing simple or forked, erect appendages, or branches, at intersections, up to 2cm long, scarlet. **Stipe:** 3–11cm long, 1.5–4cm thick; cylindrical; surface wrinkled; white to yellow, becoming pink at the apex; hollow. **Volva:** persisting as remnants of the egg at the base of the stipe. **Flesh:** fragile, porose; white to off-white. **Smell:** rotten meat odour; smell attracts flies, which disperse the spores. **Spore mass:** mucilaginous; brown-olive; spore-bearing mass borne externally on branches.

SIMILAR SPECIES: Both *Aseroë rubra* and *Clathrus archeri* have red fruit bodies and a fetid odour.

EDIBILITY: Inedible, although eggs in the early stage of development may be edible.

The thick stipe is distinctive.

Brown-olive spore mass.

The viscous spore mass is sited on the surface of the lobes.

This young specimen is identifiable by the conical head and orange-red fused columns.

Liz Popich

Lysurus cruciatus (Lepr. & Mont.) Henn. 1902

Common names: Lizard's claw stinkhorn, lantern stinkhorn
Afrikaans: Akkediskloustinkhoring

Etymology: GREEK: *lysis* = loosening, *-urus* = pertaining to;
LATIN: *cruciatus* = tormenting

Synonym(s): *Anthurus cruciatus, A. sanctae-catharinae,
Lysurus argentinus, L. australiensis, L. pusillus, L. texensis*

ECOLOGY: Saprophytic, possibly also mycorrhizal.

DISTRIBUTION: Gauteng and Mpumalanga, possibly more
widespread. Occurs in Europe, Canada, USA, Costa Rica, Brazil,
Argentina, Australia and New Zealand.

HABITAT: Grows in grass, on compost, on straw, and among leaf
litter of broadleaved trees; fruit bodies single, grouped or clustered.

DESCRIPTION: Fragile and short-lived, the species is characterised
by the cylindrical stipe supporting a cluster of pointed arms
(resembling claws), the spore mass lining their inner surfaces.
Fruit body: 3–11cm tall; emerging from a globose to egg-shaped
membraneous sac up to 6cm in diameter; egg attached below
ground by thick mycelial strands, inner layer gelatinous, surface
matted, fibrous, thin, tough, white, sac tearing irregularly at the apex
to allow for the emergence of the stipe and fruit body; fruit body
distinctly stipitate; stipe dividing at the conical apex into 4–8 vertical
columns or arms, each 1–2.5cm long, curving outward, hollow; inner
surface convex, smooth; outer surface concave, grooved; white, then
orange-red to reddish brown. **Stipe:** 3–11cm long, 1.5–2cm thick;
cylindrical; whitish to cream; spongy, hollow. **Volva:** persisting as
remnants of the egg at the base of the stipe. **Flesh:** fragile, porose,
minutely chambered; white to off-white. **Smell:** putrid odour; smell
attracts flies, which disperse the spores. **Spore mass:** mucilaginous;
olive-brown, darker when dry; borne on inner surface of arms, not
extending to outer surface.

SIMILAR SPECIES: *Lysurus borealis, L. gardneri, L. mokusin* (none
described here).

EDIBILITY: Inedible, although eggs in the early stage of development
may be edible.

> **NOTES:** Similar to other stinkhorns, the putrid smell of the spore
> mass attracts flies, which distribute the spores.

A young specimen.

The arms, once separated, remain erect.

The viscid spore mass appears on the inner surface of the arms.

The head consists of 5–8 three-sided arms.

The slender, curved stipe appears white at first, becoming faintly pinkish or tinged with orange as the fungus matures. The olive-green spore mass is borne on the upper part of the stipe.

Mutinus caninus (Huds.) Fr. 1849

Common names: Dog stinkhorn, headless stinkhorn
Afrikaans: Hondstinkhoring

Etymology: LATIN: *mutinus* = penis; *caninus-* = relating to a dog

Synonym(s): *Aedycia canina, Cynophallus caninus, Phallus caninus, P. inodorus*

The stipe has a spongy texture.

ECOLOGY: Saprophytic.

DISTRIBUTION: Gauteng, possibly more widespread. Occurs in the UK, Europe, Canada, USA, Mexico, Costa Rica, Brazil, Russia, Japan, Australia and New Zealand.

HABITAT: Grows in gardens, on lawns, woodchips and mulch, and in broadleaved and coniferous forests, often near rotting stumps; fruit bodies grouped.

DESCRIPTION: In this species, the spore-bearing tip is not a separate structure, but merges with the stipe, helping to differentiate it from other stinkhorn species. **Fruit body:** 5–10cm tall, stipe emerging from an elongate to egg-shaped, or pear-shaped, membraneous sac 1–4cm in diameter; egg attached below ground by thick mycelial strands, inner layer gelatinous, surface leathery, pale yellow or off-white, sac splitting irregularly at the apex to allow for the emergence of the stipe and fruit body; spore-bearing cap 2cm tall, conical, apex pointed, surface reticulate, mucilaginous; fertile part initially covered with spore-bearing mass, soon disappearing to reveal the red to orange tip. **Stipe:** 5–10cm long, 1–1.5cm thick; cylindrical, bluntly narrowed at the tip, slender, curved; white at first, then tinged faintly yellowish or pinkish; spongy, hollow. **Volva:** persisting as remnants of the egg at the base of the stipe. **Flesh:** fragile, thin; whitish. **Smell:** slightly fetid odour; smell attracts flies, which disperse the spores. **Spore mass:** mucilaginous; olive-green.

SIMILAR SPECIES: Similar to other stinkhorns, but this species is usually taller and more slender and can be distinguished by the appearance of the red tip once the slimy spore mass disappears. The unpleasant odour is less pronounced than in other stinkhorns.

EDIBILITY: Inedible.

Mycelial strands grow at the base of the stipe.

As the spore-bearing slime starts to disappear in the mature fungus, the red to orange tip becomes conspicous.

The spore cap, separated from the stipe by an incipient net, is pocked and covered with the greenish-yellow spore mass.

Liz Popich

Phallus duplicatus (Bosc) Fr. 1811

Common names: Skirted stinkhorn, netted stinkhorn, wood witch, short-netted stinkhorn
Afrikaans: Netrokstinkhoring

Etymology: GREEK: *phallos* = erect penis; LATIN: *duplicatus* = having two parts
Synonym(s): *Dictyophora duplicata, Hymenophallus duplicatus, Phallus impudicus* var. *pseudoduplicatus*

Immature membraneous sac, or egg.

ECOLOGY: Saprophytic.

DISTRIBUTION: First reported in South Africa in Gauteng, but may be more widespread. Occurs in Europe, USA, Costa Rica and Russia.

HABITAT: Grows in gardens, on lawns, on woodchips and in broadleaved forests; fruit bodies single.

DESCRIPTION: The fragile, skirt-like netting hanging from the stipe just below the cap makes this species easy to identify.
Fruit body: 4–7cm tall; emerging from a globose to egg-shaped membraneous sac up to 4cm in diameter; egg attached below ground by thick mycelial strands, inner layer gelatinous, surface matted, fibrous, whitish, pinkish or yellowish, becoming ochraceous; sac splitting irregularly at the apex to allow for the emergence of the stipe and spore cap; cap thimble-shaped, hollow, open at the apex, surface pitted, with cavities, covered by the glutinous spore mass, eventually dissolving into a blackish, dense liquid and revealing the white surface underneath; net with large meshes, fragile, hangs curtain-like from the cap margin to more or less halfway down the stipe, quickly disappearing. **Stipe:** 4–7cm long, 1.5–3.5cm thick; cylindrical; white; spongy, hollow. **Volva:** persisting as remnants of the egg at the base of the stipe. **Flesh:** fragile, porose; white. **Smell:** fetid odour; smell attracts flies, which disperse the spores. **Spore mass:** mucilaginous; greenish yellow becoming olivaceous yellow.

SIMILAR SPECIES: *Phallus indusiatus* (not described here) has a longer, more pronounced skirt.

EDIBILITY: Inedible.

The sac splits, allowing the fruit body to emerge.

The volva remains at the base of the stipe.

A skirt-like net hangs from the stipe apex.

The spore cap, showing the opening at the apex, rises from the splitting sac.

The bright yellow stipe and the slightly tapered spore cap, containing the viscous spore mass, distinguish this species.

Phallus rubicundus (Bosc) Fr. 1826

Common names: Yellow stinkhorn, devil's stinkhorn
Afrikaans: Geelstinkhoring

Etymology: GREEK: *phallos* = erect penis; LATIN: *rubicundus* = red, ruddy, reddish

Synonym(s): *Ithyphallus rubicundus, Leiophallus rubicundus, Satyrus rubicundus*

Inedible

ECOLOGY: Saprophytic.

DISTRIBUTION: Western Cape, Eastern Cape, Gauteng, KwaZulu-Natal and Free State, possibly more widespread. Occurs in the USA, Brazil, Central Pacific Islands and Australia.

HABITAT: Grows on lawns and among grasses; fruit bodies single or scattered, sometimes grouped.

DESCRIPTION: This distinctive fungus is readily recognised by the yellow to apricot fruit body and the brown-olive, mucilaginous spore mass, which emits a strong, unpleasant odour. **Fruit body:** up to 20cm tall; emerging from a globose to egg-shaped membraneous sac 4.5–5.5cm in diameter; egg attached below ground by thick mycelial strands, inner layer gelatinous, surface matted, fibrous, whitish, or pink to purple; sac splitting irregularly at the apex to allow for the emergence of the stipe and spore cap; cap conical to thimble-shaped, membraneous, surface with longitudinal, irregular ridges, white, covered by the dark spore mass. **Stipe:** up to 20cm long, 1–2cm thick; cylindrical or tapering slightly toward the head; yellow, buff, salmon-orange or apricot. **Volva:** persisting as remnants of the egg at the base of the stipe. **Flesh:** soft, spongy, porose; concolorous with stipe. **Smell:** strong putrid odour; smell attracts flies, which disperse the spores. **Spore mass:** mucilaginous; brown to olivaceous.

A sac emerges next to a developing specimen (visible in the background).

SIMILAR SPECIES: *Itajahya rosea, Phallus impudicus* (neither described here), *Mutinus caninus*.

EDIBILITY: Inedible.

> **NOTES:** This stinkhorn species was originally described from South Carolina, USA, by French naturalist Louis Augustin Guillaume Bosc (1759–1828), who named it *Satyrus rubicundus*.

Stipe with salmon-orange colour variation.

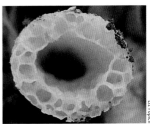

The yellow flesh is spongy and porose.

Clavulinopsis luteoalba (Rea) Corner 1950

Common name: Apricot club fungus
Afrikaans: Appelkoosknuppel

Etymology: LATIN: *clavula* = club, *-opsis* = resembling; *luteus* = golden yellow, *albus* = white
Synonym(s): *Clavaria luteoalba*, *Clavulinopsis filipes*

ECOLOGY: Saprophytic.

DISTRIBUTION: First reported in South Africa in Gauteng (Pretoria). Occurs in the UK, Europe and Russia.

HABITAT: Grows in grassy areas and forest humus and along mossy banks; fruit bodies single or grouped.

DESCRIPTION: Similar in appearance to other species in the genus, this fungus can be distinguished by the sharp, pale tip of the fruit body. **Fruit body:** 3–6cm tall, 0.1–0.4cm in diameter; rubbery, solid; spindle- or club-shaped, slender, wavy; surface vertically grooved; light to dark yellow or apricot, ochre when dry, but colour variable, tip pale or whitish. **Stipe:** absent. **Flesh:** firm; orangish. **Smell:** slight musty or sour odour. **Spores:** white.

Distinct longitudinal grooves can be seen on the surface of the fruit body.

SIMILAR SPECIES: *Clavulinopsis helvonia* (not described here) is almost indistinguishable, but the spores have prominent warts, unlike other *Clavulinopsis* species, which have smooth spores. *C. fusiformis* (not described here) is also similar, but can be distinguished by the clubs which are fused at the base. *C. helvola* and *C. laeticolor* are odourless (neither described here).

EDIBILITY: Inedible.

This club-shaped fungus can grow to about 6cm in height.

The fruit bodies occur singly or in groups.

The tips become sharply pointed.

Pterula subulata Fr. 1830

Common name: Angel hair coral
Afrikaans: Engelhaarkoraal

Etymology: GREEK: *pteron* = feather, wing, *-ula* = diminutive;
LATIN: *subula* = awl, *-ata* = resembling
Synonym(s): *Merisima subulatum*

ECOLOGY: Saprophytic.

DISTRIBUTION: First reported in South Africa in Gauteng (Pretoria), but may be more widespread. Occurs in the UK, Europe, Canada, USA, Russia and Japan.

HABITAT: Grows on dead or decaying branches, twigs, bark and leaves; fruit bodies in dense groups.

DESCRIPTION: This fungus is readily recognised by its white to amber coloration and the thin, multitiered branches that end in pointed tips. **Fruit body:** 1–6cm tall; shrub-like, tufts densely branched; branches 0.03–0.1cm wide, slender, cylindrical, erect, tapering upward, forming a thread-like, conical tip; surface waxy, becoming horny when dry; branches subdividing into several finer branches, whitish to pale brown or flesh-coloured. **Stipe:** 0.2–0.6cm long, 0.1–0.3cm thick; short, slender, somewhat flattened; flesh-coloured, drying black-brown. **Flesh:** tough, horny to cartilaginous. **Smell:** no distinctive odour. **Spores:** brown to cinnamon-brown or rusty brown.

EDIBILITY: Inedible.

A short, slender stipe supports the fruit body.

This species appears in dense groups.

The fruit body is densely branched, subdividing into multiple hair-like offshoots.

The branches taper upward.

The cylindrical branches are pinkish ochraceous to orangish pink; they later become powdery with maturing spores.

Ramaria formosa (Pers.) Quél. 1888

Common names: Salmon coral, beautiful clavaria, handsome clavaria, yellow-tipped coral fungus, pink coral fungus
Afrikaans: Koraalswam

Etymology: LATIN: *ramus* = branch, *-aria* = pertaining to; *formosus* = of beautiful form
Synonym(s): *Clavaria formosa, Corallium formosum, Merisma formosum*

Poisonous

ECOLOGY: Mycorrhizal.

DISTRIBUTION: Western Cape and Gauteng, possibly more widespread. Occurs in Europe, Canada, USA, Russia, Japan, Australia and New Zealand.

HABITAT: Grows in humus on the forest floor, particularly under broadleaved trees; fruit bodies single, scattered or grouped.

DESCRIPTION: Although the salmon-pink branches of this species are striking, it is very similar in appearance to other coral fungi; identification is best verified microscopically. **Fruit body:** 2–10cm tall, up to 12cm in diameter; fleshy; shrub-like, consisting of numerous branches; branches cylindrical, crowded, smooth at first, then becoming powdery with spores; pinkish ochraceous to orangish pink with yellowish tips, later brownish. **Stipe:** 1–3cm long, 0.2–0.6cm thick; fleshy; branched, smooth; whitish orange-pink, with a white base. **Flesh:** soft, dry, crumbly; white, tinged with pale orange, darkening slowly when exposed to air. **Smell:** no distinctive odour. **Spores:** ochraceous to pale yellow.

EDIBILITY: Poisonous; causes severe nausea, vomiting, diarrhoea and colicky pain when eaten.

Typical of coral fungi, the fruit body is shrub-like in appearance.

The branches of old, decaying specimens are hard and amber-coloured.

This species grows in humus-rich soil, particularly under broadleaved trees.

Hundreds of orange-yellow fruit bodies grouped on a decyaing log make for an impressive sight.

Calocera cornea (Batsch) Fr. 1827

Common names: Small stag's horn, tuning-fork jelly horn
Afrikaans: Stemvurkjelliehoring

Etymology: GREEK: *kalós* = beautiful, *cerae* = horn, projection, antenna; LATIN: *corneus* = horny
Synonym(s): *Calocera cornes, Corynoides cornea*

ECOLOGY: Saprophytic.

DISTRIBUTION: Western Cape, Eastern Cape, Gauteng, KwaZulu-Natal and Mpumalanga, possibly more widespread. Occurs in the UK, Europe, Canada, USA, Mexico, Costa Rica, Venezuela, Colombia, Ecuador, Brazil, Peru, Bolivia, Paraguay, Chile, Uruguay, Argentina, Russia, Japan, Papua New Guinea, Australia, New Zealand and Tenerife.

HABITAT: Grows on rotting and dead tree stumps and branches; fruit bodies grouped, occasionally clustered.

DESCRIPTION: When clustered or grouped in large numbers, the colour of the bright orange-yellow fruit bodies and the pointed tips, which are sometimes forked, make this species easy to identify.
Fruit body: 0.4–1cm tall; gelatinous-tough; horn- or awl-shaped, slender, erect, occasionally forked, often two or more fruit bodies appearing partially joined at their bases; bright orange-yellow, drying brownish orange and horny; dry fruit body can rehydrate when wet.
Flesh: gelatinous, elastic, slightly sticky; orangish yellow. **Smell:** no distinctive odour. **Spores:** white.

SIMILAR SPECIES: *Dacryopinax spathularia.*

EDIBILITY: Inedible.

The short branches are occasionally forked at the tips.

Two or more fruit bodies may become joined at their bases.

The resemblance of the fruit body to the antlers of a deer gives this fungus its common name of 'small stag's horn'.

The fruit bodies occur on dead stumps and branches.

Microscopic spores give the surface of the fruit body a white appearance.

When dry, this fungus becomes leathery, its colour changing from orange-yellow to orange-red.

Dacryopinax spathularia (Schwein.) G.W. Martin 1948

Common names: Fan-shaped jelly fungus, extruded jelly, yellow fingers, spatula-shaped yellow jelly
Afrikaans: Waaierjellieswam

Etymology: GREEK: *dacry* = tear, *pinax* = plank, tablet; LATIN: *spathula* = spatula or flat, broad knife, *-aria* = pertaining to

Synonym(s): *Catharellus spathularius, Guepinia spathularia, Guepiniopsis spathularia, Merulinus spathularius*

ECOLOGY: Saprophytic.

DISTRIBUTION: Western Cape and Gauteng, possibly more widespread. Occurs in the USA, Mexico, Costa Rica, Colombia, Ecuador, Brazil, India, Cambodia, Malaysia, Taiwan, Japan, South Korea, the Philippines, Indonesia, Australia, New Zealand, Kermadec Islands, Nigeria, Democratic Republic of the Congo, Ethiopia, Kenya and Zambia.

HABITAT: Grows on dead or decaying logs and stumps that have been stripped of their bark; fruit bodies grouped or clustered.

DESCRIPTION: This fungus is readily recognised by the spatulate shape of the fruit body. It can be distinguished microscopically from similar-looking species by its spore characters. **Fruit body:** 0.5–2.5cm tall, up to 1cm in diameter; gelatinous; spatula- to fan-shaped to spoon-like valves, simple or branched, flattened; yellow-orange to orange, drying to orange-red and becoming leathery. **Stipe:** 0.05–0.3cm in diameter; lateral; cylindrical to flattened; bright pale yellow to dark orange. **Flesh:** gelatinous, soft when wet, hard when dry; orange when fresh, darkening to orangish red when dry. **Smell:** no distinctive odour. **Spores:** white to pallid yellow.

SIMILAR SPECIES: *Calocera cornea.*

EDIBILITY: Edible; used in Chinese cuisine.

The fan shape of the fruit body is typical of this brightly coloured species.

Dacryopinax spathularia fruits on dead or decaying logs and stumps where it may form dense rows.

The spore-producing hymenium is borne on the external surface of the fruit body.

When wet, the fruit body becomes soft and jelly-like.

Sebacina schweinitzii (Peck) Oberw. 2017

Common names: False coral, jellied false coral
Afrikaans: Vals koraalswam

Etymology: LATIN: *sebum* = grease, tallow, wax; *-ina* = resembling; *schweinitzii* = after American botanist and mycologist Lewis David von Schweinitz (1780–1834), founder of North American mycological science

Synonym(s): *Sebacina pallida, Thelephora pallida, T. schweinitzii, Tremellodendron pallidum*

ECOLOGY: Mycorrhizal.

DISTRIBUTION: First reported in South Africa in Gauteng (Pretoria), but may be more widespread. Occurs in Canada, USA, Mexico, Honduras, Puerto Rico, Bolivia, China and Thailand.

HABITAT: Grows on bare soil in broadleaved forests; fruit bodies single or clustered.

DESCRIPTION: Resembling coral but classified as a jelly fungus, this species can be distinguished by the rubbery, branched fruit body, which is white in younger specimens and pale tan in older ones. **Fruit body:** 3–10cm tall, 5–15cm in diameter; tough-rubbery; coral-like, with numerous branches; branches round at first, then flattened, fused laterally at the bases; white or buff, turning yellowish or pale tan with age. **Stipe**: comprising multiple fused branches; arising from matted mycelium. **Flesh:** tough, pliant, solid; concolorous with fruit body. **Smell:** no distinctive odour. **Spores:** white.

EDIBILITY: Unknown.

NOTES: Although similar in appearance to coral fungi, *Sebacina schweinitzii* has been reclassified as a jelly fungus on the basis of its microscopic spore-bearing structure (basidium) being morphologically closer to that of jelly fungi. This has given rise to its common name 'false coral'.

Unknown

The branches become yellowish or pale tan with age.

Specimens cluster on bare soil under broadleaved trees.

The stipe supports multiple fused branches of the same colour.

Phaeotremella foliacea (Pers.) Wedin, J.C. Zamora & Millanes 2016

Common names: Leafy brain, jelly leaf, brown witch's butter
Afrikaans: Bruinheksebotter

Etymology: GREEK: *phaeo* = dark, dusky, *trema* = female pudendum, *-ella* = diminutive; LATIN: *folium* = leaf, *-acea* = resembling

Synonym(s): *Phaeotremella neofoliacea, P. skinneri, Tremella foliacea, T. neofoliacea*

ECOLOGY: Parasitic.

DISTRIBUTION: First reported in South Africa in Gauteng and KwaZulu-Natal, but may be more widespread. Occurs in the UK, Europe, Canada, USA, Russia, China, Japan, Australia and New Zealand.

HABITAT: Grows on stumps, logs and fallen branches of broadleaved and occasionally conifer trees; fruit bodies single or grouped.

DESCRIPTION: The reddish-brown colour and the flattened, undulating lobes make this fungus readily recognisable. **Fruit body:** 3–7cm tall, 4–12cm in diameter; flabby; comprising a complicated mass of wavy or leaf-like folds and lobes; glossy in fresh specimens, gelatinous and translucent when wet, bone hard and shrunken when dry, water can rehydrate desiccated specimens; reddish cinnamon to brown, vinaceous brown or tinged purple, paler when waterlogged. **Stipe:** absent. **Flesh:** gelatinous; concolorous with fruit body or slightly lighter. **Smell:** no distinctive odour. **Spores:** white to yellowish.

SIMILAR SPECIES: *Auricularia auricula-judae* is more solid and has fewer lobes. *Tremella fuciformisa* (not described here) can be distinguished by its white appearance and *Tremella mesenterica* by its yellow coloration.

EDIBILITY: Edible; considered flavourless, but can be used in soups.

The fruit body may become paler when wet.

A mass of wavy or leaf-like folds characterises this species.

The coloration of *Sirobasidium magnum* typically ranges from whitish or cream to orange-brown, finally becoming reddish brown.

Liz Popich

Sirobasidium magnum Boed. 1934

Common name: Jelly tube fungus
Afrikaans: Jelliebuisswam

Etymology: GREEK: *siros* = a pit for storing corn, trench,
LATIN: *basidium* = small pedestal; LATIN: *magnus* = great

Synonym(s): None

When wet, the lobes become transparent.

ECOLOGY: Saprophytic.

DISTRIBUTION: Gauteng, but may be more widespread. Occurs in Europe, Brazil, Thailand, Taiwan, Japan and the Philippines.

HABITAT: Grows on dead wood and plant litter; fruit bodies single, clustered or grouped.

DESCRIPTION: This small, gelatinous fungus can be distinguished by its whitish to reddish-brown fruit body, which is almost translucent.
Fruit body: 1–7cm in diameter; gelatinous, almost transparent when wet; resembling leaves; whitish to cream to light brown to orange-brown to reddish brown. **Stipe:** absent. **Flesh:** gelatinous; concolorous with the fruit body or slightly lighter. **Smell:** no distinctive odour. **Spores:** glassy and translucent in appearance.

EDIBILITY: Unknown.

The colour of old specimens tends to fade.

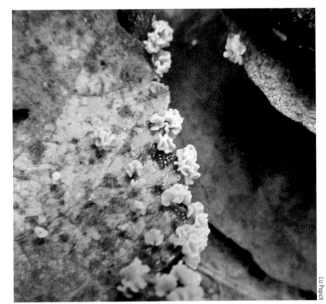

A group of fungi living on decayed wood.

The fruit body grows to about 7cm in width.

Tremella fuciformis Berk. 1856

Common names: Snow fungus, snow ear, snow wood ear, white tree ear, silver ear fungus, white mushroom
Afrikaans: Witjellieswam

Etymology: GREEK: *trema* = female pudendum, *-ella* = diminutive; LATIN: *fucus* = a kind of rock lichen, *-forma* = shape

Synonym(s): *Nakaiomyces nipponicus*

Edible

ECOLOGY: Parasitic.

DISTRIBUTION: First reported in South Africa in Gauteng and KwaZulu-Natal, but may be more widespread. Occurs in the USA, Mexico, Guatemala, Costa Rica, Panama, Brazil, Paraguay, Russia, Taiwan, China, Japan, the Philippines, Australia, New Zealand, Mauritania, Democratic Republic of the Congo and Mayotte Island.

HABITAT: Grows on dead wood of broadleaved trees where it is believed to parasitise *Hypoxylon*, a genus of ascomycetes; fruit bodies single, scattered or in small groups.

DESCRIPTION: The white, almost transparent, multilobed fruit body of this species makes it readily recognisable in rainy weather. When dry, it shrinks and may become leathery, making it more difficult to identify. **Fruit body:** 0.5–4cm tall, 1.5–7cm in diameter; comprising numerous convoluted lobes, forming a relatively rounded, ball-like mass that is attached by mycelial threads to the substrate, lobes often crisp at the edges; surface shiny, smooth, gelatinous when wet, shrivelling as it dries, sometimes becoming leathery; whitish or nearly translucent; spores develop over the entire surface of the lobes. **Stipe:** absent. **Flesh:** gelatinous; translucent white. **Smell:** no distinctive odour. **Spores:** white.

EDIBILITY: Edible; considered tasteless, but valued for its somewhat crunchy texture. It is popular in China where it traditionally features in sweet dishes.

MEDICINAL: *Tremella fuciformis* is primarily used in traditional Chinese medicine to increase fluids in the body and to treat conditions such as dry coughs, heart palpitations and high blood pressure. In Japan it is used to prevent atherosclerosis. *T. fuciformis* has been proven to contain anti-wrinkle properties, and extracts of this fungus are used in skincare products.

A wet specimen, showing the gelatinous, convoluted lobes.

The white to translucent colour is typical.

Tremella mesenterica (Schaeff.) Retz., Kongl. Vet. Acad. Handl. 1769

Common names: Witch's butter, yellow brain, jelly brain, golden jelly, yellow trembler
Afrikaans: Geeljellieswam

Etymology: GREEK: *trema* = female pudendum, *-ella* = diminutive; *mes-* = middle, *enteron* = intestine, *-ica* = pertaining to

Synonym(s): *Tremella lutescens*, *T. quercina*

ECOLOGY: Parasitic.

DISTRIBUTION: Western Cape, Gauteng and KwaZulu-Natal. Occurs in the UK, Europe, Canada, USA, Mexico, Costa Rica, Colombia, French Guiana, Argentina, Russia, India, Taiwan, China, Japan, Indonesia, New Caledonia, Australia and New Zealand.

HABITAT: Grows on dead and decaying wood of broadleaved trees where it parasitises the mycelium of wood-decomposing crust fungi; fruit bodies single or scattered.

The fruit body consists of a mass of irregular, soft, flabby lobes.

DESCRIPTION: The fruit body of this species is conspicuous only during or immediately after rainy weather when it absorbs water and swells to its full size. In dry weather it is dark, shrunken, hard and dormant. **Fruit body:** 0.5–4cm tall, 1–6cm in diameter; comprising a mass of irregular, soft, smooth lobes, attached to the substrate by mycelial threads; gelatinous and transparent when wet, horny and brittle when dry, rehydrating in rain; pale yellow to orange-yellow to golden yellow, paler when old, dark orange when dry; may occasionally produce true albino forms; spores produced on the surface, giving a powdery appearance. **Stipe:** absent.
Flesh: jelly-like when wet, brittle when dry; translucent to white to yellow. **Smell:** no distinctive odour. **Spores:** white to pale yellowish.

SIMILAR SPECIES: Unlike *Tremella mesenterica*, *T. aurantia* (not described here) has a stipe, and parasitises the mycelium of crust fungi such as *Stereum hirsutum*. Fruit bodies may resemble *T. fuciformis*.

EDIBILITY: Edible; considered flavourless, but can be used in soups.

Tremella mesenterica grows on broadleaved trees where it parasitises the mycelium of wood-decomposing crust fungi.

MEDICINAL: Biomedical researchers have found that certain polysaccharides (a type of carbohydrate) produced by *Tremella mesenterica* could be beneficial in preventing cancer and enhancing the immune system. These compounds are also reported to have antidiabetic, antiallergic and anti-inflammatory properties.

NOTES: Like other jelly fungi, this species dries up in the sun and rehydrates in the rain.

The yellow coloration of this fungus makes it easy to see in the wild.

Liz Popich

Auricularia auricula-judae grows on decaying wood of broadleaved and conifer trees.

Liz Popich

Folds develop as the fruit body ages and eventually dries out.

Auricularia auricula-judae (Bull.) Quél. 1886

Common names: Tree ear, wood ear, jelly ear, ear fungus, Judas ear, black fungus
Afrikaans: Judasoor

Etymology: LATIN: *auricula* = ear, *-aria* = characteristic of; *auricula* = ear, *judae* = after Judas, the Jew who it is said betrayed Jesus

Synonym(s): *Exida auricula-judae, Hirneola auricula-judae, Tremella auricula-judae*

ECOLOGY: Saprophytic.

DISTRIBUTION: Western Cape, Eastern Cape, Gauteng and KwaZulu-Natal, possibly more widespread. Occurs in the UK, Europe, Canada, USA, Mexico, Nicaragua, Costa Rica, Dominican Republic, Colombia, Brazil, Bolivia, Paraguay, Russia, India, Taiwan, China, Japan, South Korea, Australia, Norfolk Island, New Zealand, Tenerife, Ghana and Cameroon.

HABITAT: Grows on decaying broadleaved and conifer branches and logs; fruit bodies single or clustered in tiers or rows.

DESCRIPTION: The ear shape and the greyish-brown to reddish-brown colour of the fruit body when young or wet make this jelly ear easy to identify. **Fruit body:** 3–15cm tall, 4–6cm in diameter; gelatinous; sessile, attached centrally or laterally to the substrate by mycelial threads; typically ear-shaped, wavy and irregular; outer (upper) surface minutely hairy, often wrinkled, ribbed or veined, yellowish brown to reddish brown or greyish brown; inner (lower) surface spore-bearing, usually facing downward, hairless, often ribbed or veined, yellowish brown to reddish brown; folds developing as the fruit body ages and dries out, becoming hard and horny. **Stipe:** absent. **Flesh:** thin, rubbery, tough when fresh, hard, brittle when dry; light brown, almost flesh-coloured. **Smell:** no distinctive odour. **Spores:** white.

EDIBILITY: Edible; generally considered tasteless but soaks up flavour. It is highly prized in the East where it is cultivated and used in soups and vegetable dishes.

MEDICINAL: Research into the medicinal value of *Auricularia* species indicates that these fungi have antitumour, anticoagulant and cholesterol-lowering properties, and may be effective in the treatment of hypoglycaemia.

NOTES: Desiccated *Auricularia* fungi are capable of revival in wet weather and can continue to produce spores.

Edible

The spore-producing lower surface of the fruit body usually faces downward.

The upper surface is covered in downy hairs.

Liz Popich

The hairless inner surface of this fungus contains large cavities that form a honeycomb-like pattern.

Jean Stephenson

The fruit bodies are closely attached to the bark on which they grow.

Auricularia delicata (Mont. ex Fr.) Henn. 1893

Common names: Jelly ear, ear fungus, jelly ear fungus
Afrikaans: None

Etymology: LATIN: *auricula* = ear, *-aria* = characteristic of; *delicatus* = tender, soft, delicate

Synonym(s): *Auricula delicata, Auricularia auricula-judae* var. *delicata, Laschia delicata*

ECOLOGY: Saprophytic.

DISTRIBUTION: Eastern Cape, Gauteng and KwaZulu-Natal, possibly more widespread. Occurs in Mexico, Costa Rica, Panama, Colombia, Brazil, Peru, Bolivia, India, Thailand, Malaysia, China, Japan, South Korea, the Philippines, Indonesia, Australia, New Zealand, Côte d'Ivoire, Ghana, Nigeria and Zambia.

HABITAT: Grows on decaying branches and logs of broadleaved trees, commonest in damp localities; fruit bodies single or clustered in tiers or rows.

DESCRIPTION: This fungus is readily recognised by the porose, net-like or veined lower surface. **Fruit body:** 1.5–8cm tall, 1–8cm in diameter; sessile, attached centrally or laterally to the substrate; wavy, irregular, typically ear-shaped; outer (upper) surface finely hairy, often wrinkled, ribbed or veined, pinkish when fresh, then yellowish brown to reddish brown or greyish brown; inner (lower) surface hairless, net-like, ribbed, veined or honeycomb-like, with cavities, spore-bearing, usually facing downward, yellowish brown to reddish brown; folds develop as the fruit body ages and dries out. **Stipe:** absent. **Flesh:** thin, translucent, gelatinous-rubbery, becoming hard and tough when dry; tan to yellow-brown, blackish when dry. **Smell:** no distinctive odour. **Spores:** white.

SIMILAR SPECIES: Several other *Auricularia* species, including *A. mesenterica* (not described here), which is more or less bracket-shaped.

EDIBILITY: Edible.

MEDICINAL: *Auricularia delicata* has reputedly been used in Manipur, India, as a remedy for various gastrointestinal and liver ailments.

Edible

This species commonly grows on decaying wood in damp areas.

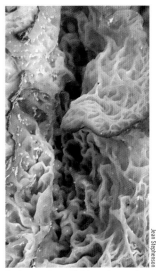

The inner surface, which faces downward, forms folds as the fruit body ages.

The outer surface is finely hairy and often wrinkled, ribbed or veined.

The edible *Auricularia polytricha* has a crunchy texture and is used in Chinese cooking. It is also available in powder form.

Auricularia polytricha (Mont.) Sacc. 1885

Common names: Cloud ear fungus, hairy wood ear, Chinese wood ear, black fungus
Afrikaans: Wolkoorswam

Etymology: LATIN: *auricula* = ear, *-aria* = characteristic of; GREEK: *poly* = many, *-tricha* = in three parts

Synonym(s): *Auricularia auricula-judae* var. *polytricha*, *Exidia polytricha*, *Hirneola polytricha*

ECOLOGY: Saprophytic.

DISTRIBUTION: Gauteng and KwaZulu-Natal, possibly more widespread. Occurs in Mexico, Costa Rica, Panama, Colombia, Brazil, Peru, Bolivia, India, Thailand, Malaysia, China, Japan, South Korea, the Philippines, Indonesia, Australia, New Zealand, Côte d'Ivoire, Ghana, Nigeria and Zambia.

HABITAT: Grows on decaying branches and logs of broadleaved trees, commonest in damp localities; fruit bodies in small groups.

DESCRIPTION: This fungus can be distinguished by the hairy ear-shaped fruit body and the purple-brown to violet colour of the spore-bearing surface. **Fruit body:** 1–6cm in diameter; sessile, attached centrally or laterally to the substrate; typically cup- or ear-shaped, thin, elastic; outer (upper) surface velvety, grey-brown to dark brown; inner (lower) surface smooth or wrinkled, spore-bearing, usually facing downward, purple-brown to violet, finally black; drying to grey-black, becoming very hard. **Stipe:** absent. **Flesh:** thin, gelatinous-rubbery, becoming hard and tough when dry; tan to yellow-brown, blackish when dry. **Smell:** no distinctive odour. **Spores:** white.

SIMILAR SPECIES: Other *Auricularia* species.

EDIBILITY: Edible.

MEDICINAL: This jelly ear has both antioxidant and antimicrobial properties. One of its compounds, vitamin K, is essential in inhibiting blood clots, thrombosis and embolism. Regular consumption can help prevent heart disease.

Edible

Fine hairs cover the outer surface.

The fungus is closely attached to the bark.

The small fruit bodies grow in damp areas on rotting logs, branches and twigs.

The lower, spore-bearing surface is typically oriented downward.

Helvella crispa (Scop.) Fr. 1822

Common names: Common white saddle, fluted white elfin saddle, common helvel
Afrikaans: Witsaalswam

Etymology: LATIN: *helvella* = a kind of pot-herb; *crispa* = curled
Synonym(s): *Costapeda crispa, Helvella alba, H. nivea, H. sulcata*

ECOLOGY: Saprophytic.

DISTRIBUTION: Gauteng and KwaZulu-Natal, possibly more widespread. Occurs in the UK, Europe, Canada, USA, Costa Rica, Russia, China, Japan and New Zealand.

HABITAT: Grows in broadleaved and coniferous forests; fruit bodies single or grouped.

DESCRIPTION: The cream to tan colour, undulating cap and robust, fluted stipe make this fungus easy to recognise. **Cap:** 1–5cm in diameter; brittle; convoluted and irregularly lobed, sometimes saddle-shaped, waxy appearance; margin free from the stipe, at first inrolled, then gradually spreading outward, often becoming wider at one end; upper surface smooth or slightly wrinkled, spore-bearing, cream to pale pinkish buff or tinged yellowish; lower surface scurfy, faintly hairy, off-white to slightly darker or greyish. **Stipe:** 3–10cm long, 0.8–3cm thick; cylindrical or tapering upward; surface smooth to wrinkled, pitted, deep, longitudinal furrows; white to off-white to tan, sometimes darkening slightly with age; chambered within; base robust, slightly rooting. **Flesh:** thin, brittle; white. **Smell:** slight mushroomy odour. **Spores:** white.

EDIBILITY: Suspect; known to cause stomach upsets when raw. This mushroom should only be eaten after being boiled in water or dried until crisp.

The stipe has deep, longitudinal furrows.

The upper surface of the cap is smooth.

A young specimen with an inrolled margin.

Several convolutions and undulations mark the cap.

Helvella lacunosa Afzel. 1783

Common names: Black elfin saddle, black helvella, slate grey saddle, common grey saddle
Afrikaans: Swartplooihoed

Etymology: LATIN: *helvella* = a kind of pot-herb; LATIN: *lucunosus* = pitted
Synonym(s): *Costapeda lacunosa, Helvella nigricans*

ECOLOGY: Saprophytic.

DISTRIBUTION: Western Cape and Gauteng, possibly more widespread. Occurs in the UK, Europe, Canada, USA, Mexico, Costa Rica, Russia, China and Japan.

HABITAT: Grows in broadleaved and conifer forests, often in open or disturbed areas near paths; fruit bodies single or scattered.

The cap margin is initially attached to the stipe at several points.

DESCRIPTION: The irregularly shaped black cap, partial fusion of the cap margin with the stipe, and deeply fluted, almost decorative, stipe make this fungus unmistakable. **Cap:** 4–8cm tall, 2–4cm in diameter; brittle; convoluted and irregularly lobed, sometimes saddle-shaped, waxy appearance; margin at first typically inrolled, then gradually spreading outward, often becoming wider at one end; upper surface smooth or wrinkled, spore-bearing, grey-black to black; lower surface smooth to faintly hairy, grey to greyish brown. **Stipe:** 4–8cm long, 1–2cm thick; cylindrical or tapering; surface smooth, with depressions, deep, longitudinal furrows; white to grey to dark grey; chambered within. **Flesh:** thin, brittle; grey to dark grey. **Smell:** no distinctive odour. **Spores:** white.

SIMILAR SPECIES: *Helvella suculata* and *H. vespertina* (not described here) also have blackish caps.

EDIBILITY: Poisonous. Many older field guides list this mushroom as edible, but more recent research indicates that it contains gyromitrin, a toxic compound that is potentially carcinogenic and can cause gastrointestinal distress in some individuals. Symptoms include vomiting, stomach cramps and diarrhoea about 6–12 hours after consumption.

NOTES: Some experts maintain that this mushroom can be detoxified and made edible by parboiling it for 3–5 minutes and then drying it before using it in cooking.

Deep grooves run down the length of the stipe.

The cap is sometimes saddle-shaped.

Morchella elata Fr. 1822

Common names: Black morel, fire morel
Afrikaans: Swart-moril

Etymology: GERMAN: *morchel* = morel mushroom; LATIN: *elatus* = elevating, to raise up

Synonym(s): None

ECOLOGY: Mycorrhizal and saprophytic.

DISTRIBUTION: First reported in South Africa in the Western Cape, Eastern Cape and KwaZulu-Natal, possibly more widespread. Occurs in the UK, Europe, Canada, USA, Mexico, Costa Rica, Peru, Argentina, Russia, Tajikistan, the Philippines, Australia and New Zealand.

HABITAT: Grows in soil (usually with a high pH value), often appearing in recently burned areas; fruit bodies single or scattered.

DESCRIPTION: The long, pointed cap, its surface covered with distinct ridges to form a honeycombed pattern, and the robust stipe help to distinguish this species from other similar-looking morels. **Cap:** 2.5–8cm tall, 2–5cm in diameter; conical, tapering at the top; pitted and with brown to black ridges, intergrown with the stipe, hollow; coloration of pits is brown to smoky grey, ridges are brown to black; yellowish brown, reddish or pink-tinged when young, becoming darker with age. **Stipe:** 2–8cm long, 1–3cm thick; surface mealy or granular; white; hollow. **Flesh:** thin, brittle; whitish. **Smell:** pleasant mushroomy odour. **Spores:** white to cream.

SIMILAR SPECIES: *Morchella augusticeps, M. conica, M. deliciosa, M. esclenta*, and *Gyromitra* and *Verpa* species (none described here).

EDIBILITY: Edible; excellent, with a crunchy texture and delicious nutty flavour. Although all *Morchella* species are edible, raw morels can cause digestive upsets and some people are allergic to them. The mushrooms are sold fresh and dried.

NOTES: *Morchella* species are distinguished from one another by their spore morphology.

The tapering conical cap is distinctive.

The pitted surface ranges from brown to smoky grey.

A basket of *Morchella elata*, prized throughout the world for its nutty flavour.

Kalaharituber pfeilii (Henn.) Trappe & Kagan-Zur 2005

Common names: Kalahari truffle, desert truffle, n'abba (Nama), haban (Khoe), hawan (Khoe)
Afrikaans: Kalahari truffel

Etymology: kalahari = after the Kalahari Desert where it was first discovered, LATIN: *tuber* = tumour, hump; *pfeilii* = after the German explorer, Count Joachim von Pfeil (1857–1924)
Synonym(s): *Terfezia pfeilii*

ECOLOGY: Mycorrhizal.

DISTRIBUTION: Northern Cape (Kalahari Desert). Native to southern Africa, occuring in the desert regions of Angola, Namibia and Botswana. Also occurs in Saudi Arabia (Arabian Desert) and Australia (Great Victoria, East Great Sandy, Tanami and Simpson deserts).

HABITAT: Grows underground in sandy soil and in the reddish sand dunes of the Kalahari and Namib deserts in southern Africa; forms a mycorrhizal relationship with a broad range of hosts, including *Citrullus lanatus* (tsamma melon), *Vachellia haematoxylon* (grey camel thorn), *Vachellia hebeclada* (candle thorn), *Senegalia mellifera* (black thorn), *Cynodon dactylon* (couch grass) and other grass species of the *Aristida, Eragrostis* and *Stipagrostis* genera; fruit bodies single or in small groups.

The pale yellow- to dark-brown fruit body is covered with a tough rind.

DESCRIPTION: The fruit body forms underground and its presence is indicated by cracks in the surface, often near tussocks of bushman grass (*Stipagrostis* species). The surface is finely velvety and may display yellowish wrinkles or cracks. **Fruit body:** 2.5–4cm in diameter, forming 5–40cm underground; subglobose, top- to pear-shaped, with a basal attachment scar, smooth; enclosed by a toughened rind (peridium); surface uneven or with vertical grooves, darkening and cracking; pale yellow-brown to dark brown. **Flesh:** soft cheese texture; white to cream, faintly marbled, turning yellow with conspicuous white, marbled veins; eventually disintegrates, leaving spores in the sand. **Smell:** strongly pleasant mushroomy odour. **Spores:** embedded in the flesh; pale brown.

Mature specimens, with a cross section showing the white flesh.

EDIBILITY: Edible; excellent, nutty flavour and texture similar to that of porcini. This species is eaten not only by humans, but also by meerkats, hyaenas, baboons and bat-eared foxes.

NOTES: *Kalaharituber pfeilii* is relatively common after the rains, from April to June. Once ripened, the fruit bodies dry out and shrivel with exposure to the sun. As they disintegrate, the spores are released and distributed by the wind, remaining dormant in years of drought. For centuries, this fungus has been collected by the San of the Kalahari Desert as part of their diet.

Harvested truffles, an excellent meal in the making.

Tuber melanosporum (Vittad.) 1831

Common names: Périgord black truffle, black winter truffle, black truffle
Afrikaans: Swart Périgord-truffel

Etymology: LATIN: *tuber* = tumour, hump; GREEK: *melana* = black, *spora* = spore, *-orum* = pertaining to
Synonym(s): None

Edible

ECOLOGY: Mycorrhizal.

DISTRIBUTION: First cultivated in South Africa in the Western Cape (Ceres, Franschhoek) and KwaZulu-Natal (Kokstad). Occurs in Spain, France, Italy, Slovenia, Croatia, Australia (Capital Territory) and New Zealand.

HABITAT: Grows in calcareous soil under Mediterranean oak species and other host trees, usually buried among roots a few centimetres beneath the surface; fruit bodies single.

DESCRIPTION: A most delicious truffle, this species is easily identified by the rough black surface, black flesh and incomparably fragrant smell. **Fruit body:** 2–8cm in diameter, but can grow bigger; averaging around 40g, but specimens of up to 250g have been found; covered with a rough rind consisting of hundreds of polygonal warts; black. **Flesh:** firm; pale at first, then turning violet-black, marbled brown with white veining which reddens when exposed to the air. **Smell:** powerful, fragrant odour. **Spore colour:** dark brown.

SIMILAR SPECIES: *Tuber aestivum* (not described here) has a similar black, polygonal, warty exterior.

EDIBILITY: Edible; the most delectable of all mushrooms and famous for its distinctive, piquant flavour. It is one of the most expensive foods in the world, with prices determined by the great demand for and short supply of this mushroom. It may be interesting to note that much of the commercial truffle oil is not made with truffles at all, but from several flavouring compounds, mixed with olive oil, to reproduce the aroma of this delicacy.

NOTES: The most royal of all truffles, this species gets its common name from the Périgord district in France. Experienced truffle hunters use the services of sow pigs and gun dogs – particularly the Italian dog breed Lagotto Romagnolo – to find these delicacies. *Tuber melanosporum* is now commercially available as inoculated seedlings, and is cultivated in evergreen oak or hazelnut plantations.

The rough black rind consists of hundreds of polygonal warts.

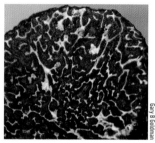

A cross section shows the marbled flesh.

A delicacy, *Tuber melanosporum* is one of the most expensive mushrooms in the world.

Daldinia concentrica (Bolton) Ces. & De Not. 1863

Common names: Cramp ball, King Alfred's cake, charcoal ball, carbon ball, tinder fungus, coal fungus
Afrikaans: Houtknoetsswam

Etymology: *daldinia* = after mycologist, cryptogamic botanist, and Swiss monk Agostino Daldini (1817–1895); LATIN: *concentricus* = concentric

Synonym(s): *Hemisphaeria concentrica, Hypoxilon concentricum, Stomatosphaeria concentrica*

ECOLOGY: Saprophytic.

DISTRIBUTION: Widespread in South Africa. Occurs in the UK, Europe, Canada, USA, Argentina, Russia, Japan, Australia and New Zealand.

HABITAT: Grows on old, dead logs and stumps of broadleaved trees, occasionally on bark of dying trees; fruit bodies single or grouped.

DESCRIPTION: The hard, rounded fruit body, which resembles charcoal, and the concentric silvery rings of the flesh are characteristic of this species. **Fruit body:** 2–5cm in diameter; tough, woody, older specimens brittle or crumbly and often cracked; broadly attached; hemispherical to round, lumpy or irregular; surface shiny, covered by tiny raised protrusions; reddish brown when young, becoming carbon-black. **Stipe:** absent. **Flesh:** hard, wooden; purplish brown with alternating silver-grey and black concentric zones; resembling charcoal in appearance and texture. **Smell:** no distinctive odour. **Spores:** black.

SIMILAR SPECIES: *Daldinia grandis* (not described here), also commonly known as 'cramp ball' and 'carbon ball', has similar concentric silvery zones, but it is usually shinier with purple tints, and its pores are slightly smaller. *D. vernicosa* (not described here) has a narrowed base and dark-brown and white, or sometimes grey, concentric zones.

EDIBILITY: Inedible.

MEDICINAL: A powder made from this fungus mixed with equal amounts of honey is said to be a remedy for chronic cough. One teaspoon of the mixture should be taken twice a day.

NOTES: While the common names 'charcoal ball', 'carbon ball', 'tinder fungus' and 'coal fungus' all allude to the fungus's appearance and ability to burn like charcoal when exposed to a flame, some of its other names are derived from folklore. The name 'cramp ball' has its origin in an ancient belief that the fungus could ward off cramps if carried on one's person.

Inedible

A young specimen, identifiable by the reddish-brown surface.

The fruit body turns carbon-black with age.

Cross section showing the concentric zones.

Isaria sinclairii (Berk.) Lloyd 1923

Common name: Vegetable cicada
Afrikaans: None

Etymology: GREEK: *isos* = equal, *-aria* = pertaining to; *sinclairii* = after the British surgeon, botanist and second colonial secretary of New Zealand, Andrew Sinclair (1794–1861)

Synonym(s): *Cordyceps caespitose, C. sinclairii, Torrubia caespitose*

Inedible

ECOLOGY: Parasitic.

DISTRIBUTION: First reported in South Africa in Gauteng (Pretoria), but may be more widespread. Occurs in Canada, China, Japan, South Korea, North Korea and New Zealand.

HABITAT: Emerges from cicada larvae just beneath the surface of the soil, which it parasitises and kills; fruit bodies single or in small groups.

DESCRIPTION: The white fruit body appears as a slender stipe, the tip of which is covered with white, tufted structures that contain the powdery spores. **Fruit body:** 2–4cm tall, 0.2–0.4cm in diameter; stipe with tufts on the upper part emerges from larvae buried shallowly in the soil; tufts containing powdery spores are borne on specialised stipes called conidiophores; white. **Stipe:** attached to remnant of parasitised pupae or larvae host; branched or unbranched; orange or yellow, brown toward the base. **Flesh:** thin, fibrous. **Smell:** no distinctive odour. **Spores:** white.

SIMILAR SPECIES: *Isaria fumosorosea* (not described here) occurs on buried larvae and pupae of more than 25 insect families, usually in open grassy areas or under trees.

EDIBILITY: Inedible.

MEDICINAL: *Isaria sinclairii* produces myriocin, which has powerful immunosuppressive properties. A synthetic derivative of this chemical compound, fingolimod, was approved by the US Food and Drug Administration (FDA) for use in the treatment of multiple sclerosis. Extracts of this mushroom are also used in traditional Chinese and Tibetan medicine.

> **NOTES:** *Isaria sinclairii* is an entomopathogenic fungus, meaning that it can disable or kill its insect host, specifically a cicada larva, by parasitising it. It does this by infecting the host, which is lodged just below the surface of the soil, with its spores. The fungus grows inside the host until it completely fills the cavity with fungal mycelium. Once the larva is dead, a stipe, carrying white spore-bearing structures at its apex, rises from the soil. The cycle is repeated when the mature fungus releases white, powdery spores, which fall to the ground, ready to infect other cicada larvae.

The fruit bodies arise from the larvae of cicadas buried in soil.

The apex is covered with powdery, white tufted structures containing the spores.

The stipe is slender, ending at the apex in tufted branches.

Poronia oedipus (Mont.) Mont. 1856

Common names: Nail fungus, black dung button, small dung button
Afrikaans: Spykerswam

Etymology: GREEK: *poros* = callus, soft stone, *-onia* = pertaining to; GREEK: *oidipous* = swollen foot

Synonym(s): *Hypoxylon oedipus*

Inedible

ECOLOGY: Saprophytic.

DISTRIBUTION: First reported in South Africa in Gauteng, but may be more widespread. Occurs in Mexico, Panama, Galápagos Islands, Ecuador, French Guiana, Bolivia, Chile, Brazil, Australia and New Zealand.

HABITAT: Grows on herbivore dung; fruit bodies single or grouped.

DESCRIPTION: Resembling a nail, this fungus can be identified by the dark-grey to black surface colour, tapering stipe and apical disc that is studded with tiny spore chambers. **Fruit body:** 0.85–3.25cm tall; tough, hard, not woody; apical disc flat or dish-shaped; upper surface slightly raised, studded with perithecia (tiny spore chambers), pale grey to pinkish when fresh, drying darker; perithecia punctuated with small black holes (ostioles) through which spores are released; ostiole slightly protuberant; lower surface smooth, dark grey-brown. **Stipe:** 0.85–3.25cm long, 0.1–0.2cm thick; tiny, club-shaped, broadening toward the base. **Smell:** unknown. **Spore mass:** blackish brown.

SIMILAR SPECIES: *Poronia punctata* (not described here) is larger.

EDIBILITY: Inedible.

This species grows only on herbivore dung.

This tiny mushroom, with its cylindrical stipe and disc-like cap, has the appearance of a nail.

The cap surface is studded with small black holes through which the spores escape.

Xylaria hypoxylon (L.) Grev. 1824

Common names: Candle-snuff fungus, stag's horn
Afrikaans: Takbokgeweiswam

Etymology: GREEK: *xyl* = wood, LATIN: *-aria* = pertaining to;
GREEK: *hypo-* = under, *xylon* = pertaining to wood

Synonym(s): *Clavaria hypoxylon, Sphaeria hypoxylon,
Xylosphaera hypoxylon*

ECOLOGY: Saprophytic.

DISTRIBUTION: Gauteng and KwaZulu-Natal, possibly more
widespread. Occurs in the UK, Europe, USA, Mexico, Costa Rica,
Panama, Brazil, Russia, India, Japan, Australia and New Zealand.

HABITAT: Grows on dead wood and on rotting logs and stumps of
coniferous and broadleaved trees; fruit bodies grouped.

DESCRIPTION: Growing in small, conspicuous groups, this fungus
is easily identified by its flattened stipe, which usually, although not
always, branches into several pointed, antler-like extensions. **Fruit
body:** 1–6cm tall, 0.1–0.4cm in diameter; tough, hard; cylindrical or
narrowly club-like, erect, slender; emerges vertically as a flattened
stipe, forking into 2–5 extensions, antler-like; asci (microscopic
sac-like structures containing spores) borne in flask-like structures
in the fruit body (usually in the upper portion); white and powdery
when young, eventually becoming black and minutely roughened.
Stipe: downy, base hairy; dark brown, base black. **Flesh:** leathery;
white to whitish. **Smell:** no distinctive odour. **Spores:** black.

SIMILAR SPECIES: *Xylaria polymorpha* produces thicker, finger-like
clubs. Some coral fungi, such as those of the genus *Clavaria*, can
produce similar slender, forked fruiting bodies.

EDIBILITY: Inedible; too small and tough.

The flattened stipe sometimes divides into
several antler-like branches at the apex.

The slender fruit bodies grow on
decaying wood.

The cross section of a mature fungus, showing the
white flesh in which the asci are embedded.

A young specimen appears greyish and
powdery due to the formation of spores.

Xylaria polymorpha (Pers.) Grev. 1824

Common names: Dead man's fingers, devil's fingers
Afrikaans: Swartknuppelswam

Etymology: GREEK: *xyl* = wood, LATIN: *-aria* = pertaining to; GREEK: *poly* = many, *morphé* = shape, form

Synonym(s): *Hypoxylon polymorphum*, *Sphaeria polymorpha*, *Xylosphaera polymorpha*

ECOLOGY: Saprophytic.

DISTRIBUTION: Gauteng, KwaZulu-Natal and Mpumalanga. Occurs in the UK, Europe, USA, Mexico, Costa Rica, Cuba, Colombia, Brazil, Russia, India, Japan, Australia, New Zealand, Nigeria and Tanzania.

HABITAT: Grows on rotting wood, including roots and buried wood; fruit bodies scattered or grouped, sometimes clustered.

DESCRIPTION: This small, black, finger-like fungus is difficult to tell apart from other species in the *Xylaria* genus, and may only be differentiated on microscopic features. **Fruit body:** 3–8cm tall, 1–3cm in diameter; tough, woody, hard; erect, finger-like or club-shaped, sometimes twisted or irregular, single-stemmed or branched, with 2–5 branches clustered together; surface pimpled where fruiting bodies protrude from the substrate; asci (microscopic sac-like structures containing spores) borne in flask-like structures embedded in the fruit body; covered with a whitish to greyish or brownish powder when young, sometimes with greenish or bluish tinges, black when mature. **Stipe:** short, narrow; black. **Flesh:** corky, hard; white. **Smell:** no distinctive odour. **Spores:** black.

SIMILAR SPECIES: *Xylaria longipes* (not described here) is similar but the finger-like extensions are more slender.

EDIBILITY: Inedible; too hard and woody.

NOTES: The white to grey or brown powder that coats *Xylaria* fruit bodies is easily rubbed off once the specimens mature.

The fruit body arises from a substrate of rotting wood.

The outer surface is hard and crust-like.

A fine powder covers the young fruit bodies.

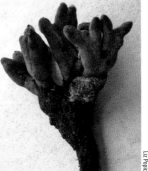

A cluster of freshly dug-up fruit bodies.

The fruit body turns black with age.

Peziza vesiculosa Bull. 1790

Common names: Bladder cup fungus, blistered cup fungus, bladder elf cup, common dung cup
Afrikaans: Miskomswam

Etymology: GREEK: *pezis* = sessile mushroom; LATIN: *vesicula* = blister, bladder, *-osa* = denoting abundance
Synonym(s): *Aleuria isochroa, A. vesiculosa, Galactinia vesiculosa*

Suspect

ECOLOGY: Saprophytic.

DISTRIBUTION: Gauteng (Pretoria), possibly more widespread. Occurs in the UK, Europe, USA, Brazil, Russia, Japan, Australia and New Zealand.

HABITAT: Grows on herbivore dung, old straw and well-manured or composted soil; fruit bodies single or grouped, sometimes clustered.

DESCRIPTION: This pale-brown fungus is readily recognised by its distinctive bladder-like shape and tightly rolled, curved margin.
Fruit body: 1–4cm tall, 1–8cm in diameter; fleshy; more or less spherical at first, then opening to cup-shaped; margin inrolled, intricately folded, twisted, or coiled; outer surface mealy, granular, whitish to pale buff; inner surface smooth or wrinkled toward the centre, yellowish to yellow-brown to pale ochraceous yellow, translucent when wet, darker brown with age. **Stipe:** absent or present as a narrowed, basal point of attachment extending into the substrate. **Flesh:** brittle, fragile, soft; light buff. **Smell:** no distinctive odour. **Spores:** white.

SIMILAR SPECIES: *Peziza domiciliana* (not described here) is not as rounded.

EDIBILITY: Suspect; poisonous when raw. Some field guides list this mushroom as edible if well cooked.

The outer surface is granular and has a mealy appearance.

Dung is one of the preferred habitats of this fungus.

If present, the stipe appears as a narrowed, basal point of attachment.

The inner surface is smooth and translucent when wet.

Scutellinia scutellata (L.) Lambotte 1887

Common names: Eyelash cup, molly eye-winker, scarlet elf cap, eyelash fungus
Afrikaans: Gewimperde kommetjieswam

Etymology: LATIN: *scutella* = dish, *-inia* = relating to; *scutellata* = covered with small plates

Synonym(s): *Ciliaria scutellata, Patella scutellata, Peziza aurantiaca, P. scutellata*

ECOLOGY: Saprophytic.

DISTRIBUTION: Gauteng and KwaZulu-Natal, possibly more widespread. Occurs in the UK, Europe, USA, Argentina, Russia, Japan, Australia, New Zealand and Tenerife.

HABITAT: Grows on moist logs of broadleaved trees, sometimes near water or marshy places, and on herbivore dung, sometimes attached to old bracket fungi; fruit bodies grouped or clustered.

DESCRIPTION: The orange-red colour and the long, dark-brown hairs along the margin of the cup distinguish this species. **Fruit body:** up to 0.2cm tall, 0.2–1cm in diameter; sessile; initially somewhat concave, flattening to a shallow cup, eventually disc-shaped; margin with stiff, dark-brown hairs that turn inward when immature and outward when fully mature; semitranslucent; inner (upper) surface smooth, produces spores, bright orange-red; outer (lower) surface pale orange-brown. **Stipe:** absent. **Flesh:** thin, fragile; pale brown. **Smell:** no distinctive odour. **Spores:** white.

SIMILAR SPECIES: *Anthracobia melaloma* is similar in colour, but is much smaller.

EDIBILITY: Inedible; too small to be of culinary interest.

NOTES: The pigment carotene, important for photosynthesis in plants and fruits, is responsible for the orange-red colour of this fungus.

This species grows on moist logs, sometimes near water or marshy places.

A dense row of stiff, dark-brown hairs grows along the rim of the cup.

A bright orange-red fungus, *Scutellinia scutellata* is initially somewhat concave, before flattening out to become disc-shaped.

This fungus reaches about 1cm in diameter.

Anthracobia melaloma (Alb. & Schwein.) Arnould, Bull. 1893

Common names: Burn site ochre cup, charcoal eyelash
Afrikaans: Gewimperde koolkommetjieswam

Etymology: GREEK: *anthrac* = coal, carbon; *mela* = black, *loma* = fringe, margin

Synonym(s): *Humaria melaloma, Humariella melaloma, Lachnea melaloma, Patella melaloma*

ECOLOGY: Saprophytic.

DISTRIBUTION: First reported in South Africa in Gauteng (Pretoria), but may be more widespread. Occurs in the UK, Europe, Canada, USA, Brazil, Argentina, British Virgin Islands, Russia, India, Australia and New Zealand.

HABITAT: Grows on burned ground and burned wood, and sometimes in recent charcoal beds; fruit bodies grouped.

DESCRIPTION: The tiny orange cups, appearing in abundance after a fire, are characteristic. **Fruit body:** 0.1–0.3cm in diameter; sessile; shallowly cup- to disc-shaped, then flattened; inner (upper) surface bright yellowish orange; outer (lower) surface studded with tiny holes, brownish hairs around the edge. **Stipe:** absent. **Flesh:** thin; orange, base paler. **Smell:** no distinctive odour. **Spores:** white.

EDIBILITY: Suspect.

> **NOTES:** The appearance of this fungus after fires helps to stabilise the soil by profuse growth of the mycelium. The mycelial mats appear to play a role in binding soil particles, which minimises movement in the substrate and may prevent erosion in damaged areas.

Tufts of short, brownish hairs appear around the edge and on the lower surface of the cup.

The tiny orange fruit bodies are cup-shaped before becoming plane.

This brightly coloured species is conspicuous on soil or wood damaged by fire.

The luminous yellow-orange colour of this species makes it easy to identify.

Chlorociboria aeruginosa (Oeder) Seaver ex C.S. Ramamurthi, Korf & L.R. Batra 1958

Common names: Blue-green elf cup, blue-green wood stain
Afrikaans: Groenhoutkomswam

Etymology: GREEK: *chloros* = green, greenish yellow, *cibor* = drinking cup; LATIN: *aereuginis* = made of copper, *-osa* = denoting abundance

Synonym(s): *Chlorosplenium aeruginascens*, *C. discoideum*, *Peziza aeruginascens*

ECOLOGY: Saprophytic.

DISTRIBUTION: Mpumalanga, possibly more widespread. Occurs in the UK, Europe, Canada, USA, Mexico, Costa Rica, Brazil, Argentina, Russia, Japan, Papua New Guinea, South Korea and Australia.

HABITAT: Grows mostly on the rotting or dead wood of pine trees; fruit bodies scattered in colonies.

DESCRIPTION: The striking, bluish-green colour of this species, imparted to the wood on which it grows, makes it instantly recognisable. Even when it is not fruiting, the blue-green stains on the substrate advertise its presence. **Fruit body:** 0.1–1.2cm in diameter; goblet- to cup- to disc-shaped, becoming flattened with age; margin becoming wavy or irregular; verdigris, turquoise to greenish or olivaceous, lower surface lighter in colour. **Stipe:** up to 0.6cm long, 0.1–0.2cm thick; central to slightly excentric; concolorous with cup. **Flesh:** thin; orange-yellow. **Smell:** no distinctive odour. **Spores:** white.

SIMILAR SPECIES: *Chlorociboria aeruginascens* (not described here) can only reliably be distinguished by microscopic examination.

EDIBILITY: Inedible.

NOTES: The mycelium of this fungus imparts a greenish to turquoise colour to the substrate on which it grows. The wood stained in this manner is sought after for use in decorative woodwork such as marquetry. It is also a feature of Tunbridge ware, a form of delicate inlaid woodwork (mostly in the form of boxes) created between 1830 and 1900 in the Tonbridge area in Kent, Britain.

A thick, central to somewhat excentric stipe attaches the mushroom to the substrate.

A colony of *Chlorociboria aeruginosa* carpets a substrate of dead wood.

Young specimens, showing a smooth inner surface and relatively wavy margins.

Wood stained green or turquoise by *Chlorociboria aeruginosa* is highly prized by wood-turners.

Liz Popich

Pilobolus crystallinus grows in the dung of plant-eating mammals.

Liz Popich

The dark spore capsule sits atop a small fluid-filled sac at the tip of the hypha, a special type of thread-like filament. The spore capsule is discharged when the sac ruptures, shooting the capsule into the air.

Pilobolus crystallinus (H.F. Wigg.) Tode 1784

Common names: Hat-thrower fungus, dung cannon, cap throwing fungus
Afrikaans: Hoedgooiswam

Etymology: GREEK: *pilos* = a hair, *bôlos* = lump; LATIN: *crystallus* = clear ice, glass, *-inus* = resembling

Synonym(s): *Pilobolus crystallinus* var. *hyalosporus*, *P. crystallinus* var. *kleinii*

Inedible

ECOLOGY: Saprophytic.

DISTRIBUTION: Widespread in South Africa. Occurs in the UK, Europe, Canada, USA, Brazil and New Zealand.

HABITAT: Grows in dung of herbivores; fruit bodies in large clusters.

DESCRIPTION: The diminutive, unbranched fruit body is capped with a black spore capsule. It is only when these microfungi appear in a large mass on the substrate that they become conspicuous.
Fruit body: up to 0.5cm tall; attached in the substrate to an ovoid to globose structure (trophocyst) by a long, rhizoidal extension; a specialised hypha, or sporangiophore, emerges from the base, bearing the spore capsule (sporangium); the hypha is straight, never branched; spore capsule sited on the top of a fluid-filled sac (vesicle) at the apex, hemispherical to ovoid, with a smooth wall, black; vesicle ovoid to globose, two rings of orange pigment at the base and apex of the vesicle function to orientate the hypha toward the brightest light so that, when the capsule is discharged, it won't encounter obstructions in its path. **Spores:** yellow.

SIMILAR SPECIES: *Pilobolus hyalosporus, P. kleinii* and *P. longipes* (none described here) look very similar and can be distinguished only by means of a microscope.

EDIBILITY: Inedible.

Dung covered with tiny fruit bodies.

The fruit bodies reach a height of up to 0.5cm.

NOTES: This microfungus earns its common name 'hat-thrower fungus' from its specialised form of spore dispersal. As these fungi grow in herbivore dung, they rely on grazing mammals to consume their spores in order to complete their life cycle. The spore capsule is discharged with great velocity away from the fruit body onto the surrounding vegetation where it can be ingested by a grazing animal. Germination takes place as the spores pass through the digestive system. By the time the fungus emerges in a pile of dung, it rapidly colonises the substrate before repeating the life cycle. The fungi rarely reach 0.5cm in height, but can propel their spore capsules over a distance of at least 2m.

The dark spore capsule is borne on a fluid-filled sac called the vesicle.

MUSHROOM RECIPES

RICH CREAMY MUSHROOM SOUP
Serves 4

1 Tbsp olive oil
500g wild mushrooms, half of them sliced, the rest
    roughly chopped
3 cloves garlic, chopped
pinch of fresh thyme, finely chopped
salt and pepper
2 Tbsp butter
2 Tbsp flour
4 cups vegetable stock (or chicken)
½ cup cream
thyme or Italian parsley, finely chopped

1. In a large pot combine the olive oil, mushrooms,
   garlic, thyme and a pinch of salt and pepper. Sauté
   over medium heat until all the mushrooms' moisture
   has been released and has evaporated, and the
   mushrooms become dark brown.
2. Add the butter; stir over medium heat for 2 minutes.
3. Add the flour, stir for a few minutes but don't let
   it burn.
4. Add the vegetable stock slowly until the roux absorbs
   it all. Bring to a simmer, then stir in the cream.
5. Serve with a sprinkle of finely chopped thyme or
   Italian parsley.

Suggested mushrooms: blusher (p. 41), horse
mushroom (p. 45), pine ring (p. 133), pine bolete
(p. 190), granular stalk bolete (p. 193)

PASTA WITH WILD MUSHROOMS & GARLIC
Serves 4

200g spaghetti (or any pasta of your choice)
½ Tbsp olive oil
4 cloves garlic, finely chopped
½ onion, finely chopped
250g small wild mushrooms, whole
salt and black pepper to taste
2 Tbsp fresh cream
25g Parmesan cheese, finely grated
fresh herbs

1. Cook the pasta in boiling salted water until al dente.
   Drain, reserving a cupful of cooking water.
2. Heat the olive oil in a large nonstick frying pan; add
   the garlic, onion and mushrooms. Season with salt
   and pepper, and cook for a few minutes or until
   golden, tossing regularly.
3. Remove from the pan. Add a splash of reserved
   cooking water and the cream to the pan, then reduce
   until slightly thickened.
4. Mix the drained pasta with the mushrooms,
   thickened sauce and half the Parmesan cheese.
   Season to taste.
5. Serve sprinkled with the remaining Parmesan and a
   handful of herbs.

Suggested mushrooms: porcini (p. 177), bay bolete
(p. 181), poplar bolete (p. 183), golden bolete (p. 187),
cow bolete, (p. 191), slippery jack (p. 195)

Gary B Goldman

MUSHROOM BOURGUIGNON

Serves 4

25g butter
olive oil
100g fresh porcini mushrooms, cubed
500g mixed wild mushrooms, roughly chopped, smaller
    ones left whole
1 onion, finely chopped
2 large potatoes, peeled and cut into 1cm cubes
2 cloves garlic, peeled and chopped
6 sprigs fresh thyme
2 fresh bay leaves
1 Tbsp tomato purée
500ml red wine
cornflour (for thickening)
salt and black pepper to taste
25g Parmesan cheese, finely grated

1. Heat half the butter with 1 Tbsp oil in a pan over medium heat. Fry the mushrooms in batches until coloured but still firm; don't overcook them. Add oil between batches. Remove and set aside.
2. Heat the remaining butter in the same pan and sauté the onion till golden. Add the potatoes and garlic.
3. Add the thyme, bay leaves, tomato purée and wine.
4. Simmer for 25 minutes, or until the wine has reduced slightly and the vegetables are cooked through. Add a little cornflour to thicken if necessary.
5. Stir in the cooked mushrooms, along with any juices, heating through for a couple of minutes. Season to taste.
6. Serve with a little grated Parmesan cheese.

Suggested mushrooms: prince (p. 47), smooth parasol (p. 63), shrimp russula (p. 143), wood blewit (p. 145), porcini (p. 177), or any other edible wild mushrooms of your choice

MARINATED WILD MUSHROOMS

1kg wild mushrooms, thoroughly washed
2 Tbsp salt
3–5 bay leaves
15–20 black peppercorns
6–8 cloves
1 Tbsp dill seeds or a small bunch fresh dill
spirit vinegar

1. Place the mushrooms in a pot, just cover with water, and boil for 1 hour.
2. Add the rest of the ingredients and boil for another 30–40 mins.

Logan Scott

3. Fill two 500g sterilised glass jars with the mushroom mixture and add 1–2 Tbsp spirit vinegar before closing the jars.
4. Allow to cool, then store the jars in a cool area or in the fridge.
5. Delicious served with potato mash, cheered up with a shot of vodka.

Suggested mushrooms: Any excess edible wild mushrooms, especially blusher (p. 41), field mushroom (p. 51), pine ring (p. 133), porcini (p. 177), poplar bolete (p. 183)

GARLIC MUSHROOM KEBABS

Makes 6

2 Tbsp balsamic vinegar
2 Tbsp olive oil
3 fat cloves garlic, sliced lengthwise
1 tsp fresh oregano, chopped
1 tsp fresh basil, chopped
coarse salt and black pepper to taste
1kg assorted wild mushrooms
1 Tbsp chopped fresh parsley (or other fresh herbs
    of your choice)

1. In a large bowl, whisk together the balsamic vinegar, olive oil, garlic, oregano and basil; season with salt and pepper to taste. Stir in the mushrooms and leave for 10–15 minutes.
2. Meanwhile, heat a heavy-duty pan on the stove – not too hot.
3. Thread the mushrooms onto skewers, alternating different species, interspersed with garlic.
4. Put a little olive oil in the heated pan, then add the kebabs. Fry gently and slowly, turning regularly until brown on all sides.
5. Serve immediately, garnished with parsley or other fresh herbs.

Suggested mushrooms: Any of the edible boletes, especially the larger specimens

GLOSSARY OF TERMS

adnate broadly attached to the stipe (gills).

adnexed narrowly attached to the stipe (gills).

anastomosing forming an angular network by dividing and rejoining (ridges, gills).

apical at the tip or apex.

applanate flattened.

appressed closely pressed to the surface.

Ascomycota a major group (phylum) of fungi that produce spores in asci; includes most moulds, mildews, lichens, and yeasts and a few large forms such as cups, discs, flasks, morels, saddles and truffles.

ascus (pl. **asci**) a microscopic sac-like structure in which the spores of ascomycete fungi develop.

Basidiomycota a major group (phylum) of fungi that form spores on basidia; includes the majority of familiar cap-and-stipe mushrooms and other fungi.

basidium (pl. **basidia**) cells that produce the spores in basidiomycete fungi.

bolete fungus with a firm, dome-shaped cap and pores rather than gills.

calyptra cap; hood-like structure to which the spore mass is attached.

cartilaginous not pliant; tough-brittle; making a noise when broken.

central stipe attached at the centre of the cap.

clathroid lattice; a regularly repeated three-dimensional arrangement or pattern.

close spaced close together, between crowded and distant (gills).

concolorous having the same colour.

crenate edge with rounded teeth.

crenulate delicately crenate.

crisped finely wavy.

crowded arranged extremely close together; full (gills).

cuticle outermost layer of cap or stipe.

decurrent extending down the stipe below the point of attachment (gills).

deliquesce liquify after maturing.

depressed central part of the cap sunken.

detersile removable without leaving a residue or scar.

disc central part of the cap surface.

distant spaced far apart (gills).

effused-reflexed spreading over the surface with the margin turned away from the surface.

entire smooth and even (margin).

excentric stipe not centrally attached to the cap.

exoperidium the expanded outer layers or outermost wall of fruit bodies of puffballs, earthstars and similar fungi.

fairy ring mushrooms growing naturally in a circle.

fibril fine thread.

fibrillose covered in, or composed of, fibrils.

flexuous bent repeatedly; winding.

floccose covered with little woolly tufts.

free not attached to the stipe; not reaching the stipe (gills).

fruit body the spore-bearing structure of a fungus, the main part of which is the mycelium that lies beneath the soil, within roots and branches of trees, or within rotting matter.

gill a plate-like appendage on the underside of the cap of a mushroom and bearing the hymenium; lamella.

glabrous hairless; without ornamentation.

gleba (pl. **glebae**) the inner, fertile portion (spore-bearing mass) of the fruit body of gasteroid fungi.

glebifer organ that produces the sticky spore-filled slime (gleba) on a stinkhorn.

globose spherical or globe-shaped.

glutinous sticky; covered with a substance which turns sticky when wet.

granular covered with small particles.

hirsute covered with long hairs.

host living organism harbouring a parasite.

hygrophanous having a water-soaked appearance when wet; sometimes resulting in a colour change of the mushroom tissue, especially the cap surface.

hymenium the layer of fertile cells that produce the spores.

hymenophore a collective term for the fleshy structures that bear the hymenium; the spore-bearing structure; includes smooth surfaces, gills, folds, tubes or teeth.

hypha (pl. **hyphae**) one or more filamentous cells that make up the mycelium.

incurved curved or rolled inward toward the stipe (margin).

inrolled rolled up on the side next to the stipe, especially when young (margin).

irregular not a constant shape.

lateral at the side.

lobate lobed.

margin the edge of the cap or the gills.
membraneous thin and pliant like a membrane.
mucilaginous sticky; viscid.
mycelium the collection of hyphae (mass of threads) forming the vegetative part of a fungus.
mycorrhiza symbiotic association of a fungus with the roots of a plant.

notched indented just before reaching the stipe (gills).

ostiole small pore through which spores are discharged in flask fungi.
ovoid egg-shaped; with the broad end below.

parasitic growing on or getting sustenance from a living plant or animal.
partial veil a membraneous tissue of certain mushrooms connecting the cap margin to the stipe and remaining as the ring on the stipe after expansion of the cap.
pathogen a bacterium, virus or other microorganism that can cause disease.
pedicel short, slender stalk.
perennial living over a number of years.
peridiole the small, lens-shaped spore packets of certain gasteroid fungi.
peridium the outer wall or layer of fungal fruit bodies.
perithecium (pl. **perithecia**) in ascomycetes, the round or flask-shaped fruit body that contains the asci.
persistent lasting; not disappearing.
plane flat.
polypore fungus larger fungi in which the hymenium is borne inside tubes on the underside of the mostly tough, corky or woody fruit body.
pore opening of the spore-bearing tube of a bolete or polypore fungus; opening in the spore sac of some gasteroid fungi.
porose full of pores.
pruinose covered in white powdery granules; frosted in appearance.
pseudorhiza a root-like extension of the stipe, as in *Termitomyces*.

reflexed turned upward or backward (margin).
resupinate growing completely flat on the substrate with the hymenium on the outer (upper) surface.
reticulate divided in such a way as to resemble a net-like pattern or network.
rhizoids tightly spun hyphae.
rhizomorph a root-like aggregation of hyphae.
ring a band of tissue encircling the stem of a mushroom.

saprophyte an organism which obtains food by growing on dead organic material.

sclerotium a compact mass of hardened mycelium containing food reserves, capable of remaining dormant for long periods.
scurfy covered with scales or scurf on the surface.
sessile attached directly to the substrate; sitting; without a stipe.
sinuate with a dentation close to the attachment to the stipe (gills).
sinuous having many curves and turns.
spathulate spoon-shaped.
sporangium (pl. **sporangia**) a receptacle in which asexual spores are formed.
spore reproductive unit in fungi.
squamose covered with scales; scaly.
sterile without spore-bearing structures.
stipe stem; stalk.
stipitate having a stipe.
striate marked with fine lines, ridges or grooves.
stuffed having the inner part of a different texture to the outer layers (stipe).
subdistant between close and distant; less distant; *see also* **close** and **distant**.
subglobose almost spherical.
substrate the surface or material, such as soil or bark, to which a fungus is attached or on which it grows.

tomentose covered with long, soft, downy hairs.
toxin a metabolic product produced by one organism which is injurious to another.
tube the tubular spore-bearing structures under the caps of certain fungi, such a boletes and polypores; visibile as pores on the lower surface.

umbo a central swelling or raised part on the upper surface of the cap.
umbonate having an umbo.
undulate wavy.
unequal arrangement of gills whereby full gills are interspersed with gills of a shorter length.
universal veil a layer of tissue covering the young, developing fruit body, sometimes persisting in the form of a volva or as scales or warts on the cap.

veil a covering membrane; *see also* **partial veil** and **universal veil**.
ventricose swollen around the middle.
viscid constantly sticky; *see* **glutinous**.
volva cup-like remains of the universal veil around the base of the stipe.

warts remnants of the universal veil.

zone concentric bands of colour.

BIBLIOGRAPHY

Arora, D. 1986. *Mushrooms Demystified.* Ten Speed Press, Berkeley, CA, USA.

Coetzee, J.C. 2010. Taxonomic notes on the Clathraceae (Phallales: Phallomycetidae) *sensu* Bottomly and a new key to the species in southern Africa. *Bothalia* 40(2): 155–159.

Conlon, B.H., De Beer, Z.W., De Fine Licht, H.H., Aanen, D.K. & Poulsen, M. 2016. Phylogenetic analyses of *Podaxis* specimens from southern Africa reveal hidden diversity and new insights into associations with termites. *Fungal Biology* 120(9): 1065–76.

Crous, P.W. *et al.* 2006. How many species of fungi are there at the tip of Africa? *Studies in Mycology* 55: 13–33.

Dähncke, R.M. & Dähncke, S.M. 1989. *700 Pilze in Farbfotos.* AT Verlag, Aarau.

Dickinson, C. & Lucas, J. 1979. *The Encyclopedia of Mushrooms.* Orbis Publishing, London.

Fuhrer, B. 2005. *A Field Guide to Australian Fungi.* Blooming Books.

Gorter, G.J.M.A. & Eicker, A. 1988. Gewone Afrikaanse en Engelse name vir die meer algemene Suid-Afrikaanse sampioene en ander makroswamme. *Suid-Afrikaanse Tydskrif vir Natuurwetenskap en Tegnologie* 7(1): 55–64.

Gryzenhout, M. 2010. *Pocket Guide: Mushrooms of South Africa.* Struik Nature, Cape Town.

Hallock, R.M. 2015. *A Mushroom World Guide: Etymology, Pronunciation, and Meanings From Over 500 Mycology Words.* CreateSpace, CA, USA.

Härkönen, M., Niemelä, T. & Mwasumbi, L. 2003. *Tanzanian Mushrooms: Edible, Harmful and Other Fungi.* Finnish Museum of Natural History, Helsinki.

Jaeger, E.C. 1944. *A Source-book of Biological Names and Terms.* Charles C. Thomas, IL, USA.

Læssøe, T. & Lincoff, G. 2002. *Smithsonian Handbooks: Mushrooms.* Dorling Kindersley, London.

Lamison, J. & Polese, J. 2005. *The Great Encyclopedia of Mushrooms.* Könemann, Keulen.

Levin, H., Branch, M., Rappoport, S. & Mitchell, D. 1987. *Field Guide: Mushrooms of South Africa.* Struik Publishers, Cape Town.

Lincoff, G. 1998. *National Audubon Society Field Guide to North American Mushrooms.* Alfred A. Knopf, Inc., New York.

Luard, E. 2006. *Truffles.* Berry & Co. Ltd, London.

Pearson, A.A. 1950. Cape agaricus and boleti. *Transactions of the British Mycological Society,* 33: 276–316.

Phillips, R. 1981. *Mushrooms and Other Fungi of Great Britain & Europe: The Most Comprehensively Illustrated Book on the Subject this Century.* Macmillan, London.

Pilát, A. & Ušák, O. 1951. *Mushrooms.* Spring Books, London.

Ramsbottom, J. 1951. *A Handbook of the Larger British Fungi.* British Museum, London.

Reid, D. 1980. *Mushrooms and Toadstools.* Kingfisher Books Ltd, London.

Rinaldi, A. & Tyndalo, V. 1974. *Mushrooms and Other Fungi: An Illustrated Guide.* Crown Publishers, London.

Ryvarden, L., Piearce, G.D. & Masuka, A.J. 1994. *The Larger Fungi of Southern Africa.* Baobab Books, Harare.

Stamets, P. 2005. *Mycelium Running: How Mushrooms Can Help Save The World.* Ten Speed Press, Berkeley, CA, USA.

Stephens, E.L. & Kidd, M.M. 1953. *Longman's Field Handbook: Some South African Edible Fungi.* Longman's Southern Africa, Cape Town.

Stephens, E.L. & Kidd, M.M. 1953. *Longman's Field Handbook: Some South African Poisonous & Inedible Fungi.* Longman's Southern Africa, Cape Town.

Tchoumi, J.M.T., Coetzee, M.P.A., Rajchenberg, M., Wingfield, M.J. & Roux, J. 2018. Three *Ganoderma* species, including *Ganoderma dunense* sp. nov., associated with dying *Acacia cyclops* trees in South Africa. *Australasian Plant Pathology* 47: 431–447.

Tosco, U. 1973. *The World of Nature: The Mushrooms of the World.* Orbis Publishing, London.

Trudell, S. & Ammirati, J. 2015. *Mushrooms of the Pacific Northwest.* Timber Press, Inc. Portland, OR, USA.

Van der Westhuizen, G.C.A. & Eicker, A. 1994. *Field Guide to Mushrooms of Southern Africa.* Struik Publishers, Cape Town.

Wakefield, E.M. & Dennis, R.W.G. 1981. *Common British Fungi.* Saiga Publishing, Surrey.

Willis, K.J., (ed.). 2018. *State of the World's Fungi 2018.* Report. Royal Botanic Gardens, Kew.

Useful websites

Boletales: https://boletales.com

Encyclopedia of Life: https://eol.org

First Nature: www.first-nature.com

Global Biodiversity Information Facility: www.gbif.org

iSpot Share Nature: www.ispotnature.org

Mushroom Expert: www.mushroomexpert.com

MushroomMAP, Animal Demography Unit, Virtual Museum: http://vmus.adu.org.za

Mushroom Observer: https://mushroomobserver.org

MycoBank Database: www.mycobank.org

Studies in the Amanitaceae: http://amanitaceae.org

INDEX TO SCIENTIFIC NAMES

INDEX TO ENGLISH AND AFRIKAANS COMMON NAMES